YOUNG OFFENDERS
LAW, PRACTICE AND PROCEDURE

YOUNG OFFENDERS
LAW, PRACTICE AND PROCEDURE

Richard Ward LLB, Solicitor
Professor of Public Law and Head of the
Department of Law
De Montfort University, Leicester

JORDANS
2001

Published by
Jordan Publishing Limited
21 St Thomas Street
Bristol BS1 6JS

British Library Cataloguing-in-Publication Data
A catalogue record for this book is available from the British Library.

ISBN 0 85308 602 8

Typeset by Mendip Communications Ltd, Frome, Somerset
Printed by MPG Books, Bodmin, Cornwall

PREFACE

This book is intended to expound the law and practice relating to young persons who commit, or who are alleged to have committed, crime, for the benefit of legal practitioners and others working within the youth justice system. In one sense, of course, the title is a misnomer in that it does not confine itself to those who have already been convicted. Those who are accused but not convicted are not, of course, young offenders – we still cherish the presumption of innocence! Yet the title accurately reflects the fact that the majority of the text concerns itself with those who have admitted, or been convicted of, crime.

The book is not intended to be an analysis or critique of the policies which underpin the law. That has not in any way simplified the task of authorship. Most legal writers bemoan the ever-moving target they are seeking to hit. In the area of youth justice, the pace and amount of change is little short of manic: parts of the Youth Justice and Criminal Evidence Act 1999 were scarcely, if at all, in force before the Powers of Criminal Courts (Sentencing) Act 2000 provided a welcome consolidation. This clarity has not, however, survived the Criminal Justice and Courts Act 2000, which significantly amends the consolidating Act. More is in store in 2001 – with the Government announcing further measures in respect of curfews on young offenders. There will be those who conclude that a pause to digest and understand and evaluate what has become, since 1991, an almost unending stream of legislation would not only be welcome but is also essential.

I gratefully acknowledge the contribution of all who have assisted, directly or indirectly, in the writing of this book, in particular Professor Richard Card, De Montfort University, and Sarah Ward, NSPCC Dove Project, Derby, who have each co-authored earlier work with me, and on which, on occasion, this book builds. In addition, particular thanks are due to the excellent team at Jordans, who have not only shown their usual helpfulness, but also have remained remarkably stoic in the face of delays and ever-changing copy. Responsibility for any errors or omissions is, of course, mine alone.

Richard Ward
Leicester
March 2001

CONTENTS

TABLE OF CASES

References are to paragraph numbers.

TABLE OF STATUTES

References are to paragraph numbers.

TABLE OF STATUTORY INSTRUMENTS

References are to paragraph numbers.

TABLE OF INTERNATIONAL CONVENTIONS

References are to paragraph numbers.

TABLE OF ABBREVIATIONS

1933 Act	Children and Young Persons Act 1933
1969 Act	Children and Young Persons Act 1969
1980 Act	Magistrates' Courts Act 1980
1985 Act	Prosecution of Offences Act 1985
1991 Act	Criminal Justice Act 1991
1991 Regulations	Children (Secure Accommodation) Regulations 1991
1998 Act	Crime and Disorder Act 1998
1999 Act	Youth Justice and Criminal Evidence Act 1999
2000 Act	Powers of Criminal Courts (Sentencing) Act 2000
CJA 1982	Criminal Justice Act 1982
CJCSA 2000	Criminal Justice and Courts Services Act 2000
CPO	Community punishment order
CPRO	Community punishment and rehabilitation order (combination order)
CRO	Community rehabilitation order
DPP	Director of Public Prosecutions
European Convention on Human Rights or European Convention	Convention for the Protection of Human Rights and Fundamental Freedoms 1950
HRA 1998	Human Rights Act 1998
PACE 1984	Police and Criminal Evidence Act 1984
PCCA 1973	Powers of Criminal Courts Act 1973
PSR	pre-sentence report
YOT	youth offending team

Chapter 1

GENERAL CONSIDERATIONS

Introduction – Age – The Youth Court – The Context and Policy Background – The Aim of the Youth Justice System – Youth Justice Plans – Youth Offending Teams – Youth Offender Panels – The Youth Justice Board – Parents – The Human Rights Context

INTRODUCTION

1.1   The youth justice system, by which is meant the laws, procedures and institutions which deal with those aged under 18 and accused or convicted of crime, has been the subject of considerable evolution and change, culminating in the provisions in the Youth Justice and Criminal Evidence Act 1999 (the 1999 Act). This marked a radical departure by restricting the freedom of action of a youth court dealing with a young offender.[1] As far back as 1933, with the passage of the Children and Young Persons Act 1933 (the 1933 Act), the importance of having regard to the welfare of the child or young person was recognised.[2] The 1969 Act of the same name took matters further, and was intended to make a radical reform of youth justice with 'the intention of engineering a significant shift . . . in which the young person's welfare would be the prime consideration'.[3] If it had been fully implemented, which it was not, it would have prevented the prosecution of a child under 14 for any crime other than murder, and have restricted the prosecution of offenders under that age. It also proposed restrictions on custodial sentences.

The youth court, which deals with the vast majority of criminal charges against children and young persons,[4] came into being in October 1992, replacing the pre-existing juvenile courts. The Criminal Justice Act 1991 (the 1991 Act) introduced a range of substantive and procedural changes relating to the way young persons were dealt with. In particular, 17-year-olds were included within the jurisdiction of the youth court, and a more flexible approach to sentencing 16- and 17-year-olds was introduced to reflect their level of maturity.[5] More recently, however, the Crime and Disorder Act 1998 (the 1998 Act) and the 1999 Act have made fundamental changes to the institutions dealing with youth justice and to approaches to offending by young offenders, which overtly shift the emphasis of the youth justice system to an approach based on early interventions to prevent re-offending.[6] In particular, the purpose of the youth justice system has been put beyond doubt by the introduction of s 37 of the 1998 Act which states that the principal aim of the youth justice system is to prevent offending by children and young persons.[7] The context and policy background to these changes is discussed at paras **1.7–1.9**.

The seemingly endless changes introduced in recent years, and outlined above, have led to the existence of a legislative morass of labyrinthine complexity. The need for consolidation was recognised publicly by the Government during the passage of the 1998 Act, which introduced a wide range of detailed changes (1998 Act, Sch 7). The promised consolidation found its way through Parliament in the form of the Powers of Criminal Courts (Sentencing) Act 2000 (2000 Act). References are made at the relevant parts of this text to the consolidated statutory sources. However, any notion that this consolidation will result in a simple 'one-stop' legislative scheme in respect of sentencing law is misplaced. Already, the Criminal Justice and Courts Services Act 2000 amends the 2000 Act, by renaming certain community orders,[8] by creating new orders[9] and by a host of other amendments.

---

1   See paras **4.6–4.8**.
2   1933 Act, s 44: see para **1.9**.
3   See Cavadino and Dignan *The Penal System* (Sage Publications, 1997) p 251.
4   See para **1.3**.
5   For an evaluation of the impact of the changes, see O'Mahoney and Haines Home Office Research Study 152 *An Evaluation of the Introduction and Operation of the Youth Court* (Home Office, 1999).
6   See para **1.8**.
7   See, further, paras **1.9–1.16**.
8   Probation orders become 'community rehabilitation orders' (see para **5.59**), community service orders become 'community punishment orders' (see para **5.93**) and combination orders 'community punishment and rehabilitation orders' (see para **5.98**).
9   Exclusion orders (see para **5.1**), drug abstinence orders (see para **5.117**).

AGE

1.2   At the outset, the terminology must be clearly defined. The youth justice system applies to those under 18 years of age, although, on occasion, different age limits are relevant. The generic terms 'juvenile',[1] 'youth' and 'young offender' can be used to describe both children and young persons: a 'child' is aged between 10 and 13, and a 'young person' between 14 and 17.[2] The term 'young defendants' is also used as a generic term.[3] A person reaches a particular age at the commencement of the relevant anniversary of his or her birth.[4] It is for the court to decide whether the age of the individual is such as to give the court jurisdiction or the power to make any individual order. For this purpose, it is acceptable for a court to act on the age specified by the defendant, unless, of course, there is cogent evidence to the contrary.[5] The date at which the relevant age has to be met will vary according to the particular provision being used.[6] The jurisdiction of the youth court depends upon the age of the individual at the date of the hearing.[7]

A youth court may proceed and deal with a charge in respect of an individual who is believed to be a child or young person even though it is discovered that he is not (1933 Act, s 48(1)). It may also deal with a person aged 18 who commits a further offence during the currency of a conditional discharge made before he attained that age (1933 Act, s 48(2)).

1   This term has a more limited meaning in the context of PACE Code C1, where it applies only to those aged under 17 years: see para **2.7**.
2   Children and Young Persons Act 1933, s 107(1); Children and Young Persons Act 1969, s 70(1).
3   See *Practice Direction (Crown Court: Trial of Children and Young Persons)* (2000) *The Times*, 17 February.
4   Family Law Reform Act 1969, s 9.
5   *R v Recorder of Grimsby, ex parte Purser* [1951] 2 All ER 889, DC.
6   See, eg *R v Uxbridge Youth Court, ex parte H* (1998) 162 JP 327, DC, where the court followed *R v Amersham Juvenile Court, ex parte Wilson* [1981] 2 All ER 315, DC, and distinguished *R v Billericay Justices, ex parte Johnson* (1979) 143 JP 697, DC. In *Ex parte Johnson* in the context of the Children and Young Persons Act 1969, s 7(8), it was held that the appropriate date to determine the relevant age was when the proceedings were begun.
7   *R v Uxbridge Youth Court, ex parte H* (1998) 162 JP 327, DC.

THE YOUTH COURT

1.3   Section 45 of the Children and Young Persons Act 1933 states that the courts of summary jurisdiction constituted in accordance with the provisions of Sch 2 to that Act and sitting for the purpose of hearing any charge against a child or young person or for the purpose of exercising any other jurisdiction conferred on youth courts by or under that or any other Act, shall be known as youth courts[1] and in whatever place sitting shall be deemed to be petty sessional courts.

The reason for the existence of youth courts is the principle that children and young persons accused of crime should be dealt with separately from adults, and in a less formal way, so as to focus their offending behaviour, and avoid undesirable publicity. This principle is reflected in a series of rules relating to composition, sitting, and publicity. The composition and sitting of youth courts is governed by ss 45 to 49 of the 1933 Act, Sch 2 to that Act, and by the Youth Court (Constitution) Rules 1954.[2] The youth court should be regarded as a magistrates' court constituted for the purpose of hearing of a charge against a child or young person, or for discharging any function conferred by statute on a youth court.

1   Renamed by the Criminal Justice Act 1991, s 70(1).
2   SI 1954/1711.

1.4   Justices who sit in the youth court must be drawn from a panel of justices who are specially qualified to deal with cases involving juveniles (1933 Act, Sch 2, para 2). Special rules apply to London, where youth courts are constituted in such divisions and in such places as the Home Secretary may by order specify. Members sit on a youth court panel for a period of three years commencing on 1 January of the year following appointment (r 11(1)).

No more than three justices may sit, and three are normally required to sit (1933 Act, Sch 2, para 15; r 12(1)). Unless unforeseen circumstances have arisen, in consequence of which only men or only women are available to form a court, the court must include both a man and a woman (r 12(1)), and clearly a genuine attempt should be made to achieve this gender balance.[1] It is a mandatory requirement. In *R v Birmingham Youth Court, ex parte F (A Minor)*,[2] the applicant, who was 13 years old, pleaded not guilty to a charge of robbery. At trial, there were only two male magistrates hearing the case. No explanation was given, and no point taken by either counsel. The case was adjourned part-heard. The same bench sat one week later. The applicant was convicted and sentenced. He appealed to the Crown Court, where the bench consisted of a male recorder and two male magistrates. Counsel objected to the constitution, which was contrary to the Crown Court Rules 1982 as lacking a female member. The Crown Court realised that the youth court had been wrongly constituted. An application for judicial review of the decision of the youth court was allowed by the Divisional Court. It was quite clear that r 12(1) was mandatory and that the hearings were unlawful and without jurisdiction, unless there had been a proper exercise of discretion, under r 12(3), by the bench of two men to proceed without a woman justice. In the instant case, the bench had failed to consider r 12(3) at all, so that the proceedings before them had been a nullity. Moreover, had the members of the panel considered that it was inexpedient in the interests of justice for there to be an adjournment (see below) and, therefore, wished the court to be constituted without a woman or, as the case might be, without a man, pursuant to r 12(3) that decision had to be made in open court, after hearing submissions from all parties, in order to comply with elementary principles of fairness. It would not be enough to state that the applicant had been represented and so could have argued that the bench was improperly constituted. This decision clearly demonstrates the mandatory nature of the rules, but leaves open the question: what if the Crown Court bench had been properly constituted? Since in these circumstances the appeal is effectively a re-hearing, it could be argued that fairness of that appeal 'cures' the procedural defect inherent in the original youth court hearing, and that, whilst there has been a breach of a mandatory requirement, no remedy need be granted on judicial review. On the other hand and, arguably, more persuasively, the accused is entitled to have a valid determination at the youth court, and thus the correct constitution of the Crown Court ought not to matter. The accused is entitled to his or her 'two bites at the cherry'.

Where a court cannot be constituted as above, and it appears to the chairman that an adjournment would not be in the interests of justice, the chairman may sit with one other member (whether a man or a woman) (1933 Act, Sch 2, para 17).

A stipendiary magistrate is a member of a youth court panel *ex officio* (r 2), and, outside the London Metropolitan area, may sit alone only if he is the only member present and it is inexpedient to adjourn (r 2). However, a different rule applies within the Metropolitan area: since the implementation of s 48 of the Crime and Disorder Act 1998, a stipendiary magistrate may sit alone, or, alternatively, the court may comprise a panel of chairman and two members (in accordance with the rule stated above regarding gender) (1933 Act, Sch 2, para 15).

Justices may be transferred between youth court panels within the same commission area or to a panel in another commission area provided the justice has been first appointed as a justice to that other commission area.

---

1   See *Re JS (An Infant)* [1959] 3 All ER 856, ChD, where it was observed, albeit in a context
      not related to youth courts, that to give a woman notice to attend without inquiring
      whether she could, in fact, do so, was not to ensure her attendance.
2   [1999] All ER (D) 1053, DC.

1.5   The Government, in 1997, concluded that inadequate attention was often being given by the youth court to the need to address and change the offending behaviour,[1] a state of affairs encouraged by the court's structures and procedures. These perceived failings were addressed by the provisions of the Crime and Disorder Act 1998[2] and the Youth Justice and Criminal Evidence Act 1999.[3] A series of changes was considered necessary[4] to provide speedier decisions on guilt or innocence, much closer to the date of the offence and with less tolerance of adjournments; a system which is more open, and which commands the confidence of victims and the public; processes which engage young offenders and their parents and focus on the nature of their offending behaviour and how to change it; a stronger emphasis on using sentencing to prevent future offending; and more efficient arrangements for the scheduling and arrangement of cases. It was intended that the purpose of the youth court should change from simply deciding guilt or innocence and then issuing a sentence to the triggering of an inquiry into the circumstances and nature of the offending behaviour, leading to action to change that behaviour. This change underpins the provisions now found in Part III of the 2000 Act, requiring a youth court, in some circumstances, to refer a young offender to a youth offender panel.

---

1   *No More Excuses: New National and Local Focus on Youth Crime* (Home Office, 1997), para 9.2.
2   See paras **1.18–1.20**.
3   See paras **4.1–4.4**.
4   *No More Excuses*, op cit, para 9.

1.6   The jurisdiction of the youth court is that prescribed by statute or by rules made by the Lord Chancellor pursuant to s 145 of the 1980 Act.[1] It sits in private, and with restrictions as to who may attend.[2] These restrictions have been the subject of criticism, the Government believing that there should be more openness in respect of youth court proceedings.[3] Again, it is for this reason that significant changes were made by the Youth Justice and Criminal Evidence Act 1999.[4] As the law currently stands, no report of proceedings may be published which reveals the name, address or other identifying detail of any juvenile concerned in the proceedings, whether he be concerned as a party or merely as a witness (1933 Act, s 49(1)). The court may, however, lift the ban on publicity to the extent it considers necessary either to avoid injustice to the juvenile himself or, as respects a juvenile to whom s 49(5)(b) applies, where it is necessary to do so for the purpose of apprehending him and bringing him before a court or returning him to custody (s 49(5)). Section 49(5)(b) applies to a juvenile charged with or convicted of a violent or sexual offence or an offence punishable in the case of a person aged 21 or over with imprisonment for 14 years or more. Section 49(5) can be employed only when notice has been given by the Director of Public Prosecutions (DPP) to the juvenile's legal representative.

---

1   See Magistrates' Courts (Children and Young Persons) Rules 1992, SI 1992/2071, as amended by the Magistrates' Courts (Children and Young Persons) (Amendment) Rules 1997, SI 1997/2420 and the Magistrates' Courts (Miscellaneous Amendment) Rules 1998, SI 1998/2167.
2   See paras **3.18–3.19**.
3   *No More Excuses*, op cit, para 9.7.
4   See paras **3.25–3.27**.

THE CONTEXT AND POLICY BACKGROUND

1.7   Approaches to crime prevention and reduction have increasingly focused on the need for effective and timely responses to offending by young offenders. Home Office research shows that among 14- to 25-year-olds, one in two males and one in three females admits to having committed an offence.[1] The Audit Commission estimated that in 1996 young offenders committed 7 million offences per year, with 10- to 17-year-olds accounting for around 25% of all known offenders.[1] The same research identified the fact that a 'small hard core of persistent offenders is responsible for a disproportionate amount of crime … about 3% of young offenders commit 26% of youth crime'.[2] Even more startling is the fact that figures for 1995 showed that 0.3% of males born in 1973 had six or more court appearances by age 17 and accounted for 21% of all court appearances for that age group.[2] Of course, those statistics tell us little about the balance of commission of *serious* crime between young offenders and adult offenders, although research studies show increases in the numbers of young offenders being convicted for offences of violence against the person, robbery and drug offences.[3] The causes of that criminality are difficult to establish, but factors which are known to be relevant include being male; being brought up by a criminal parent or parents; living in a family with multiple problems; poor parenting and lack of supervision; poor discipline in the family and at school; failure to attend school; and associations with delinquents, including having siblings who offend.[4] The importance of the quality of a young person's home life, and of parenting, is, unsurprisingly, one key principle underpinning the changes made by the Crime and Disorder Act 1998. Inherent in all these changes is a recognition that the principle of restorative justice has a key role to play. This principle involves interactions between the offender, the community and the youth justice agencies and involves strategies to prevent re-offending, through:

–   attending to the victim, and offenders taking responsibility for their actions;
–   a community that supports rehabilitation of offenders; and
–   providing a means of avoiding the delays and costs of the legal system.[5]

1   *No More Excuses*, op cit, para 1.1; *Young People and Crime: Research Findings No 24* (Home Office, 1995).

2   Ibid, para 1.2; *Aspects of Crime: Young Offenders, 1995* (Home Office, 1997).

3   See *Aspects of Crime: Young Offenders, 1995*, op cit.

4   Ibid, para 1.4. For a more detailed list of known risk factors, see 'What Works in the UK?', a paper presented to the Youth Justice Board Conference, 8 March 1999, by D. Utting, and to be found at www.youthjusticeboard.gov.uk/reports.

5   For one example, see Hughes, Pilkington and Ruchira, *An Independent Evaluation of the Northamptonshire Diversion Unit* (Open University, 1996). For the background to the introduction of approaches designed to divert young persons from the court system, see Bowden and Stevens 'Justice for Juveniles – A Corporate Strategy in Northampton' (1986) 150 JPN 326 at 329, 345–347.

1.8   Another key approach is the need for effective, coordinated and timely responses by youth justice agencies. This involves the swift administration of justice so that matters are dealt with without delay; the confronting of young offenders with the consequences of their offending; punishment proportionate to the seriousness and persistence of offending; the encouragement of reparation by offenders to victims; the reinforcement of responsibilities of parents; the helping of offenders to resolve problems associated with their own offending and the development of a sense of personal responsibility.[1] Again, these factors permeate the recent legislation. In particular, a raft of measures have been introduced designed to reform the youth justice system in order to reduce delay. In 1996, it took an average of 131 days to deal with a young offender from offence to disposal.[2] In its study, *Misspent Youth*, the Audit Commission found that four out of five cases observed were adjourned at least once and that, on average, each young offender appeared in court four times during the progress of his or her case.[3] In some areas, this average increased to up to 220 days, revealing a significant discrepancy between the best and the worst areas. Following the recommendations of the *Narey Report*,[4] significant procedural changes have been introduced by the 1998 Act.

1   These factors were proposed by the Home Office Youth Justice Task Force, and adopted by the Government: *No More Excuses*, op cit, para 2.9.

2   Ibid, para 7.1. For relevant Audit Commission Reports, see *Misspent Youth: Young People and Crime* (1996); *Misspent Youth '98: The Challenge for Youth Justice* (1998).

3   See note 2, above.

4   *Review of Delay in the Criminal Justice System: A Report* (Home Office, 1997).

THE AIM OF THE YOUTH JUSTICE SYSTEM

1.9   Section 37(1) of the Crime and Disorder Act 1998 (the 1998 Act) states that the principal aim of the youth justice system is to prevent offending by children and young persons. The Government considered that 'for far too long there has been a lack of clear direction in the youth justice system'.[1] It was for this reason that the 1998 Act established a new structural framework for the management and monitoring of the delivery of youth justice services, through the creation of this new general duty (s 37(1)), the creation of a Youth Justice Board, the creation of a framework of local inter-agency partnerships to deliver a range of youth justice services to the courts and the community including, specifically, the creation of youth offending teams, and by reform of the youth court. It is the duty of all persons and bodies carrying out functions in relation to the youth justice system to have regard to that aim (s 37(2)). This approach, of stating an overall aim, is not new: as noted earlier, s 44 of the Children and Young Persons Act 1933 requires a court, in fulfilling its duties, to take account of the welfare of the child or young person before the court, and to take steps to remove him from undesirable surroundings. It must also secure proper provision for the education of the child or young person (1933 Act, s 44(1)). By contrast, the aim stated by s 37(1) of the 1998 Act does not relate the aim to the individual offender before the court. Thus an individual young offender may, quite legitimately within the principal aim stated by s 37(1), be dealt with in a way which will prevent offending generally by children and young persons, even if it does not have that effect individually.

---

1   *No More Excuses*, op cit, para 8.1.

1.10   The duty under the 1998 Act applies to all those working within the context of the youth justice system, including local authorities, health authorities, probation services, voluntary agencies, the police and the courts. A police officer, in determining whether or not to issue a reprimand or final warning,[1] will be required to have regard to this general duty; the Crown Prosecution Service will need to have regard to s 37 when determining whether a prosecution should be undertaken. A sentencing court will likewise have, as a principal aim, the prevention of re-offending. The duty will extend to defence solicitors and barristers. It does not follow from that that such bodies will be required to give effect in their decisions to that aim irrespective of other considerations. The phrase 'principal aim' identifies the overall aim of the system: individuals working within it are required to have regard to that aim, but not to the exclusion of other legitimate aims or objectives, such as the protection of the public or their own professional obligations. Thus the general duty does not detract from the duty a lawyer owes to his client, or of a Crown Prosecutor to have regard to the Code for Crown Prosecutors. If the means by which offending by an individual, or by other individuals, can be prevented, is by the imposition of a custodial order, then nothing in s 37 prevents that.

---

1   See para **2.64**.

1.11   The general duty could be described as a statement of how issues relating to youth offenders should be addressed, and is intended to achieve clarity of purpose and focus. Confusion and uncertainty have sometimes arisen as to what the purpose of the youth justice system actually is.[1] This is, perhaps, unsurprising given the changing emphases which have existed in the past.[2]

CONTRADICTION
SIMILAR TO
THAT OF PROB SERV
PUNISHMENT v REHAB

Now, following the passage of s 37 of the 1998 Act, it is beyond doubt that the welfare of the individual offender (to which the court must have regard)[3] is not the prime purpose of the criminal justice system, although almost always the welfare of the offender will be promoted by the preventing of re-offending, and a failure to address the offending behaviour might be regarded as contrary to the welfare principle.[4] For this reason, arguments put in mitigation that an offender should not be made the subject of a particular custodial order, because it might increase, rather than decrease, the potential for re-offending, are unlikely to be justifiable by reference to the general duty imposed by s 37.

However, there is a tension between this general duty and that which exists to promote the welfare of the defendant. Section 44 of the 1933 Act requires a court to have regard to the welfare of the child or young person. The importance of this is underscored by the range of provisions in international law and practice which emphasise the need to have regard to the welfare of the child.[5] In particular, the European Convention on the Rights of the Child[6] provides, in Art 3, that in all actions concerning children their best interests are to be a primary consideration. This principle has been recognised both by the European Court of Human Rights[7] and by English courts.[8] It is unclear how the differences in emphasis between s 44 of the 1933 Act (and of the international obligations to like effect) and the general duty in s 37(1) of the 1998 Act are to be resolved. Although the two may in many circumstances be compatible, on occasion they might not be. Approaches to issues in respect of publicity, or particular orders, may well be appropriate to prevent offending generally, for example by sending a message designed to deter young persons from committing certain types of crime, yet not particularly in the interests of the welfare of the individual young person. The answer is perhaps that there is a clear obligation on courts, and others, to act in a way consistent with the welfare of the child. Within that, however, in determining which one of a range of available options should be chosen, a court should focus on taking decisions that are designed to prevent re-offending.

Note should also be taken of the provisions of s 2 of the Criminal Justice and Courts Services Act 2000. This Act creates, inter alia, a new National Probation Service. Section 2 states that the Home Secretary, local probation boards and probation officers must, when performing their various functions under the Act, have regard to the following aims:

(1) the protection of the public;
(2) the reduction of re-offending; and
(3) the proper punishment of offenders.

Again, however, the fact that regard must be had to these aims does not mean that these aims are the only relevant aims, or that they must inevitably prevail.

---

1   Alun Michael, MP, Minister of State, Home Office, HC Committee B, April–July 1998, cols 375–376.
2   See Cavadino and Dignan *The Penal System* pp 150–250.
3   Children and Young Persons Act 1933, s 44: see para **1.1**.
4   Alun Michael, MP, Minister of State, Home Office, HC Committee B, op cit, col 37.

5   See para **1.27**.
6   TS No 44 (No 2), Cm 1796, adopted by the United Nations General Assembly, 20 November 1989.
7   *T v United Kingdom; V v United Kingdom* (1999) *The Times*, 17 December: see para **1.37**.
8   See, eg, *McKerry v Teesdale and Wear Valley Justices*, (2000) *The Times*, 20 February.

1.12   The 1998 Act made significant changes to the management of the criminal justice process, by creating a new framework for the development and management of crime and disorder strategies, and through a new system for managing the youth justice system. Through these two initiatives, the Government sought to develop an approach to the prevention of crime, and the management of crime, based on inter-agency initiatives and co-operation. Further, by s 17, a new duty was imposed on local authorities, requiring them to take account of the crime and disorder implications of their actions and of the need to do all that they can to prevent crime and disorder in their area. The significance of s 17 has yet to be fully tested in respect of the extent it provides the potential for legal action against a local authority and other agencies.[1] Arguably, it will be a relevant consideration to which regard may, and should, be had in the exercise of any statutory power or more specific duty, and, perhaps, a failure to have regard to which would be challengeable on an application for judicial review on normal judicial review principles.[2] The context of the Human Rights Act 1998 should also be borne in mind. A public body may be under a positive duty to secure the protection of the rights of individuals. This is because, under Art 1 of the Convention, signatory States are under an obligation to secure the protection of Convention rights,[3] that protection being real and effective, not theoretical and illusory.[4] Given the broad scope of the statutory duty, it may take a significant disregard of this general duty, or a failure to address the authorities' mind to the matter, before the matter provides an effective and realistic basis for legal action, but in a case involving such a failure leading to loss of life, or interference with property rights by criminals,[5] Convention arguments may come into play.

1   See the analysis of Bullock, Moss and Smith: *Anticipating the Impact of Section 17 of the Crime and Disorder Act* Home Office Briefing Note 11/00, available at www.homeoffice.gov.uk.
2   See *Associated Provincial Picture Houses Ltd v Wednesbury Corporation* [1948] 1 KB 223.
3   Although Art 1 is not a 'Convention right' for the purpose of the Human Rights Act 1998, s 1, this positive duty is recognised in the case-law of the Court of Human Rights (see note 4, below) to which a court must have regard (Human Rights Act 1998, s 3).
4   *Artico v Italy* (1981) 3 EHRR 1, ECHR; *X and Y v Netherlands* (1986) 8 EHRR 235, ECHR; *A v United Kingdom (Human Rights: Punishment of Child)* [1998] 2 FLR 959, ECHR; *KL v United Kingdom* (1998) 26 EHRR 113, ECHR.
5   See Art 1, Protocol 1 (right to property); Art 8 of the Convention (respect for private and family life, home and correspondence).

1.13   In 1997, the Government published a White Paper, *Getting to Grips with Crime: A New Framework for Local Action.*[1] The White Paper identified the fact that there is a realisation generally that the police cannot be expected to fight crime alone, and identified a wide range of partnership arrangements then operating up and down the country, involving different agencies from the public and voluntary sectors at all levels. These ranged from multi-agency umbrella groups covering whole police force areas, to close collaboration between a beat officer and local Neighbourhood Watch groups.[2] This approach was very much based on the recommendations of the Morgan Report, which was published in 1991.[3] Much of the current thinking on the importance of partnership and on the most effective mechanisms for delivering it stems from the publication of that report, which was the work of an independent working group convened by the then Home Office Standing Conference on Crime Prevention.

1   Home Office Consultation Paper (1997).
2   Ibid, para 2.3.
3   *Safer Communities: the Local Delivery of Crime Prevention through the Partnership Approach* (Home Office, 1991).

1.14   The Morgan Committee examined in detail the opportunities and problems which existed for those wanting to work in partnerships to prevent and reduce crime. The Report underlined the need for broadly based, multi-agency approaches to crime prevention and reduction, within which agencies could co-operate as well as deliver their own contribution. It highlighted the importance of involving the voluntary and business sectors as partners in this work; it identified structural barriers to success such as differing operational areas between police service, local authority and probation service boundaries; and expressed the view that a factual analysis of local problems was an essential first step in the development of a successful local crime prevention partnership. *Getting to Grips with Crime* identified the fact that the police and local authorities have embraced the concept of multi-agency work and identified the results of a survey of local authorities.[1] Some 90% of authorities which participated in the survey recognised community safety as an area of work relevant to them, and 84% had reported on it to the relevant committee within the two preceding years; 62% of authorities were engaged in independent multi-agency partnerships, with 32% also involved in other types of partnership; 62% undertook local crime pattern analysis, and over one-third did crime audits; 51% had a separate budget for community safety; 37% have appointed their own community safety officer; and 67% run diversionary holiday schemes for young people.

There were also some less encouraging findings. Various factors restricting further development of the work were identified, including the attitude of central government, the internal priority attached to the subject and the effects of local government reorganisation. One of the biggest barriers to progress was seen as the lack of a statutory role for local authorities.

1   See 'Survey of Community Safety Activities in Local Government in England and Wales' (Home Office, 1996).

1.15   The provisions of Part III of the 1998 Act implemented Government proposals to improve the delivery of work with young offenders in the community. This inter-agency approach is particularly important in the context of the delivery of youth justice. The Criminal Justice Act 1991, and Home Office Circular 30/1992, both encouraged joint initiatives in relation to 16- and 17-year-old offenders.[1] Existing responsibility for such offenders is split between local authority social service departments, who generally have prime responsibility for offenders aged under 16, and for those aged 16 known to them, and the probation service which generally deals with offenders aged 17, but also some offenders aged 16 and a few younger offenders.[2] The details of this division of responsibility are a matter for local negotiation and agreement. Some parts of England and Wales have inter-agency teams which deal with young offenders, but the precise arrangements varied widely and were not consistent.[3] The rationale for change was explained in *No More Excuses* as follows:[4]

> 'The Government believes that action is needed to bring about greater consistency in the approach to work with young offenders in the community and to ensure that all the relevant local agencies play a full part. Such action will need to be built on the best of existing work but, to ensure that youth justice is given proper priority by the relevant agencies and is clearly focused on challenging offending behaviour, the Government believes that a more structured approach is required. This will involve clear and specific duties on those agencies and greater openness and accountability concerning the way in which those duties are discharged.'

It was for that reason that the 1998 Act sought to define the general aim of the youth justice system, discussed at para **1.11**.

---

1   *No More Excuses: New National and Local Focus on Youth Crime* (Home Office, 1997), paras 11–14.
2   See para **5.11**.
3   *No More Excuses*, para 13.
4   Ibid, para 14.

1.16   To achieve this general duty, each local authority[1] is under a duty to secure that, to such extent as is appropriate for their area, all youth justice services are available there (s 38(1)). These services have to be provided in accordance with national standards drawn up by the Youth Justice Board created by the Crime and Disorder Act 1998.[2] The duty is to be performed in co-operation with the appropriate chief constable and police authorities, probation committee and health authority (s 38(1), (2)), and such bodies are under a statutory duty to co-operate in the discharge of that duty by the local authority.

'Youth justice services' are defined by s 38(4) as any of the following:

> '(a)   the provision of persons to act as appropriate adults[3] to safeguard the interests of children and young persons detained or questioned by police officers;
> (b)   the assessment of children and young persons, and the provision for them of rehabilitation programmes, for the purposes of section 66(2) below;[4]
> (c)   the provision of support for children and young persons remanded or committed on bail while awaiting trial or sentence;

(d) the placement in local authority accommodation of children and young persons remanded or committed to such accommodation under section 23 of the Children and Young Persons Act 1969 ("the 1969 Act");[5]

(e) the provision of reports or other information required by courts in criminal proceedings against children and young persons;

(f) the provision of persons to act as responsible officers in relation to parenting orders, child safety orders, reparation orders and action plan orders;[6]

(g) the supervision of young persons sentenced to a probation order, a community service order or a combination order;[7]

(h) the supervision of children and young persons sentenced to a detention and training order[8] or a supervision order;[9]

(i) the post-release supervision of children and young persons under section 37(4A) or section 65 of the 1991 Act or section 31 of the Crime (Sentences) Act 1997 ("the 1997 Act").

(j) under subsection (1) of section 102 of the Powers of Criminal Courts (Sentencing) Act 2000 (period of detention and training under detention and training order by such persons as may be authorised by the [Home Secretary] under that subsection;[10]

(k) the implementation of referral orders within the meaning of the Powers of Criminal Courts (Sentencing) Act 2000.'

The Home Secretary may from time to time amend this definition so as to extend, restrict or otherwise alter it, by order (s 38(4)).

---

1   A local authority is for this purpose defined widely to include county councils, district council (where the district does not form part of an area that has a county council) London borough council or the Common Council of the City of London (s 42(1)).

2   See para **1.23**.

3   See para **2.12**.

4   See paras **4.25** *et seq.*

5   See paras **3.41–3.44**.

6   See para **5.43** for action plan.

7   Under the Criminal Justice and Courts Services Act 2000, to be known as community rehabilitation orders, community punishment orders and community punishment and rehabilitation orders respectively: see, generally, Chapter 5.

8   See para **6.3**.

9   See para **5.7**.

10 See paras **6.3** *et seq.*

Youth justice plans

1.17 Each local authority will, each year, formulate and implement a youth justice plan. This plan, which will be published, must set out (s 37(1)):

(a) how youth justice services in their area are to be provided and funded; and

(b) how the youth offending team(s), referred to below, are to be composed and funded, how they are to operate and what functions they are to carry out.

These provisions are similar to other statutory provisions. Section 6 of the 1998 Act imposes a duty on a local authority (which is usually a different local authority from that under a duty to publish a youth justice plan)[1] to prepare a community safety and crime reduction strategy. The Children Act 1989 imposes a duty on a local authority to produce a children services plan. Police authorities are under a duty, imposed by s 8 of the Police Act 1996, to produce an annual policing plan. Section 9 of the Education Act 1997 requires the publication of a plan setting out the proposed arrangements for dealing with pupils with behavioural difficulties, including persistent non-attenders and excluded pupils. Clearly, a measure of coordination and dialogue is required if plans are not to end up being contradictory, but each of these plans will have different overall objectives. That of the youth justice plan is to prevent re-offending by children and young persons.

The youth justice plan identifies the local infrastructure of youth justice services, and provides the context in which youth offending teams will work. The plan must include[2] appropriate arrangements for bail supervision and support, arrangements for supervision work in support of the final warning system created by the 1998 Act,[3] arrangements for the supervision of the range of community sentences available in respect of young offenders, and for the management of parenting and child safety orders. The plan should not concern itself with the operation or administration of the courts; that said, such plans should address the timeliness and efficiency of the court process, and can include provisions for 'fast tracking' persistent young offenders, for the preparation of pre-sentence and other reports, and liaison with the Crown Prosecution Service.

---

1   See 1998 Act, s 5(4), which defines a local authority for the purposes of s 5.
2   *No More Excuses: New National and Local Focus on Youth Crime*, op cit, para 32.
3   See paras **2.64–2.76**.

Youth offending teams

1.18   Central to the provision of youth justice services are youth offending teams (YOTs). The concept of multi-agency teams takes forward in a practical form the broad objectives identified by the Morgan Committee.[1] The 1998 Act introduced YOTs. Following initial pilots,[2] youth offending teams were introduced throughout England and Wales on 1 April 2000.[3]

These YOTs are under a duty to coordinate the provision of youth justice services within the local authority area, and to carry out such functions as are assigned to the team in the local authority's youth justice plan made under s 40 (s 39(7)). These teams 'should pull together all the relevant local agencies in delivering community-based interventions with, and supervision of, young offenders'.[3] The right local infrastructure should exist on which youth offending teams can draw, and the courts should have access to appropriate bail support arrangements in dealing with young people. Not all functions are necessarily performed by the youth offending teams themselves; their work may in fact draw on programmes and activities provided by local agencies or by the voluntary sector. One detailed example of this is the fact that, whilst wider preventative and family support work might be undertaken by the local authority social services department, it may be appropriate in some instances for orders such as parenting orders to be supervised by members of the team (eg where the order is imposed on the parents of a young offender). Again, a team might supervise a child safety order if the team was involved locally in preventative work or if the family concerned was known to it.[4]

It is crucial, however, that the team does not lose sight of its criminal justice objectives. Thus, the primary functions are likely to be the assessment and intervention work in support of the final warning (including work with the offender to bring about behavioural change, reparation work with victims, supervised leisure activities and work with parents), supervision of community sentences (if appropriate drawing on agencies and projects outside the team) ensuring that there is an 'appropriate adult' service available for police interviews, provision of bail information to assist the courts in making decisions about juveniles, bail supervision and support, the placement of young people in open or secure accommodation, remand fostering, or approved accommo-dation, court work and the preparation of reports, and through-care during, and undertaking post-release supervision following, a custodial sentence. The Government also proposes a role for youth offending teams in relation to parenting and child safety orders.

---

1   See paras **1.14** and **1.15**.
2   *New National and Local Focus on Youth Crime*, op cit. See further para **1.21**.
3   For discussion of the findings of the pilot schemes, see para **1.21**.
4   *New National and Local Focus on Youth Crime*, op cit, para 20.

Composition
1.19   Each local authority must establish at least one YOT, in co-operataion with relevant police authorities, probation committees and health authorities (s 39(1), (3)). Two or more authorities may choose to act together to establish one or more youth offending team for their areas: the 1998 Act entitles them to do so (s 39(2)). Each team will include at least one probation officer, local authority social worker, police officer, nominee of a health authority and of the local education authority (s 39(4)). The precise composition of teams or the roles of individual members is not prescribed. Nor is the list in s 39(4) intended to be exhaustive. After consultation with the police authority, probation committee and health authority, the local authority may include on the youth offending team such other person as it thinks appropriate (s 39(5)). The key consideration in determining the composition of each of them is the need for the work of such teams to be clearly directed towards tackling offending behaviour and to challenge young offenders to change behaviour and attitudes.[1] The composition should be such as to reflect this objective. Clearly, social workers will be key members of the team. The young offender, or his family, may be known to social services or receiving support or other social services intervention. The young offender may be, or have been, in care.

Probation officers will likewise be key players, the 1998 Act having removed the restriction on the supervision by probation officers of 10- to 12-year-olds.[2] The supervisor of a person under a supervision order should be a member of a YOT within whose area it appears to a court that the supervised person resides or will reside. The most appropriate person will supervise the offender.

---

1   Children and Young Persons Act 1969, s 131(2).
2   Schedule 9, paras 12–14. See also s 71(5) for the selection of supervision for supervision orders.

1.20   Other participants in the YOT include police officers, the local authority education department and health authority staff. Police officers are expected to ensure good liaison with police colleagues dealing with the final warning under s 65,[1] to highlight to the offender the consequences of offending on victims and of a criminal record, to help supervise more persistent young offenders (eg by checking curfews and attendance at projects) and to promote wider community safety and crime reduction schemes (eg supervised leisure activities). Local authority education department workers will be able to ensure that educational and training issues and needs are addressed, and be involved in work with truants or excluded pupils. Health authority staff will be able to liaise in respect of local alcohol and drug misuse and psychiatric provision, feeding in, perhaps, to the rehabilitation programme that accompanies the final warning and envisaged by s 66. Whether all or any such individuals need be full-time members of the YOT is a matter for local decision. Individuals from other agencies and organisations, such as the local authority youth service, or voluntary agencies may be involved directly, or more indirectly through partnership arrangements. So, too, may representatives from the business community.

---

1   See paras **2.64–2.75**.

1.21   The pilot schemes outlined above have been the subject of on-going evaluation.[1] Experience suggests that agreement of protocols with the court about key areas of YOT activity is particularly important. Close liaison with the courts is regarded as an important element in the development of youth offending services. In several of the pilot areas, justices' clerks have been represented for liaison purposes on YOT Steering Committees, who have also benefited from discussions with local magistrates. One particular aspect of the pilots has been a reluctance on behalf of the courts to commission the reports associated with the reparation order and action plan order, and instead to commission full pre-sentence reports. The courts should consider, for the purposes of avoiding unnecessary delay and for the appropriate use of resources, whether the circumstances of the case, and the sentence which they consider reasonably to be in prospect given its seriousness, might not better warrant the commissioning of a report with a view to the making of a reparation or action plan order.

1   *Delivering the Aim – News From the Youth Justice Pilots, Issue 2* (Home Office, May 1999), to be
     found at www.homeoffice.gov.uk/yousys.

Youth offender panels

1.22 Youth offender panels were established by the Youth Justice and
Criminal Evidence Act 1999. These are discussed later.[1]

1   See paras **4.19–4.20**. For the current statutory source, see the 2000 Act, s 21.

The Youth Justice Board

1.23 The Youth Justice Board was created by s 41 of the 1998 Act. Under the
terms of s 41(3), 10, 11 or 12 members, who must include persons with
extensive recent experience of the youth justice system (s 41(3), (4)), may be
appointed by the Home Secretary. In particular, persons with experience of the
courts in dealing with young offenders and with experience of services for
victims are among those who will be represented on the Board.[1] The initial
appointments to the Board comprised 12 members.[2]

Detailed provisions relating to membership, procedure and financial arrangements are contained in Sch 2. An individual is appointed for a fixed period (no
longer than five years), and may be re-appointed (even more than once)
provided his total length of service does not exceed 10 years (Sch 2, para 2(5)).
A member may be removed from membership where the conditions of
appointment so permit, where there has been a failure (without reasonable
excuse) to discharge functions for a continuous period of three months,
beginning not earlier than six months before the removal, upon conviction for
a criminal offence, the making of a bankruptcy or similar order, or where the
individual is unfit to discharge the functions of a member (Sch 2, para 9).
Members may be paid, in accordance with terms set out by the Home Secretary.
The Board is chaired by one member appointed by the Home Secretary as
chairman (Sch 2, para 1), and will determine its own procedure (Sch 2, para 7).
The Board is under a duty to publish an Annual Report and accounts (Sch 2,
para 8).

1   Alun Michael, MP, Minister of State, Home Office, HC Committee B April–July 1998,
     col 393.
2   The range of appointments includes appointees from local authority social services (Lord
     Warner of Brockley, chairman), probation, police forensic psychology, justices of the
     peace, the voluntary sector and the media. For details of the Board, see
     www.youthjusticeboard.gov.uk/reports.

1.24 The functions of the Board are set out in s 41(5) of the 1998 Act, as
follows:

'(a) to monitor the operation of the youth justice system and the provision of
      youth justice services;

(b)   to advise the Secretary of State on the following matters, namely –

   (i)   the operation of that system and the provision of such services;
   (ii)   how the principal aim of that system might most effectively be pursued;
   (iii) the content of any national standards he may see fit to set with respect to the provision of such services, or the accommodation in which children and young persons are kept in custody; and
   (iv)   the steps that might be taken to prevent offending by children and young persons;

(c)   to monitor the extent to which that aim is being achieved and any such standards met;
(d)   for the purposes of paragraphs (a), (b) and (c) above, to obtain information from relevant authorities;
(e)   to publish information so obtained;
(f)   to identify, to make known and to promote good practice in the following matters, namely –

   (i)   the operation of the youth justice system and the provision of youth justice services;
   (ii)   the prevention of offending by children and young persons; and
   (iii) working with children and young persons who are or are at risk of becoming offenders;

(g)   to make grants, with the approval of the Secretary of State, to local authorities or other bodies for them to develop such practice, or to commission research in connection with such practice; and
(h)   themselves to commission research in connection with such practice.'

In particular, in fulfilment of these functions, the Board provides benchmarks for the work of the various inspectorates that oversee, or might oversee, the work of the youth offending teams.

The work of the Board thus provides the framework, context and information base within, and upon which, local authorities and youth offending teams operate. One important aspect of this is to advise the Government on the drawing up of National Standards for the work of YOTs and the provision of youth justice services, focusing on the particular needs and objectives of work with young people. The existing National Standards for the Supervision of Offenders in the Community are primarily focused on adult offenders. New National Standards extend the scope of guidance so as to embrace the range of issues inherent in working with young offenders. The Board has taken the view[1] that the effective police work is undone by delays in the youth justice system. The pressure on court time means that it frequently takes months for a case to come to court. One of the six key objectives in supporting the prevention of offending behaviour is the swift administration of justice. The Board has set a target of halving the average time from arrest to sentence from the current average of 142 days to 71. Initiatives to achieve this include the issue of a guide identifying issues that need to be considered in all areas to reduce delays in dealing with young offenders coming to court; consultancy support to assist in the implementation of the suggestions in the guide; organisation of joint professional development workshops for all youth justice stakeholders; and requiring each Youth Court User Group to create joint performance improvement plans. League tables showing which areas still need to make an improvement are to be published.

1   See Lord Warner *Tackling Delay in Youth Justice: A Practical Approach* (1999) 163 JP 42. See generally the Circular *Reducing Delay in Committing Youth Cases to the Crown Court* (Home Office, 10 May 2000).

Parents

1.25   This book is concerned with the law and procedure relating to youth justice. Inherent in that is the role and importance of parents. It has been noted earlier[1] that parents have a particularly important role in respect of responsibility for the young offender and the prevention of re-offending. Research shows that some 42% of young offenders who have a low or medium level of parental supervision had offended, a figure that reduces to 29% in respect of those who had benefited from high degrees of supervision. The quality of the relationship is also crucial in predicting whether or not a juvenile is likely to offend, and that parents who offend are twice as likely to have children who offend.[2]

1   See paras **1.7**, **1.8**.
2   See Card and Ward *Crime and Disorder Act 1998* (Jordans, 1998), para 3.31, citing *Young People and Crime* Home Office Research Study No 145 (1995).

1.26   It is in this context that various powers relating to parents should be noted:

–   s 34A of the Children and Young Persons Act 1933 empowers, and in some cases requires, a court to require the parent of a child or young person to attend (see para **3.20**);
–   s 55 of the Children and Young Persons Act 1933[1] imposes a duty on a court to order the payment of a fine, compensation or costs to be paid by the parent of the child or young person (see para **3.63**);
–   s 8 of the Crime and Disorder Act 1998 creates a Parenting Order.

Each of these is discussed at appropriate parts of the text.

1   See now Powers of Criminal Courts (Sentencing) Act 2000, s 137.

THE HUMAN RIGHTS CONTEXT

1.27   One of the most important contexts within which the youth justice system has to operate is that provided by the various international provisions relating to the rights of children and young persons. The European Convention on Human Rights is, of course, at the forefront of these, and is discussed below.[1] However, there are other relevant provisions. Amongst these are the United Nations Standard Minimum Rules for the Administration of Juvenile Justice (the Beijing Rules).[2] These provide, inter alia:

– that the age of criminal responsibility[3] shall not be fixed at too low an age, bearing in mind the facts in respect of emotional, mental and intellectual maturity;
– that a juvenile's privacy must be respected at all stages in order to avoid harm being caused to the juvenile by undue publicity or by the process of labelling;[4]
– that, in dealing with the juvenile the well-being of the juvenile shall be the guiding factor in the consideration of the case;[5] and
– that the reaction should be proportionate and restrictions on the personal liberty of the juvenile should be imposed to the minimum necessary.[6]

The United Nations Convention on the Rights of the Child[7] again requires the best interest of the child to be a primary consideration. Article 37(a) and (b) provides:

'(a) No child shall be subjected to torture or other cruel, inhuman or degrading treatment or punishment. Neither capital punishment nor life imprisonment without the possibility of release shall be imposed for offences committed by persons below eighteen years of age.[8]
(b) No child shall be deprived of his liberty unlawfully or arbitrarily. The arrest, detention or imprisonment of a child shall be in conformity with the law and shall be used as a measure of last resort and for the shortest appropriate period of time.'

Article 40 provides that a State must recognise the right of every child alleged to have, accused of having, or recognised as having infringed the penal law to be treated in a manner consistent with the promotion of the child's sense of dignity and worth, in a manner which reinforces the child's respect for the human rights and fundamental freedoms of others, which takes into account the child's age and the desirability of promoting re-integration and the child assuming a constructive role in society. In pursuance of this, Art 40 requires States to ensure that the privacy of the child is fully respected at all stages of the proceedings, and a State must ensure that appropriate laws, procedures, authorities and institutions are in place, including a minimum age of criminal responsibility and measures for dealing with children without resorting to judicial proceedings.

Finally, in the setting of this wider context, the terms of Art 14 of the International Covenant on Civil and Political Rights 1966 should be noted: Art 14(4) approximates to Art 6 of the European Convention on Human Rights,[9] and states that the procedure shall be such as will take into account their age, and the desirability of promoting their rehabilitation.[10]

---

1   See para **1.28–1.35**.
2   Adopted by General Assembly of UN, 29 November 1985.
3   See paras **2.1–2.2**.
4   For the general protection needed by the European Convention on Human Rights, see para **3.15**.
5   See paras **1.10–1.11**.
6   See para **1.37**.
7   See n 2, above.
8   See para **1.2**.
9   See para **1.35**.
10 See, further, para **1.11**.

European Convention on Human Rights and the Human Rights Act 1998

1.28 The United Kingdom is a signatory to the European Convention on Human Rights, being one of the ten original signatories to the Convention on 5 May 1949. The Convention came into force on 3 September 1953. The UK recognised rights of individual petition in 1966, but, until the Human Rights Act 1998 came into force on 2 October 2000, the Convention was not directly enforceable[1] in the domestic courts. It contains a variety of provisions directly relevant to the content, and use, of the criminal justice system as it applies to children and young persons. In particular, the provisions of Art 3 (the right not to be subject to inhuman or degrading treatment, or torture), Art 5 (the right to liberty and security of the person), Art 6 (the right to a fair trial) and Art 8 (respect for a person's private and family life) may each impact on aspects of the relevant powers, or their use. The Human Rights Act 1998 makes issues under the Convention directly relevant to any court.

---

1   This phrase should be read in context: the 1998 Act does not simply directly incorporate the Convention into English law, although that may be the effective result: see para **1.31**.

1.29 Section 2(1) of the HRA 1998 provides that a court or tribunal must have regard to the statements of the law emanating from the court and institutions of the Convention. The key words here are 'have regard', in that it will be open to the UK courts to adapt and develop the jurisprudence under the Convention to meet the particular needs of the domestic jurisdiction. It is safe to assume, however, that English courts will seek to apply the principles as closely as possible to the approach adopted by the European Court of Human Rights. To do otherwise would largely defeat the purpose of the passage of the HRA 1998, namely, to remove the need for complainants of breaches of the Convention to have to apply to the European Court of Human Rights outside the normal domestic jurisdiction.

A court or tribunal determining any question which has arisen under the Human Rights Act 1998, s 2(2) in connection with a Convention right must take into account any:

'(a) judgment, decision, declaration or advisory opinion of the European Court of Human Rights;
(b) opinion of the Commission given in a report adopted under Article 1 of the Convention;
(c) decision of the Commission in connection with Article 26 or 27(2) of the Convention; or
(d) decision of the Committee of Ministers taken under Article 46 of the Convention.'

1.30 Section 3(1) provides that an Act of Parliament or subordinate legislation, whenever enacted, must, *so far as it is possible to do so*, be read and given effect in a way which is compatible with Convention rights. This does not affect the validity, continuing operation and enforcement of any incompatible primary legislation, nor of any incompatible subordinate legislation if (disregarding any possibility of revocation) primary legislation prevents removal of the incompatibility (s 3(2)). In this context, it should be noted that there is a clear principle of statutory interpretation that Parliament intends to legislate in compliance with its international obligations.[1] In the context of legislation passed after the commencement of the HRA 1998, parliamentary intention will be easy to ascertain: s 19(1) of the 1998 Act states that a Minister in charge of a Bill in either House of Parliament must, before the Second Reading of the Bill:

'(a) make a statement to the effect that in his view the provisions of the Bill are compatible with the Convention rights ("a statement of compatibility"); or

(b) make a statement to the effect that although he is unable to make a statement of compatibility the Government nevertheless wishes the House to proceed with the Bill.

The statement must be in writing and be published in such manner as the Minister making it considers appropriate.'

As noted above, if a court in any proceedings determines that a provision is incompatible with a Convention right, it may make a statement of incompatibility. Such a power does not, however, extend to a youth court, magistrates' court, Crown Court, county court or family court.

---

1   *Saloman v Customs and Excise Commissioners* [1996] 3 All ER 871, CA.

1.31   The HRA 1998 does not specifically require a court to give effect to the Convention in developing the common law. This duty is, however, created more indirectly, by s 6, which states that it is unlawful for a public authority to act in a way which is incompatible with one or more of the Convention rights. The term 'public authority' includes a court or tribunal which exercises functions in relation to legal proceedings, and any person certain of whose functions are functions of a public nature. A court will not be acting unlawfully if (s 6(2)):

'(a) as the result of one or more provisions of primary legislation, the authority could not have acted differently; or

(b) in the case of one or more provisions of, or made under, primary legislation which cannot be read or given effect in a way which is compatible with the Convention rights, the authority was acting so as to give effect to or enforce those provisions.'

By s 7(1), a person who is a 'victim', who is able to claim that a public authority has acted, or proposes to act, in a way which is contrary to any of the rights contained in the Convention, may:

'(a) bring proceedings against the authority under this Act in the appropriate court or tribunal, or

(b) rely on the Convention right or rights concerned in any legal proceedings,'

The term 'victim' bears the same meaning as under Art 25 ('person, non-governmental organisation or groups of individuals claiming to be the victim of a violation'). A victim will be directly affected in some way.[1] A defendant in criminal proceedings will clearly be a victim. A party to a case who believes that a court decision or ruling is contrary to the Convention may make application to the court if the case is still before that court. Thus, if a matter of procedure or evidence is still before that court, the Convention right can be relied on in any submissions made on that matter. If a case has been concluded, an appeal can be based on the fact that the court deciding the case acted unlawfully, or the decision can be challenged by way of judicial review (s 7).

---

1   See *Hilton v United Kingdom* (1988) 57 D&R 108; *Klass v Federal Republic of Germany* (1979–1980) 2 EHRR 214.

1.32   It will be clear from the above that until the 1998 Act took effect, a claim or application *directly* seeking to rely on a Convention right was likely to fail. In *R v Secretary of State for the Home Department, ex parte Brind*,[1] the House of Lords declined to impose a duty on the Home Secretary to have regard to the Convention in exercising a statutory discretion. More recent authority, since the enactment of the 1998 Act, has stressed that the Convention was not part of English law,[2] and, indeed, in *R v North West Lancashire Health Authority, ex parte Can*,[3] Buxton LJ observed that 'it is important to ensure that Convention rights are not asserted in inappropriate circumstances'.

It should not be concluded, however, that the Convention had no legal significance even prior to the coming into force of the HRA 1998. In *R v Khan (Sultan)*,[4] it was accepted that breach of Convention rights might be a relevant consideration in determining whether evidence should be excluded under s 78 of the Police and Criminal Evidence Act 1984. More recently, in *R v Secretary of State for the Home Department, ex parte Simms*,[5] a magistrate excluded evidence under s 78, being of the view that the admission of evidence of entrapment caused a breach of the fair trial provisions of Art 6 of the Convention. In allowing the appeal, the court did not deny the general proposition that the Convention was relevant, but doubted whether, on the facts, there was a breach of Art 6. Again, in *Nottingham City Council v Amin*,[6] the magistrates' court had excluded evidence on a charge of plying for hire with an unlicensed vehicle, contrary to Town Police Clauses Act 1847, s 39. This evidence was that of a police officer who had flagged-down the defendant's unmarked vehicle. This was considered to amount to entrapment, and contrary to Art 6 of the Convention for the Protection of Human Rights and Fundamental Freedoms. In allowing the appeal, the court, whilst noting the decision of the European Court of Human Rights in *Teixera de Castro v Portugal*,[7] did not consider it to be wholly applicable to English proceedings. In *Teixera de Castro*, the applicant complained that he had been deprived of a fair trial due to the conviction being based mainly on statements of two police officers who had incited the commission of that offence. The Court of Human Rights, in finding there to be a breach of Art 6, stated that, although admissibility of evidence is primarily a matter for regulation by national law, the role of the officers in this case had gone beyond that of undercover agents. They had instigated the offence, and there was nothing to suggest that without their intervention the applicant would have committed the offence. There was no evidence to suggest that the applicant was predisposed to commit the offence. By contrast, in *Ludi v Switzerland,*[8] there was such a predisposition, evidenced by the fact that there was pre-existing evidence. There was, on the facts, no breach of Art 6.

---

1   [1991] 1 All ER 720, HL. The House cited with approval the dicta of Lord Denning MR in
     R v Chief Immigration Officer, ex parte Bibi [1976] 3 All ER 843, CA. The case would, after 2
     October 2000, be decided differently: see HRA 1998, s 6(1).
2   See para **1.34**, n 2.
3   [1999] All ER (D), DC. See also *R v Legal Aid Board, ex parte W and Others* [2000] 2 FLR 154.
4   [1996] 3 WLR 162, HL.
5   [1999] All ER (D) 751, HL.
6   [1999] All ER (D) 1269, DC.
7   (1999) 28 EHRR 101.
8   A 238 (1992), cited by Cheney, Dickson, Fitzpatrick and Uglow, *Criminal Justice and the
     Human Rights Act 1998* (Jordans, 1999).

1.33   Of particular importance is the decision of the House of Lords in *R v Director of Public Prosecutions, ex parte Kebilene,*[1] where the defendants were seeking to challenge the decision of the DPP to consent to the institution of proceedings against them, under the Prevention of Terrorism (Temporary Provisions) Act 1989. Their challenge was based on the Convention for the Protection of Human Rights and Fundamental Freedoms and the enactment of the Human Rights Act 1998. At the conclusion of the adducing of evidence at trial, counsel for the applicants submitted that s 16A, under which these applicants had been prosecuted, was in conflict with Art 6(2) of the Convention. The applicants sought to rely on a legitimate expectation entertained by them that the Director will exercise his prosecutorial discretion in accordance with the Convention following enactment of the Human Rights Act 1998 and pending the bringing into force of its central provisions. Such expectation was said to derive from the ratification of the Convention by the UK; from enactment of the Human Rights Act 1998 and, in particular, s 22(4) of the 1998 Act. Section 7(1) of the 1998 Act provides, inter alia, that:

> 'A person who claims that a public authority[2] has acted (or proposes to act) in a way which is made unlawful by section 6(1)[3], may –
>
> (a)   bring proceedings against the authority under this Act in the appropriate court or tribunal, or
> (b)   rely on the Convention right or rights concerned in any legal proceedings,
>
> but only if he is (or would be) a victim[4] of the unlawful act.'

Further, s 22(4) states that:

> 'Paragraph (b) of subsection (1) of section 7 applies to proceedings brought by or at the instigation of a public authority whenever the act in question took place; but otherwise that subsection does not apply to an act taking place before the coming into force of that section.'[5]

The Divisional Court had held that the DPP had acted unlawfully in continuing to consent to the prosecutions under s 16A, because that provision infringed Art 6(2). This conclusion was reversed by the House of Lords.

The House of Lords, in dealing with the question of whether the DPP was duty bound to have regard to the Convention in determining whether to give his consent to proceedings under s 16A, recognised that, although the HRA 1998 was not in force, he had, in the exercise of his discretion, to direct himself properly.[6] In an earlier case,[7] Lord Hope had observed:

> 'If the respondent is to have an effective remedy against a decision [on extradition] which is flawed because the decision-maker has misdirected himself on the Convention which he himself says he took into account, it must surely be right to examine the substance of the argument.'

This dictum was approved. However, the submission that there was in this case a legitimate expectation that consent would not be granted was misconceived, as being contrary to the 1998 Act.

The House then turned to the substantive issue. It concluded that the decision of the DPP as to whether to consent to prosecution was not amenable to judicial review, because of the effect of s 29(3) of the Supreme Court Act 1980.[8] Now the 1998 Act is in force, such a matter relating to the Convention would be dealt with in the trial process or on appeal, not on judicial review. In any event, it was by no means clear that s 16A of the 1989 Act infringed Art 6 of the Convention; even if it might be argued that it was clear, by the time of any appeal against any conviction that might arise on trial, the HRA 1998 would be in force and it would be possible to apply s 3 of the 1998 Act. Section 3(1) requires a court, when considering legislation, to construe it in a way compatible with Convention rights, so far as it is possible to do so. For these reasons the application for judicial review failed, the appeal being allowed.

---

1   [1999] 4 All ER 801, HL.
2   By 1998 Act, s 6(3) 'public authority' includes: (a) a court or tribunal, and (b) any person certain of whose functions are functions of a public nature.
3   Section 6(1) states: 'It is unlawful for a public authority to act in a way which is incompatible with a Convention right.'
4   By 1998 Act, s 7(7), a person is a victim of an unlawful act only if he would be a victim for the purposes of Art 34 of the Convention if proceedings were brought in the European Court of Human Rights in respect of that Act.
5   2 October 2000.
6   See Lord Steyn at [1999] 4 All ER at p 832e.
7   *R v Secretary of State for the Home Department, ex parte Launder* [1997] 3 All ER 961, at 989.
8   Because it related to matters relating to trial on indictment.

1.34 The Convention is therefore now a relevant consideration for a public body to take into account, and, on this basis, a case such as *R v Secretary of State for the Home Department, ex parte Brind*[1] may need to be reconsidered. Nevertheless, it could not be *directly* enforced until the date of commencement, and, further, regard should be had to the comments of the Law Lords in *R v Director of Public Prosecutions, ex parte Kebilene* that it is vitally important that the application of the 1998 Act in domestic law should take place in an orderly manner which recognises the desirability, in the criminal context, of challenges based on the Convention being made at trial or on appeal, not on judicial review.

---

1   See para **1.32**.

1.35   The Convention provides a significant context within which the youth justice system has to operate.

First, the Convention has already had an impact on the development of the law and procedure in criminal justice matters. One example is the treatment of life prisoners. An offender convicted of murder and who was aged under 18 at the time of the commission of the offence must be sentenced to be detained at Her Majesty's pleasure (1933 Act, s 53(1)).[1] In the light of *Hussain v United Kingdom; Singh v United Kingdom,*[2] the procedure for consideration of the cases of such offenders changed. That review is now in the form of an oral hearing at which prisoners are entitled to legal representation and to examine and cross-examine witnesses. Prisoners normally receive full disclosure of all relevant material. Section 28 of the Crime (Sentences) Act 1997 now provides that once an offender serving a term of detention has served the tariff period set by the Home Secretary, the Parole Board decides whether it is safe to release the offender on licence. In *Singh* and *Hussain,* the European Court of Human Rights held that a sentence of detention at Her Majesty's pleasure for convicted young persons could be justified only by considerations which centred on an assessment of the young offender's character and mental state and of his or her resulting danger to society, which had to take into account any developments of the young offender's personality and attitude as he or she grows older. The court considered that the sentence was imposed because of the presence of factors which were susceptible to change over time, namely the mental instability and dangerousness of the offender. Accordingly, it held that prisoners serving detention at Her Majesty's pleasure were entitled to take proceedings at reasonable intervals to have the legality of their detention decided by a court once the tariff periods for their offence had expired.

---

1   See para **6.1**.
2   (1996) 22 EHRR 1.

1.36   Secondly, the Convention is now a relevant consideration in all courts, including the youth court, although the youth court is not able to issue declarations of incompatibility under s 4 of the 1998 Act. Thus, this will apply in respect of any question of the interpretation of legislation, admission or exclusion of evidence or the making of any order or passing of any sentence.

1.37   Thirdly, there is clear evidence that the Convention will give rise to possible arguments in a wide variety of situations. One of the most fundamental is the question of trial of a child in an adult court.[1] In *T v United Kingdom,*[2] and *V v United Kingdom*[3] T and V each complained that their trial for murder in an adult court contravened the provisions of the Convention. The main submissions on the substantive issues were as follows:

– that the cumulative effect of the age of criminal responsibility, the accusatorial nature of the trial, the adult proceedings in a public courtroom, the length of the trial, the jury of 12 adult strangers, the physical lay-out of the courtroom, the presence of the media and public, the attacks by the public on the prison van which occurred and the disclosure of their identities together gave rise to a breach of Art 3 (inhuman or degrading treatment);
– that there was a breach of Art 6 (the 'fair trial' provision) in that the accused could not participate effectively in the conduct of their cases;
– that the age of criminal responsibility was contrary to the Convention;
– that the sentence of detention during Her Majesty's Pleasure contravened Art 3 and Art 5 (no deprivation of liberty except by due process);
– that the fixing of the tariff by the Home Secretary amounted to a breach of Art 6, in that it was not by an independent judicial authority;
– that there was no opportunity to have the continued lawfulness of the detention determined by a judicial body, contrary to Art 5.

The Court of Human Rights upheld the complaints of T and V, although not on all the grounds submitted, and summarised above.[4] In particular, the Court concluded that the nature of the proceedings against each of the accused was a breach of Art 6, in that the applicants were, in the context of a public hearing in the Crown Court, unable to participate effectively in the criminal proceedings. It also was of the view that the procedure for determining and reviewing the tariff for the length of the indeterminate sentence was unfair, and infringed both Art 5 and Art 6.

These decisions are of fundamental importance, in respect of many aspects of the treatment of children and young persons accused of crime. They are considered in more detail in various parts of this book[5] but throw up for discussion and possible change major questions as to how juveniles are dealt with by the criminal justice system.

The possible areas of challenge are many. Where real likelihood of a Convention argument arises, it is dealt with at the appropriate part of this text.[6] Amongst the possible area of challenge are the imprisonment of juveniles,[7] certain aspects of community orders[8] and anti-social behaviour orders.[9]

Inherent in the case-law of the Convention is the concept of proportionality. In essence, this means that a measure imposes no greater restriction on a Convention right than is absolutely necessary to achieve its objectives.[10] It is based on the philosophy that there should be a fair balance between the needs of the community and the requirement that the rights of the individual should be respected.[11] The interference with a right must correspond with a 'pressing social need' and be proportionate to the legitimate aim pursued.[12]

Proportionality will therefore impact across the range of powers dealt with in this book. Few, if any, of the current powers are likely to fall foul of the Convention, but much more open to challenge is their application. A disproportionate application, for example by the imposition of conditions or restrictions, or interference with liberty by such means as electronic tagging, or a sex offender order, will be potentially challengeable.

1   See paras **3.10** *et seq.*
2   (1998) 25 EHRR CD 11. For the English proceedings, see *R v Thompson and Venables.*
3   (1999) *The Times,* 17 December.
4   See paras **3.10** *et seq.*
5   For general discussion, see Cheney, Dickson, Fitzpatrick and Uglow *Criminal Justice and the Human Rights Act 1998* (Jordans, 1999).
6   See, in particular, paras **3.10** *et seq.*
7   See Chapter 6.
8   See Chapter 5.
9   See para **3.72**.
10   *Vogt v Germany* (1996) 21 EHRR 205.
11   *Soering v United Kingdom* (1989) 11 EHRR 439.
12   *Silver v United Kingdom* (1983) 5 EHRR 344.

Chapter 2

INVESTIGATION AND PRE-TRIAL POWERS

Doli Incapax – Police Powers – Arrest – Detention after Arrest – Access to Appropriate Adult and Legal Advice – Search – Intimate and Non Intimate Samples – Fingerprints – Detention – Remand – Bail – Cautioning, Reprimands and Final Warnings – Discretion to Prosecute – Detention Time-limits

THE CAPACITY OF A CHILD OR YOUNG PERSON TO COMMIT CRIME – *DOLI INCAPAX*

2.1 A child under the age of 10 years is irrebutably presumed to be *doli incapax*, ie incapable in law of committing a criminal offence. Until the commencement of s 34 of the Crime and Disorder Act 1998,[1] there was also a rebuttable presumption in respect of children aged 10 or over, but under the age of 14. At common law, it was presumed that such a child was incapable of committing an offence, unless evidence was adduced that the child knew that what was being done was seriously wrong.[2] Following widespread criticism of that presumption,[3] it was abolished by s 34, in respect of acts done on or after commencement.[4] The case-law on *doli incapax* therefore remains relevant, although that relevance will diminish with the passage of time.

At common law, it is presumed that the child is not criminally liable unless the child knew that the act the subject of the criminal charge was wrong. This is to be proved to the criminal standard of proof, by evidence which shows that the accused knew that the act was wrong as opposed to it being an act of naughtiness or mischief.[5] The proof of the doing of the act charged is not itself enough to prove guilty knowledge.[6] That guilty knowledge can be proved by what was said or done before or after the act. For example, running away might in some circumstances be probative, if indicative of guilt rather than fear of being told off for naughtiness. Circumstances surrounding the offence could prove guilty knowledge: in *A v DPP*,[7] the taking of the girl complainant to a remote place and evidence of an earlier assault and of threats were sufficient to prove guilty knowledge. The fact that the principal to an offence is *doli incapax* does not prevent others from being capable of being parties to that offence.[8] In *Graham v Director of Public Prosecutions*,[9] it was held that in order to rebut the presumption of *doli incapax* a youth court was entitled to allow the prosecution to adduce evidence of an internal disciplinary hearing involving the defendant which was held at school prior to the events that led to a charge of indecent assault. A submission that the evidence was prejudicial and lacked probative value was rejected. The dictum of Lord Lowry in *C v DPP*[10] that a child ought to be in no worse a position than an adult and therefore previous convictions ought not to be admitted unless admissible under a generally applicable principle was distinguished, on the grounds that evidence of such a hearing was not equivalent to a conviction.

---

1   30 September 1998.
2   *C v DPP* [1995] 2 All ER 43, HL.
3   Ibid; *JBH and JH (Minors) v O'Connell* (1981, unreported), DC.
4   1998 Act, s 34 and Sch 9.
5   *R v Gloria* (1919) 83 JP 136 ('very clear and compelling evidence'); *B v R* (1958) 44 Cr App R 1 ('the evidence to that effect must be clear and beyond all possibility of doubt').
6   *R v Smith* (1845) 1 Cox CC 260; *R v Kershaw* (1902) 18 LLR 357.
7   *Ward v DPP* (1995, unreported); *A v DPP* [1997] 1 Cr App R 27 (DC).
8   *A v DPP* (above).
9   (1997) 162 JP 62, DC.
10   [1995] 2 All ER 43, HL.

2.2   Except where the common law relating to *doli incapax* remains relevant, the criminal liability of the child will therefore be determined in accordance with the normal principles applicable to the specific offence, although clearly extreme youth, perhaps coupled with educational or emotional immaturity, may be relevant in determining questions relating to intent. Criticisms have been levelled at the age at which criminal liability begins.[1] The question therefore arises as to whether the current state of the law complies with the Convention for the Protection of Human Rights and Fundamental Freedoms, and whether the potential for successful challenge exists now the Human Rights Act 1998 is in force.[2] In the light of the judgment of the Court of Human Rights in *T v United Kingdom; V v United Kingdom*[3] challenge to the minimum age of criminal responsibility is unlikely to succeed in the foreseeable future. T and V in those cases each argued that the age of responsibility in England and Wales was low compared with almost all European countries.[4] The trend internationally towards a higher age of criminal responsibility was noted.[5] The Court, in rejecting the submission that the age of criminal responsibility, taken cumulatively with the other factors relating to the form and conduct of the trial, amounted to a breach of Art 3 of the Convention ('inhuman or degrading treatment or torture'), observed that in determining that matter the Court had regard to the standards prevailing among the member States of the Council of Europe[4] and did not consider that there was any clear common standard amongst those member States. Even if the threshold of the age of 10 applicable in England and Wales was low, it could not be said to be so disproportionate from the minimum age limit adopted by other member States. It did not, of itself, give rise to a breach of Art 3. However, age, coupled with issues relating to the fairness of the trial, may give rise to wider issues. The procedures, substantive law and orders of the court must be appropriate to the age of the child or young person. In particular, the application of adult modes of trial, or adult procedures, in respect of offences which should be tried on indictment in the Crown Court[6] will almost inevitably lead to a breach of Art 6 of the Convention. This is discussed later.[7]

1   See *Family Policy Studies Centre Briefing Paper No 3*, 1998.
2   2 October 2000.
3   See para **1.37**.
4   The age of criminal responsibility is 7 in Cyprus, Ireland, Switzerland and Liechtenstein; 8
     in Scotland; 13 in France; 14 in Germany, Austria, Italy and some Eastern European
     countries; 15 in Scandinavian countries; 16 in Portugal, Poland and Andorra, and 18 in
     Spain, Belgium and Luxembourg.
5   See Beijing Rules, Art 4, para **1.27**.
6   See para **3.1**.
7   See para **3.12**.

POLICE POWERS

2.3   General police powers apply equally to children and young persons as they do to adults. Thus a police officer has the same power to stop and search a suspect, to arrest a suspect and to search, irrespective of whether the suspect is an adult, child or young person. Nevertheless, the age of the suspect may be a relevant factor to take into account in determining whether powers that in fact exist should be exercised. Further, the law gives special protections to children, young persons and other vulnerable persons. The scope and exercise of these powers must in each case be considered in the context of the Convention issues that may arise in the light of the Human Rights Act 1998, bearing in mind that the question in each case is whether the Convention rights of the individual have been infringed. Inherent in any Convention issue is the fact that it is, in the context of any qualified right, important to recognise the Convention as a living instrument, and that it is, for the most part, legitimate to take account of the standards prevailing in the member States of the Council of Europe.[1] Where a right is qualified the court will need to consider the balance between the right and any practical limitation or potential limitation of that right. However, there is, in our context, an important limitation. It is clear from the decisions of the European Court of Human Rights in *T v United Kingdom; V v United Kingdom*[2] that a court will have to consider not only whether the processes, procedures and actions to which the child or young person were subject were those prescribed by law, or by the relevant Code of Practice, but also whether their exercise in the particular case was appropriate, and in a way that was appropriate, to the particular suspect.

Issues may arise under several of the Convention Articles. Article 3 protects against inhuman or degrading treatment or torture.[3] Any physical force against an individual which has not been made strictly necessary by his or her own conduct is likely to amount to a breach of Art 3. The length or conditions of detention, the persons with whom the juvenile is detained or kept and the clothing required to be worn may all provide the basis for possible challenge under Art 3. Detention, and interference with liberty, must be justifiable under Art 5. Claims may be made that the detention, or restrictions on liberty, interfere with the private and family life of the individual and thus potentially infringe Art 8. The availability of legal advice, the ability to utilise it, and to maintain the right not to self-incriminate are all real issues in the context of the fair trial provisions of Art 6.

---

1   *Soering v United Kingdom* (1989) 11 EHRR 439, ECHR; *Dudgeon v United Kingdom* (1981) 5 EHRR 573, ECHR; *X, Y and Z v United Kingdom* (1997) 24 EHRR 143, ECHR.
2   See paras **1.37**, **2.2** and **3.12**.
3   For the meaning of these phrases, see *Ireland v United Kingdom* (1979–1980) 2 EHRR 25, ECHR.

Arrest or detention?

2.4 Powers of arrest exist, either at common law[1] under the Police and Criminal Evidence Act 1984 (PACE 1984),[2] or under specific other statutory provision. It should be noted that the power of arrest exists in order to commence the criminal process. If that is not the purpose for which the power of arrest is in fact used, the arrest will be unlawful. Thus in *R v Brewin*[3] an arrest was held to be unlawful where it was made in order to take the arrested person to his parent to be dealt with. This situation should be distinguished from that where specific authority for similar action is granted by statute. For example, s 16 of the Crime and Disorder Act 1998 provides that, when a direction has been given by a local authority under s 16(2) of the 1988 Act, a police officer may remove a juvenile of compulsory school age whom he has cause to believe to be absent from a school without lawful authority to designated premises or to the juvenile's school. Again, by s 15(3) of the 1998 Act, a police officer who has reasonable cause to believe that a child is in contravention of a ban imposed by a curfew order made under s 14 of that Act may remove the child to the child's place of residence unless he has reasonable cause to believe that the child would, if removed to that place, be likely to suffer significant harm. A final example is s 46 of the Children Act 1989, which provides that where a constable has reasonable grounds to believe that a child would otherwise be likely to suffer significant harm, he may:

'(a)   remove the child to suitable accommodation and keep him there; or
(b)   take such steps as are reasonable to ensure that the child's removal from any hospital, or other place, in which he is then being accommodated is prevented.'

These are not, in the context of the discussion about powers and consequences that follow, to be regarded as powers of arrest.

Code C (the Code of Practice for the Detention, Treatment and Questioning of Persons by Police Officers), made pursuant to s 66, applies in respect of statutory powers[4] of arrest, detention, treatment, questioning, search and seizure, and failure to comply with it will be relevant to any question to be determined in any proceedings (PACE 1984, s 67(11)).[5] It refers to 'juveniles' and for that reason that term is used in this part of the book.[6] Although no statutory restriction exists as to where a juvenile can be arrested, it is preferable that a juvenile is not arrested at his place of education unless this is unavoidable.[7] Where a juvenile is arrested at his place of education, the principal of the school or college (or his nominee) must be informed.[8]

---

1   To prevent the continuance of a breach of the peace, or the occurrence of such a breach which is imminent. See *R v Howell (Errol)* [1981] 3 All ER 383, CA. The use of this power must be reasonable: *Redmond-Bate v DPP* [1999] Crim LR 998, DC. The power to bind over an individual to be of good behaviour may be open to challenge on the grounds of breadth and vagueness. In *Steel and Others v United Kingdom* (1999) 28 EHRR 603, ECHR, the European Court of Human Rights described such orders as 'particularly imprecise and offered little guidance to the persons bound over as to the type of conduct which would amount to a breach of the order' (at p 641). The particular orders under challenge in that case complied with Art 5(1) of the Convention because in each case there had been a finding of a breach of the peace, and the conduct being restrained by the order was sufficiently clear. It is clear from the decision that the use of the power must be proportionate to the conduct giving rise to the application or use of the power.
2   See PACE 1984, s 24. See also Criminal Justice and Public Order Act 1994, s 137; Children and Young Persons Act 1969, s 23A (power to arrest young offenders who are in breach of remand conditions).
3   [1976] Crim LR 742, CA.
4   Although the terms of PACE 1984, s 66, confine the role of the Codes to the use of statutory powers, arguably they should be applied in all circumstances where powers are being used.
5   See para **3.61**.
6   See para **2.7**.
7   Code C, Note for Guidance 11C.
8   Ibid.

Detention after arrest

2.5   On arrest, the juvenile will be detained in accordance with normal principles, and subject to the normal rules relating to how an arrest is effected, and to the requirement for the statement, as soon as practicable, of the fact and the reasons for arrest, even if those reasons are obvious (PACE 1984, s 28).[1] The juvenile must be cautioned.[2] The arrested person should be taken to the police station as soon as practicable after arrest (PACE 1984, s 30). Section 30(10) does permit an officer to delay taking to the police station a person who has been arrested if the presence of that person elsewhere is necessary in order to carry out such investigations as is reasonable to carry out immediately, such as the recovery of discarded evidence or the immediate verification of an explanation or possible identification.[3] This power should be used with extreme caution in respect of juvenile offenders, given that Code C provides specific and additional safeguards for juveniles and vulnerable suspects. In *R v Keane*,[4] the court observed that the youth of the suspect might be a relevant factor in determining whether the failure to take the suspect to the police station immediately, under s 30, had an adverse affect on the fairness of the proceedings. Arguably, one use of the s 30(10) power might be to take the juvenile from the place of arrest to his home, to make contact with parent or guardian prior to detention at the police station. That might be stretching the meaning of 'carrying out such investigations ...' but one which might be an appropriate use of the statutory power if the effect of it was to enhance, and not detract from, the protections given to the suspect by Code C.

1   The arrest is unlawful until the grounds of arrest are given: *Lewis v Chief Constable of the South Wales Constabulary* [1991] 1 All ER 206, QBD. If it is not practicable to state reasons at the time of arrest they must be stated as soon as practicable thereafter: PACE 1984, s 28(5). If they are not, the arrest becomes unlawful from the time when it was so practicable but the failure occurred: *DPP v Hawkins* [1988] 1 WLR 1116, DC.
2   Code C, para 10.1. The caution is in the following terms: 'You do not have to say anything. But it may harm your defence if you do not mention when questioned something which you later rely on in court. Anything you do say may be given in evidence'.
3   For the relevant principles, see *McCarrick v Oxford* [1982] Crim LR 750, DC; *R v Keane* [1992] Crim LR 306, CA; *R v Khan* [1993] Crim LR 54, CA.
4   [1992] Crim LR 306, CA.

2.6   If a person is reasonably suspected of having committed an offence he must be cautioned before he may be asked questions about it. If that suspicion is created by answers to previous questions, the suspect must be cautioned before questioning continues. These principles apply in respect of questioning regarding his involvement, or suspected involvement, in that offence, if his answers (or failure to answer or answer satisfactorily) may be given in evidence in court. He therefore need not be cautioned if questions are put for other purposes, for example, solely to establish his identify or his ownership of any vehicle or to obtain information in accordance with any relevant statutory requirement (see para 10.5C) or in furtherance of the proper and effective conduct of a search (eg to determine the need to search in the exercise of powers of stop and search or to seek co-operation whilst carrying out a search) or to seek verification of a written record of interview.

2.7   The general provisions of Code C of the PACE 1984 Codes apply equally to juveniles as they do to adults. For this purpose, a juvenile is defined by Code C as a person under 17 years of age which, of course, differs from the definition of 'juvenile' for other purposes. If the suspect appears to be under the age of 17 then he must be treated as a juvenile for the purposes of Code C in the absence of clear evidence to show that he is older. The protections of Code C relating to juveniles do not apply to those aged 17, who are technically young persons, unless they appear to be under 17. Thus, for the purposes of Code C, 17-year-olds are to be treated as adults. These propositions must, however, be considered subject to the provisions of Code C, para 1.4: if an officer has any suspicion, or is told in good faith, that a person of any age may be mentally disordered or mentally handicapped,[1] or mentally incapable of understanding the significance of questions put to him or his replies, then that person shall be treated as a mentally disordered or mentally handicapped person for the purposes of Code C. There might be circumstances where, because of youth and intellectual or emotional immaturity, the suspect has the mental inability identified in Code C, para 1.4. In those circumstances, the suspect falls to be treated as a mentally handicapped person.

1   By Code C, Note for Guidance 1G, 'mental disorder' is defined in s 1(2) of the Mental Health Act 1983 as 'mental illness, arrested or incomplete development of mind, psychopathic disorder and any other disorder or disability of mind'. It should be noted that 'mental disorder' is different from 'mental handicap' although the two are dealt with similarly throughout Code C. Where the custody officer has any doubt as to the mental state or capacity of a person detained, an appropriate adult should be called. For definition of 'appropriate adult' see para **2.12**.

2.8   Code C applies to people who are in custody at police stations in England and Wales whether or not they have been arrested for an offence.[1] By para 1.1, all persons in custody[2] must be dealt with expeditiously, and released as soon as the need for detention has ceased to apply. A custody officer is required to perform the functions specified in Code C as soon as is practicable (para 1.1A) but will not be in breach of the Code in the event of delay provided that the delay is justifiable and that every reasonable step is taken to prevent unnecessary delay. A record of any delay should be noted on the custody record. Those juveniles at the police station who are there voluntarily to give a statement should be treated as if they were in custody.[3]

1   And to those who have been removed to a police station as a place of safety under ss 135 and 136 of the Mental Health Act 1983. Section 15 (reviews and extensions of detention) applies solely to people in police detention, for example those who have been brought to a police station under arrest for an offence or have been arrested at a police station for an offence after attending there voluntarily.
2   Although certain sections of Code C (eg section 9 – treatment of detained persons) apply specifically to people in custody at police stations, those there voluntarily to assist with an investigation should be treated with no less consideration (eg offered refreshments at appropriate times) and enjoy an absolute right to obtain legal advice or communicate with anyone outside the police station.
3   This raises problems in the context of when a juvenile may be questioned in the absence of an appropriate adult: see para **2.12**.

Summary of relevant provisions of Code C

2.9   Once at the police station the following provisions of Code C should specifically be noted.

PACE 1984

Opening of custody record.	Code C, para 2.1
All information which has to be recorded must be so recorded as soon as practicable.	
Medical treatment to be sought if needed at any stage.	Code C, para 9.2
Suspect to be informed of right:	Code C, para 3.1

(a) to have someone informed of fact of arrest;
(b) the right to consult with a solicitor free of charge.

PACE 1984

Should not be delayed until appropropriate adult
arrives.

Custody officer must if practicable, ascertain person   Code C, para 3.7
responsible for welfare of juvenile, and inform that
person of arrest, grounds of arrest and place of
detention.

Appropriate adult to be similarly informed and asked   Code C, para 3.9
to attend police station.

Custody officer must contact supervising officer of any   Code C, para 3.8
juvenile known to be subject to a supervision order.

Search of person and property.   Code C, para 4.1

Interview, if any, in accordance with Code C in   Code C, para 11
presence of appropriate adult, and, if requested,
solicitor.

Review of detention.   Code C, para 15

The effect of breach of any of the provisions of Code C is discussed at para **3.61**.

Information about arrest to be given to certain persons

2.10   Of fundamental importance are the provisions which require the police
to inform the person responsible for the welfare of the juvenile of the fact of
arrest of the juvenile, and the obligation to contact the 'appropriate adult'. At
the outset, the custody officer is under a duty to inform certain persons of
information about the arrest. In the case of a juvenile, the custody officer must,
if it is practicable, ascertain the identity of a person responsible for the
juvenile's welfare (Code C, para 3.7). That person may be his or her parent or
guardian (or, if he or she is in care, the care authority or voluntary organisation,
or any other person who has, for the time being, assumed responsibility for his
welfare). Often, but not always, that person will also be the 'appropriate adult'.
The person identified as responsible for the welfare of the juvenile person must
be informed as soon as practicable that the juvenile has been arrested, why he
has been arrested and where he is detained. This right is in addition to the
juvenile's right in Code C, para 5, not to be held incommunicado (ie to have

another person informed of his presence at the police station).[1] Further, in the case of a juvenile who is known to be subject to a supervision order, reasonable steps must also be taken to notify the person supervising him (Code C, Note 3C). If the juvenile is in the care of a local authority or voluntary organisation but is living with his parents or other adults responsible for his welfare, although there is no legal obligation on the police to inform them, the parents as well as the authority or organisation should normally be contacted unless suspected of involvement in the offence concerned. Even if a juvenile in care is not living with his parents, consideration should be given to informing them as well. In none of these matters does the juvenile have a veto. These are obligations placed on the police, although no doubt the police might, and possibly should, have regard to the wishes of the juvenile if the parents are not persons whom they are obliged to inform.

---

1   See para **2.11**.

2.11   Any person arrested and held in custody at a police station or other premises may *on request* have one person known to him or who is likely to take an interest in his welfare informed at public expense of his whereabouts as soon as practicable. This right applies equally to a juvenile as it does to an adult, and, as noted above, is independent of the obligation that Code C places on the police. If the nominated person cannot be contacted, the person who has made the request may choose up to two alternatives. If they too cannot be contacted, the person in charge of detention or of the investigation has discretion to allow further attempts until the information has been conveyed.[1]

There appears to be no veto in the hands of the police to prevent contact which they consider to be undesirable, or contrary to the welfare or best interests of the juvenile. However, before any letter or message is sent, or telephone call made, the person must be informed that what he says in any letter, call or message (other than in the case of a communication to a solicitor) may be read or listened to as appropriate and may be given in evidence.[2] There is therefore no reason to prevent the police passing appropriate information to the person who is responsible for the welfare of the juvenile, or his or her supervisor. A telephone call may also be terminated if it is being abused. The costs can be at public expense at the discretion of the custody officer.

A potential Convention issue may arise, in that in any or all of the circumstances set out above there may prima facie be a breach of Art 8 of the Convention. Article 8 protects the right to respect for private and family life, home and correspondence. Any interference with, or monitoring of, conversations, telephone calls or correspondence amounts to a breach of Art 8(1).[3] The onus will then fall, under Art 8(2), upon the public authority to demonstrate the fact that the interference with the right was both necessary and proportionate to the objective of the interests of national security, public safety or the economic well-being of the country, for the protection of disorder or crime, for the protection of health or morals, or for the protection of the rights and freedoms of others (Art 8(2)). Monitoring to prevent escape, to prevent harm to the juvenile or to others, or to prevent an investigation being frustrated or evidence destroyed are all legitimate aims, and unlikely to be easily challengeable. The same could not be said in respect of any monitoring of correspondence or communication between a juvenile and legal adviser, which would raise issues not only under Art 8 but also under the fair trial provisions of Art 6: access to legal advice is not only recognised as a fundamental right in England and Wales[4] but also under the Convention.[5]

---

1   See Code C, Notes for Guidance 5C and 5D.
2   See Code C, para 5.7.
3   For support for this approach see, eg, *ADT v United Kingdom* [2000] 2 FLR 697, ECHR; *Halford v United Kingdom* (1997) 24 EHRR 523, ECHR; *Scott v United Kingdom* [2000] 1 FLR 958, ECHR.
4   *R v Samuel (Cornelius Joseph)* (1998) 87 Cr App R 232, CA: see also note 1 to para **2.19**.
5   *Benham v United Kingdom* (1996) 22 EHRR 293, ECHR.

Appropriate adult

2.12   In addition to the above, an 'appropriate adult' must be contacted. The purpose of the appropriate adult is to ensure that the interests and well-being of the juvenile are looked after. The term 'appropriate adult' is defined by Code C, para 1.7 as:

(a)   in the case of a juvenile:

   (i)   his parent or guardian (or, if he is in care, the care authority or voluntary organisation. The term 'in care' is used in Code C to cover all cases in which a juvenile is 'looked after' by a local authority under the terms of the Children Act 1989);
   (ii) a social worker;
   (iii) failing either of the above, another responsible adult aged 18 or over who is not a police officer or employed by the police;

(b)   in the case of a person who is mentally disordered or mentally handicapped:

   (i)   a relative, guardian or other person responsible for his care or custody;
   (ii) someone who has experience of dealing with mentally disordered or mentally handicapped people but is not a police officer or employed by the police (such as an approved social worker as defined by the Mental Health Act 1983 or a specialist social worker); or
   (iii) failing either of the above, some other responsible adult aged 18 or over who is not a police officer or employed by the police.

Two points should be noted at the outset. First, whilst the police are only under an obligation to seek *an* appropriate adult, frequently it may be best to ask both parents to attend, assuming that it is the parents who are responsible for the welfare of the juvenile. Secondly, the person who is responsible for the welfare of the juvenile can act also as the appropriate adult, although, as noted below, it might not always be acceptable for them to do so.

A person, including a parent or guardian, should not be an appropriate adult if he is suspected of involvement in the offence in question, is the victim, is a witness, is involved in the investigation or has received admissions prior to attending to act as the appropriate adult. If the parent of a juvenile is estranged from the juvenile, he should not be asked to act as the appropriate adult if the juvenile expressly and specifically objects to his presence. In *R v Jefferson (Andrew Steven)*,[1] the father of K, who was aged 15 when he was interviewed twice by the police about his part in public order offences, intervened robustly from time to time, sometimes joining in the questioning of his son and challenging his exculpatory account of certain incidents. On one occasion, in the first interview, he actually contradicted K. On appeal, K submitted, inter alia, that the father was inappropriate to play the role of the appropriate adult. The court considered but distinguished two earlier cases. The first was *DPP v Blake*,[2] where the court held that the estranged father of a juvenile, whom the juvenile did not wish to attend her interview, was not an appropriate adult, because it put at risk the object of Note 13C of the Code, of ensuring a fair interview and of assisting if necessary. The second was *R v Morse*.[3] In that case the judge observed that the father of the juvenile was of such low intelligence that he could not have fulfilled the role of advising the juvenile. By contrast, in *R v Jefferson*, K's father was not estranged, or unwanted at the interview, nor was he unable to perform the role. The fact that he was at times a critical observer and participant did not prevent him from fulfilling any of the three functions, namely of advising, observing that the interviews were fairly conducted and making sure that the police and the juvenile understood one another. He had no duty to protect his son from fair and proper questioning, for example by advising him to remain silent or by refraining to intervene to encourage him to be truthful, and thus the appeal against conviction was dismissed.

Encouragement by an appropriate adult of a juvenile who is being fairly interviewed to tell the truth should not normally be stigmatised as a failure of the adult to fulfil his duty to 'advise' the juvenile. In *R v W and Another*,[4] the mother of the juvenile was mentally handicapped within the meaning of s 77(3) of PACE 1984, and it was argued that she was not, for that reason, capable of acting as an appropriate adult. In dismissing an appeal against conviction that there was no breach of the Code, the trial judge observed that 'there was nothing to alert a busy custody officer that there was anything wrong with the mother'. This was a misdirection because it was for the court, not for the police, to ultimately decide whether the mother was an appropriate adult. This the judge had in fact done. Whilst she was herself psychotic and therefore suffering some intellectual deficit, her paranoid delusions were confined to her neighbours and her thought processes were rational in discussing her family. She was quite capable of dealing rationally with current events. Even if the judge had concluded otherwise, the court considered that the interview had been fairly and properly conducted, was not overlong and W had not been put under pressure. If there had, in fact, been a breach of the Code, the record of the interview would not have been excluded: there was no unfairness to the proceedings to justify exclusion under s 78.[5]

1   [1994] 1 All ER 270, CA.
2   [1989] 1 WLR 432, DC.
3   [1991] Crim LR 195, CC.
4   [1994] Crim LR 130, CA.
5   See para **3.61**.

2.13 A suspect should not generally be interviewed except, in accordance with Code C, at the police station and in the presence of the appropriate adult. However, a juvenile may make an admission in other circumstances. If a juvenile admits an offence to or in the presence of a social worker other than during the time that the social worker is acting as the appropriate adult for that juvenile, another social worker should be the appropriate adult in the interest of fairness.[1]

In the case of people who are mentally disordered or mentally handicapped, it may in certain circumstances be more satisfactory for all concerned if the appropriate adult is someone who has experience or training in their care rather than a relative lacking such qualifications. But if the person himself prefers a relative to a better qualified stranger or objects to a particular person as the appropriate adult, his wishes should, if practicable, be respected.[2]

1   Code C, Notes for Guidance 1D.
2   Code C, Notes for Guidance 1E.

2.14 A solicitor or lay visitor who is present at the police station in that capacity may not act as the appropriate adult. Further, a suspect should always be given an opportunity, when an appropriate adult is called to the police station, to consult privately with a solicitor in the absence of the appropriate adult if they wish to do so. It may generally be in the interests of the juvenile, and of the solicitor, to ensure that instructions and advice are in fact given in the absence of an appropriate adult. The reasons for this are that legal professional privilege will not extend to others who are present, unless the view is taken that any communication between solicitor and client which fulfils the criteria for legal professional privilege is protected from disclosure irrespective of the role of the person who is present. Whilst social workers and others may benefit from obligations of confidence, they are not absolute, and will not, ultimately, prevent a court from requiring questions to be answered.[1] Whether a court would conclude that it would be fair to so require is, of course, a very different question.

1   See *R v K (DT) (Evidence)* (1993) 97 Cr App R 342, CA; *R v Thompson* (1992) LEXIS, 4 June.

2.15 If the suspect is a juvenile, is mentally handicapped or appears to be suffering from a mental disorder, the custody officer must, as soon as practicable, inform the appropriate adult (who in the case of a juvenile may or may not be a person responsible for his welfare) of the grounds for his detention and his whereabouts, and ask that adult to come to the police station to see the suspect.[1]

---

1   Code C, para 3.9.

2.16   If the appropriate adult is already at the police station, then information about the juvenile's rights, and as to whether he wishes to request legal advice must be given to the juvenile in the presence of the appropriate adult. If the appropriate adult is not at the police station when that information is given to the suspect, then it must be given to the suspect again in the presence of the appropriate adult once that person arrives.[1]

---

1   Code C, para 3.11.

The role of the appropriate adult

2.17   The juvenile must be advised by the custody officer that the appropriate adult (where applicable) is there to assist and advise him and that he can consult privately with the appropriate adult at any time. Arguably, the right time for the juvenile to be told this is when the appropriate adult is present, not before he or she arrives.

If, having been informed of the right to legal advice, either the appropriate adult or the person detained wishes legal advice to be taken, then s 58 of PACE 1984 and Code C, para 6 apply. The juvenile is entitled to that legal advice, unless the limited circumstances in which a suspect can be denied access to legal advice apply.[1] It is extremely unlikely that in the case of a juvenile the grounds to deny access to a lawyer will exist, and doing so may create the potential for arguing that there is a breach of Art 6 of the Convention for the Protection of Human Rights and Fundamental Freedoms.[2] It is inherent in the special protection for juveniles in Code C that they are a vulnerable group of suspects. It could scarcely be in the best interests of a juvenile to deprive him or her of the protection that is fundamental to all suspects, and which is a basic right recognised by Art 6 of the European Convention on Human Rights. If the juvenile expresses a wish to receive legal advice before the appropriate adult arrives, the appropriate action should be taken straight away; it is not open to the police to delay action until such time as the appropriate adult arrives.

---

1   See PACE 1984, s 58(6).
2   See para **1.37**.

2.18   The purpose of Code C, para 3.13 is to protect the rights of a juvenile, mentally disordered or mentally handicapped person who may not understand the significance of what is being said to him. If such a person wishes to exercise the right to legal advice, the appropriate action should be taken straightaway and not delayed until the appropriate adult arrives. The provisions of paras 6.6 to 6.10 of Code C apply.

The right to legal advice

2.19   Subject to the provisos in s 58(6) of PACE 1984, and Annex B of Code C, all people in police detention must be informed that they may at any time consult and communicate privately, whether in person, in writing or by telephone, with a solicitor, and that independent legal advice is available free of charge from the duty solicitor. This right to legal advice is fundamental, and breach of it is likely (although not inevitably) to lead to exclusion of any confession evidence obtained while the police were in breach of this right.[1]

If, on being informed or reminded of the right to legal advice, the person declines to speak to a solicitor in person, the officer must point out that the right to legal advice includes the right to speak with a solicitor on the telephone and ask him if he wishes to do so.

---

1   See, eg, *R v Samuel (Cornelius Joseph)* (1988) 87 Cr App R 232, CA; *R v Walsh (Gerald Frederick)* (1991) 91 Cr App R 228, CA; *R v Oliphant* [1992] Crim LR 40, CA; *R v Dunford* (1990) 91 Cr App R 150, CA.

2.20   No police officer should at any time do or say anything with the intention of dissuading a person in detention from obtaining legal advice. Whenever legal advice is requested (and unless the limitations to access to legal advice apply), the custody officer must act without delay to secure the right (Code C, para 6.7).

2.21   Where a person has been permitted to consult a solicitor and the solicitor is available (ie present at the station or on his way to the station or easily contactable by telephone) at the time the interview begins or is in progress, the solicitor must be allowed to be present while he is interviewed. The solicitor may be required to leave the interview only if his conduct is such that the investigating officer is unable properly to put questions to the suspect.[1] If the person continues to waive his right to legal advice the officer must ask him the reasons for doing so, and any reasons shall be recorded on the custody record or the interview record as appropriate. Once it is clear that the juvenile neither wishes to speak to a solicitor in person nor by telephone, he should cease to be asked his reasons.

---

1   See Code C, Notes for Guidance 6D and 6E.

2.22   By Code C, para 6.6 a juvenile who wants legal advice may not be interviewed or continue to be interviewed until he has received it unless:

(a)   the restriction on access to legal advice applies; or
(b)   an officer of the rank of superintendent or above has reasonable grounds for believing that:

    (i)   delay will involve an immediate risk of harm to persons or serious loss of, or damage to, property; or
    (ii)   where a solicitor, including a duty solicitor, has been contacted and has agreed to attend, awaiting his arrival would cause unreasonable delay to the process of investigation; or

(c) the solicitor nominated by the person, or selected by him from a list:

    (i) cannot be contacted; or

    (ii) has previously indicated that he does not wish to be contacted; or

    (iii) having been contacted, has declined to attend.

In each of (i), (ii) or (iii) above the person must have been advised of the Duty Solicitor Scheme but has declined to ask for the duty solicitor, or the duty solicitor is unavailable. (In these circumstances, the interview may be started or continued without further delay provided that an officer of the rank of inspector or above has given agreement for the interview to proceed in those circumstances);

(d) the person who wanted legal advice changes his mind.

In these circumstances, the interview may be started or continued without further delay provided that the juvenile has given his agreement in writing[1] or on tape to being interviewed without receiving legal advice and that an officer of the rank of inspector or above, having inquired into the person's reasons for his change of mind, has given authority for the interview to proceed. Confirmation of the person's agreement, his change of mind, his reasons given and the name of the authorising officer must be recorded in the taped or written interview record at the beginning or recommencement of interview.[2]

---

1   For the necessity of the agreement of the appropriate adult, see para **2.13**.
2   See Code C, para 6.6.

2.23 A solicitor or appropriate adult must be permitted to consult the custody record of a person detained as soon as practicable after their arrival at the police station (Code C, para 2.4). When a person leaves police detention or is taken before a court, he or his legal representative or his appropriate adult must be supplied on request with a copy of the custody record as soon as practicable. This entitlement lasts for 12 months after his release.

The person who has been detained, the appropriate adult, or the legal representative is permitted to inspect the original custody record after the person has left police detention provided they give reasonable notice of their request (Code C, para 2.5).

2.24 If a solicitor arrives at the station to see a particular person, that person must (unless Annex B applies) be informed of the solicitor's arrival whether or not he is being interviewed and asked whether he would like to see him. This applies even if the person concerned has already declined legal advice or, having requested it, subsequently agreed to be interviewed without having received advice. The solicitor's attendance and the detained person's decision must be noted in the custody record.

Cautions

2.25 If a juvenile or a person who is mentally disordered or mentally handicapped is cautioned in the absence of the appropriate adult, the caution must be repeated in the adult's presence (Code C, para 10.6). Further, the juvenile must not be interviewed in the absence of the appropriate adult.

Interviews

2.26 Interviews are subject to significant regulation by Code C. For this purpose, an interview is the questioning of a person regarding his involvement or suspected involvement in a criminal offence or offences which, by virtue of para 10.1 of Code C, is required to be carried out under caution. Procedures undertaken pursuant to s 7 of the Road Traffic Act 1988 (provision of specimen for analysis) do not constitute an interview.

By Code 11.1, following a decision to arrest a suspect, he must not be interviewed about the relevant offence except at a police station or other authorised place of detention unless the consequent delay would be likely:

'(a)   to lead to interference with or harm to evidence connected with an offence or interference with or physical harm to other people; or

(b)   to lead to the alerting of other people suspected of having committed an offence but not yet arrested for it; or

(c)   to hinder the recovery of property obtained in consequence of the commission of an offence.'

Interviewing in any of these circumstances must cease once the relevant risk has been averted or the necessary questions have been put in order to attempt to avert that risk. Further, the juvenile must not be interviewed in the absence of the appropriate adult. A juvenile or a person who is mentally disordered or mentally handicapped, whether suspected or not, must not be interviewed or asked to provide or sign a written statement in the absence of the appropriate adult. Juveniles may be interviewed at their places of education only in exceptional circumstances and then only where the principal or his nominee agrees. Every effort should be made to notify both the parent(s) or other person responsible for the juvenile's welfare and the appropriate adult (if this is a different person) that the police want to interview the juvenile and reasonable time should be allowed to enable the appropriate adult to be present at the interview. Where waiting for the appropriate adult would cause unreasonable delay and unless the interviewee is suspected of an offence against the educational establishment, the principal of an educational establishment or his nominee can act as the appropriate adult for the purposes of the interview (Code C, para 11.15).

2.27 Except in the limited circumstances outlined earlier, interviews prior to arrival at the police station are not allowed. On the other hand, the investigator is entitled to ask questions designed to find out whether an offence has been committed. The crucial question is whether, pursuant to Code C, para 10.1, the questioning must be under caution. Paragraph 10.1 of Code C states:

'A person whom there are grounds to suspect of an offence must be cautioned before any questions about it (or further questions if it is his answers to previous questions which provide the grounds for suspicion) are put to him regarding his involvement or suspected involvement in that offence if his answers or his silence (ie failure or refusal to answer a question or to answer satisfactorily) may be given in evidence to a court in a prosecution. He therefore need not be cautioned if questions are put for other purposes, for example, solely to establish his identity or his ownership of any vehicle or to obtain information in accordance with any relevant statutory requirement ... or in furtherance of the proper and effective conduct of search, or in verification of a written record pursuant to Code C, para 11.13.'

The application of this principle is not always easy. The key test is whether the suspect is being asked to incriminate himself.[1] Spontaneous statements do not amount to interviews, but answers in response to questions may well be, and may turn what initially is not an interview into what amounts to an interview. Even questions designed to eliminate the suspect may on the particular facts amount to an interview.[2] In *R v Weekes (Trevor Dave)*,[3] the question arose as to whether an enquiry made of a 16-year-old had become an interview, and thus was required to be conducted in the presence of an appropriate adult. In allowing the appeal, the court considered that the essence of the matter was whether fairness demanded the implementation of the provisions of the Code. A distinction had to be drawn between an enquiry that an officer has to make on the spot, when he asks a suspect to account for his movements, and the more formal type of interview which should take place at the police station. Whether an interview or not, a key feature of the Code C provisions is that adequate records exist as to comments or responses made by suspects. It is for this reason that para 11.13 provides that a written record must be made of any comments made by a suspected person, including unsolicited comments, which are made outside the context of an interview but which might be relevant to the offence. That record must contain a note of the time, and be signed by the maker of the comment. Where practicable, the suspect must be given the opportunity to read that record and to either sign it as correct or to indicate the respects in which it is considered inaccurate. Any refusal to sign should likewise be recorded. It is implicit in this scheme relating to juveniles that this should be in the presence of the appropriate adult or solicitor.

These issues are also relevant where there is questioning by persons other than police officers, such as social workers, schoolteachers, or store detectives. Such persons are subject to the provisions of Code C if they are 'charged with the duty of investigation of offences or charging offenders ...' (PACE 1984, s 67(9)). Such persons may or may not fall within the ambit of s 67(10), depending on the particular factual circumstance, and it is not dependent upon a duty being imposed by law.[4] It may, on appropriate facts, include those such as store detectives,[5] but not, probably, a headteacher or other school-teacher. In *DPP v G*,[6] the court found that, in the context of PACE 1984, a headteacher was under no duty to investigate offences. Any duty to investigate was a duty to enquire into fact or incidents, not to investigate offences. Similar conclusions might be reached in respect of inquiries by social workers. The matter, however, does not end there, because Code C (and the other PACE 1984 Codes) are there to provide protections for, in this context, vulnerable suspects, and to ensure fair treatment.[7] Any attempt to conduct what amounts to an 'interview' may result in exclusion of any admissions made therein, pursuant to s 76 or s 78 of PACE 1984.[8]

1   *Batley v DPP* (1988) *The Times*, 5 March.
2   *R v Hunt* [1992] Crim LR 582, CA.
3   (1993) 97 Cr App R 222; See also *R v Fogah* [1989] Crim LR 141; *R v Maloney (Michael)*; *R v Doherty (Francis)* [1988] Crim LR 523.
4   *R v Bayliss (Roy)* (1994) 98 Cr App R 25.
5   *Joy v Federation against Copyright Theft Ltd* [1993] Crim LR 588, DC. See generally, *R v Twaites (Jacqueline Anne)* (1991) 92 Crim LR 106, CA, where commercial investigators were held to be persons charged with a duty to investigate offences for the purpose of s 67(10).
6   (1997) *The Times*, 24 November. See, for discussion thereof, Marston and Thompson 'PACE Codes of Practice and the investigation of incidents in schools' (1998) 10 *Education and the Law* 101 *et seq.*
7   *R v Smith* (1993) Cr App R 233, CA.
8   See para **3.61**.

2.28   Where the juvenile is a ward of court, the leave of the court is required prior to that juvenile being interviewed.[1]

1   *Practice Direction (Ward: Witness at Trial)* [1987] 1 WLR 1739.

2.29   Immediately prior to the commencement or recommencement of any interview at a police station or other authorised place of detention, the interviewing officer must remind the suspect of his entitlement to free legal advice and that the interview can be delayed for him to obtain legal advice (Code C, para 11.2). It is the responsibility of the interviewing officer to ensure that all such reminders are noted in the record of interview.

By Code C, para 11.2A, at the beginning of an interview carried out in a police station, the interviewing officer, after cautioning the suspect, must put to him any significant statement or silence which occurred before his arrival at the police station, and shall ask him whether he confirms or denies that earlier statement or silence and whether he wishes to add anything. A 'significant' statement or silence is one which appears capable of being used in evidence against the suspect, in particular a direct admission of guilt, or failure or refusal to answer a question or to answer it satisfactorily, which might give rise to an inference under Part III of the Criminal Justice and Public Order Act 1994.

2.30   The questions put in an interview must be appropriate to the age and emotional state of the juvenile. Questioning which is not appropriate runs the risk of being considered to be 'oppressive', and potentially problems of admissibility will be faced by those seeking to adduce any confession in court.[1] Further, questions which are likely to cause any statement to be unreliable may have a similar effect. These matters are dealt with in Chapter 3.[1]

1   See para **3.60**.

2.31   As soon as a police officer who is making enquiries of any person about an offence believes that a prosecution should be brought against him and that there is sufficient evidence for it to succeed, he should ask the person if he has anything further to say. If the person indicates that he has nothing more to say, the officer must without delay cease to question him about that offence.

2.32   The principle of proper recording has already been noted.[1] Adequate records have to be kept of any interview (Code C, para 11.5). An accurate record must be made of each interview with a person suspected of an offence, whether or not the interview takes place at a police station. The record must state the place of the interview, the time it begins and ends, the time the record is made (if different), any breaks in the interview and the names of all those present and must be made on the forms provided for this purpose or in the officer's pocket-book or in accordance with the code of practice for the tape-recording of police interviews with suspects (Code E). The record must be made during the course of the interview, unless in the investigating officer's view this would not be practicable or would interfere with the conduct of the interview, and must constitute either a verbatim record of what has been said or, failing this, an account of the interview which adequately and accurately summarises it.

---

1   See para **2.29**.

2.33   Where the appropriate adult is present at an interview, he should be informed that he is not expected to act simply as an observer and also that the purposes of his presence are, first, to advise the person being questioned and to observe whether or not the interview is being conducted properly and fairly, and secondly, to facilitate communication with the person being interviewed (Code C, para 11.16). It is important to bear in mind that, although juveniles are often capable of providing reliable evidence, they may, without knowing or wishing to do so, be particularly prone in certain circumstances to provide information which is unreliable, misleading or self-incriminating. Special care should therefore always be exercised in questioning such a person, and the appropriate adult should be involved, if there is any doubt about a person's age, mental state or capacity. Because of the risk of unreliable evidence, it is also important to obtain corroboration of any facts admitted whenever possible.

Frequency of interviews

2.34   By Code C, para 12.2, in any period of 24 hours, a detained juvenile must be allowed a continuous period of at least 8 hours for rest, free from questioning, travel or any interruption by police officers in connection with the investigation concerned. In the application of para 12.2, and the other provisions relating to welfare issues in respect of the juvenile, regard must be had to the age and maturity of that juvenile. It has already been noted[1] that the European Court of Human Rights in *T v United Kingdom; V v United Kingdom* had regard to whether a particular accused had received a fair trial. The same principle applies generally: the younger or more vulnerable the juvenile, the more important it will be that periods of questioning, rest and refreshment are appropriately structured. This period should normally be at night. The period of rest may not be interrupted or delayed, except at the request of the person, his appropriate adult or his legal representative, unless there are reasonable grounds for believing that it would:

(a) involve a risk of harm to persons or serious loss of, or damage to, property; or

(b) delay unnecessarily the person's release from custody; or

(c) otherwise prejudice the outcome of the investigation.

If a juvenile is arrested at a police station after going there voluntarily, the period of 24 hours runs from the time of his arrest and not the time of arrival at the police station. Any action which is required to be taken in accordance with para 8 of the Code (which deals with actions needing to be taken about conditions of detention), or in accordance with medical advice or at the request of the detained person, his appropriate adult or his legal representative, does not constitute an interruption to the rest period such that a fresh period must be allowed.

---

1   See para **3.15**.

2.35   By Code C, para 12.4, as far as practicable, interviews must take place in interview rooms which must be adequately heated, lit and ventilated. A juvenile being questioned or making statements must not be required to stand. Before the commencement of an interview, each interviewing officer must identify himself and other officers present by name and rank to the person being interviewed.

2.36   Code C, para 12.7 provides that breaks from interviewing must be made at recognised meal times. Short breaks for refreshment shall also be provided at intervals of approximately two hours, subject to the interviewing officer's discretion to delay a break if there are reasonable grounds for believing that it would:

(a) involve a risk of harm to people or serious loss of, or damage to, property;

(b) delay unnecessarily the person's release from custody; or

(c) otherwise prejudice the outcome of the investigation.

Searches

2.37   PACE 1984 contains various provisions applicable to search while in custody. It will be noted that the consent of the suspect is needed in many, although not all, situations. This is dealt with by para 1.11 of Code D, which governs the taking of samples. Paragraph 1.11 states that in the case of any procedure requiring a person's consent, the consent of parent or guardian of a juvenile is required as well as his own (unless he is aged under 14, in which case the consent of his parent or guardian is sufficient in its own right). The term 'appropriate adult' bears the same meaning as in respect of Code C.[1] Further, if information has to be given to the juvenile, it must be given or sought in the presence of the appropriate adult (para 1.13), and any procedure which requires the participation of the juvenile must take place in the presence of the appropriate adult (para 1.14).

1   See para **2.12**.

Intimate searches

2.38   Under s 55, an intimate search[1] may be undertaken only on the authority of an officer of at least the rank of superintendent, and then only when he has reasonable grounds for believing:

(a) that an arrested person in police detention may have concealed on him anything which he could use to cause physical injury to himself or others, and he might so use it whilst he is in police detention or in due custody of a court; or

(b) that such person may have a Class A drug[2] concealed on him and was in possession of it with the appropriate criminal intent before his arrest.

An intimate search may not be authorised unless the authorising officer has reasonable grounds for believing that the articles for which the search is being made cannot be found without an intimate search being carried out (PACE 1984, s 55(2)). The reasons why an intimate search is considered necessary must be explained to the person before the search takes place.

1   Defined by PACE 1984, s 118, as a search which consists of the physical examination of a person's body orifices other than the mouth.
2   'Class A drug' has the meaning given to it by the Misuse of Drugs Act 1971, s 2(1)(b). The list of substances which fall within Class A is a long one: for the full list, see Archbold, *Criminal Pleading, Evidence and Practice*, para 26.6.

2.39   An intimate search may be carried out only by a registered medical practitioner or registered nurse, unless an officer of at least the rank of superintendent considers that this is not practicable and the search is a search for concealed items of the type described in para (a) above. An intimate search for such items may take place only at a hospital, surgery, other medical premises or police station. An intimate search for Class A drugs may take place only at a hospital, surgery or other medical premises. An intimate search at a police station of a juvenile or a mentally disordered or mentally handicapped person may take place only in the presence of an appropriate adult of the same sex (unless the person specifically requests the presence of a particular adult of the opposite sex who is readily available). In the case of a juvenile, the search may take place in the absence of the appropriate adult only if the juvenile signifies in the presence of the appropriate adult that he prefers the search to be done in his absence and the appropriate adult agrees. A record must be made of the juvenile's decision and signed by the appropriate adult.

Where an intimate search for concealed items as described in para (a) above is carried out by a police officer, the officer must be of the same sex as the person searched. No person of the opposite sex who is not a medical practitioner or nurse must be present, nor shall anyone whose presence is unnecessary; but a minimum of two people, other than the person searched, must be present during the search. The search must be conducted with proper regard to the sensitivity and vulnerability of the person in these circumstances.

2.40   In the case of an intimate search, the custody officer must, as soon as practicable, record which parts of the person's body were searched, who carried out the search, who was present, the reasons for the search and its result. If an intimate search is carried out by a police officer, the reason why it was impracticable for a suitably qualified person to conduct it must be recorded.

Strip searches

2.41   A juvenile may also be subject to a strip search, defined by Annex A, para 9, as a search involving the removal of more than outer clothing. A strip search may take place only if it is considered necessary to remove an article which a person would not be allowed to keep, and the officer reasonably considers that the person might have concealed such an article. Strip searches must not be routinely carried out where there is no reason to consider that articles have been concealed.

Where such a search occurs, a police officer carrying out a strip search must be of the same sex as the person searched. The search must take place in an area where the person being searched cannot be seen by anyone who does not need to be present, nor by a member of the opposite sex (except an appropriate adult who has been specifically requested by the juvenile being searched) except in cases of urgency, where there is a risk of serious harm to the person detained or to others. Whenever a strip search involves exposure of intimate parts of the body, there must be at least two people present other than the person searched, one of whom must be the appropriate adult. Except in urgent cases as above, a search of a juvenile may take place in the absence of the appropriate adult only if the juvenile signifies in the presence of the appropriate adult that he prefers the search to be done in his absence and the appropriate adult agrees. A record must be made of the juvenile's decision and signed by the appropriate adult. The presence of more than two people, other than an appropriate adult, must be permitted only in the most exceptional circumstances. The search must be conducted with proper regard to the sensitivity and vulnerability of the person in these circumstances and every reasonable effort must be made to secure the person's co-operation and minimise embarrassment.

Suspects who are searched should not normally be required to have all their clothes removed at the same time, for example a boy must be allowed to put on his shirt before removing his trousers, and a girl must be allowed to put on her blouse and upper garments before further clothing is removed. Where necessary to assist the search, the person may be required to hold his or her arms in the air or to stand with is or her legs apart and to bend forward so that a visual examination may be made of the genital and anal areas provided that no physical contact is made with any body orifice. If, during a search, articles are found, the person shall be asked to hand them over. If articles are found within any body orifice other than the mouth, and the person refuses to hand them over, their removal would constitute an intimate search, which must be carried out in accordance with the provisions set out above. A strip search must be conducted as quickly as possible, and the person searched allowed to dress as soon as the procedure is complete. A record must be made on the custody record of a strip search including the reason it was considered necessary to undertake it, those present and any result.

In all these matters, care must be taken, in that grossly intrusive or humilitating procedures may fall foul of Art 3 of the Convention for the Protection of Human Rights and Fundamental Freedoms ('inhuman or degrading treatment'). For there to be a breach of Art 3 it is not necessary to demonstrate physical maltreatment. Conduct can be inhuman or degrading if it arouses in its victim feelings of fear, anguish and inferiority, capable of humiliating or debasing the victim and possibly breaking their physical or moral resistance.[1] The fact that a strip search is conducted might not of itself constitute a breach of Art 3, but its nature, intrusiveness, length, the persons present and the age of the juvenile will all be relevant factors to which a court will have to have regard, as will, indeed, the purpose of the search. If it were shown that the purpose was that of humiliation, a strong case arises for arguing that a breach of Art 3 has occurred.[2] The lack of such intent does not, however, negate completely such a claim.[3]

---

1   *Soering v United Kingdom* (1989) 11 EHRR 439; *Ireland v United Kingdom* (1978) 2 EHRR 25; *T v United Kingdom; V v United Kingdom* (1999) *The Times*, 17 December.
2   *Raninen v Finland* (1998) 26 EHRR 563.
3   *T v United Kingdom; V v United Kingdom* (1999) *The Times*, 17 December.

Intimate samples

2.42   By s 62(1) of PACE 1984, an intimate sample may be taken from a person in police detention only:

> '(a)   if a police officer of at least the rank of superintendent authorises it to be taken; and
> (b)   if the appropriate consent is given.'

By s 62(1A), an intimate sample may be taken from a person *not* in police detention if:

> '... in the course of the investigation of the offence, two or more non-intimate samples suitable for the same means of analysis have been taken which have proved insufficient –
>
> (a)   if a police officer of at least the rank of superintendent authorises it to be taken; and
> (b)   the appropriate consent is given.'[1]

Section 62(1A) requires the two non-intimate samples to have been given as part of the same investigation. It is not clear whether it has to be the same investigation as that for which the intimate sample is sought: they might have been sought for an unrelated offence. However, the use of the words 'an offence' gives some support to an argument that a completely different offence will suffice. However, it is probably more in accord with the scheme of PACE 1984 to relate it to an investigation in respect of the same offence or series of offences.

The sample must be suitable for the same means of analysis, and it will not be suitable if it is insufficient, a term defined by s 58(4) of the Criminal Justice and

Public Order Act 1994 as meaning insufficient (in point of quantity or quality) for the purpose of enabling information to be produced by means of analysis used or to be used in relation to the sample (ie the same scientific or forensic process).

---

1   As amended by the Criminal Justice and Public Order Act 1994.

Non-intimate samples

2.43   Non-intimate samples may be taken pursuant to s 63(3) of PACE 1984. That subsection allows the taking of a non-intimate sample where:

(a) the authorising officer has reasonable grounds for suspecting the involvement of the person from whom the sample is being sought in a recordable offence; and

(b) the authorising officer has reasonable grounds to believe that the sample will tend to confirm or disprove the involvement of the person from whom the sample is to be taken.

A non-intimate sample may also be taken in respect of a person:

(a) who has been charged with a recordable offence, or informed that he will be reported for such an offence; and

(b) who has not had a non-intimate sample taken from him in the course of the investigation of the offence by the police or who has had a non-intimate sample taken from him but either it was not suitable for the same means of analysis or, although so suitable, the sample proved insufficient.

This power, which does not require consent, does not cover situations where the police have no reasonable suspicion of involvement but wish to prove, or disprove, involvement.

A non-intimate sample may also be taken without consent from any person convicted of a recordable offence (PACE 1984, s 63(3B)).

Hair samples

2.44   Section 63A(2) permits samples of hair (other than pubic) to be taken, either:

> '... by cutting hairs or by plucking hairs with their roots so long as no more are plucked than the person taking the sample reasonably considers to be necessary for a sufficient sample.'

Attendance for the purposes of the taking of samples

2.45   By s 63A(4), a constable may, within the 'allowed period', require a person who is neither in police detention nor held in custody by the police on the authority of a court to attend at a police station in order to have a sample taken, provided the criteria in s 63A(4)(a) or (b) are satisfied. These are:

(a) a person is either charged with, reported for, or convicted of a reportable offence, and one of (b), (c) or (d) applies;

(b) no sample has been taken during the investigation for that offence; or

(c) the sample was not suitable for the same method of analysis; or

(d) the sample proved insufficient.

There is a power of arrest without warrant where a person fails to comply (s 63A(7)), but it should be noted that s 63A does not of itself confer any power to search or take a sample; that is governed by the normal substantive powers set out above. The 'allowed period' is defined by s 63A(5) as one month from the date of the charge or conviction, or from the date when the appropriate officer is informed of the fact that the sample is not so suitable or has proved insufficient. It should be noted that the period of one month is the period during which the demand may be made, not the period during which attendance must occur. That is dealt with by s 63A(6): the requirement must give a person at least seven days within which he must so attend, and may direct him to attend at a specified time of day or between specified times of day.

Testing persons in police detention for drugs

2.46   Section 48 of the Criminal Justice and Courts Services Act 2000 will, when in force, introduce a new power to test for the presence of Class A drugs. It does so by amending PACE 1984, by inserting into it a new s 63B and s 63C. As noted later, the power applies only to those aged at least 18 when the request for a sample is made. However, it is age at the date of request that is important, and nothing prevents an officer from making a request in respect of an individual who was a juvenile when the offence was allegedly committed, or who attains the age of 18 after arrest but before charge. The purpose of the provision is to ascertain the presence or otherwise of such drugs, so that those who are found to have committed drug offences, or drug-related offences, can be made the subject of a relevant order, such as a drug treatment and testing order under the 1998 Act,[1] or applications for bail can be informed by evidence of drug misuse where it exists.[2]

---

1   See para **5.103**. The relevant statutory provisions are ss 52 to 58 of the Powers of Criminal Courts (Sentencing) Act 2000.

2   See Criminal Justice and Courts Act 2000, s 49.

2.47   Section 63B of PACE 1984 will provide that a sample of urine or a non-intimate sample may be taken from a person in police detention for the purposes of ascertaining whether the detainee has any specified Class A drug in his body. There are three preconditions which must be satisfied.

The first is contained in s 63B(2). The person concerned:

'(a) must have been charged with a trigger offence (defined by Sch 5 to the Act)[1]; or

(b) must have been charged with an offence (of whatever kind, and irrespective of whether it is a "trigger offence") and a police officer of at least the rank of inspector has reasonable grounds to suspect that the misuse by that person of a Class A drug caused or contributed to the offence, and gives his authorisation for the taking of the sample.'

The second is that the person concerned has attained the age of 18 (s 63B(3)). Thus, the new power does not apply to juveniles, although the offence might well actually have been committed at a time when the detainee was in fact a juvenile.

The third is that a police officer must have requested the detainee to give the sample (s 63B(4)). This cannot accurately be described as requiring consent: failure without good cause to give a sample renders the individual liable to prosecution for a new offence created by s 63C.

---

1   'Trigger' offences are defined by Sch 5 as any of the following offences under the Theft Act 1968: s 1 (theft); s 8 (robbery); s 9 (burglary); s 10 (aggravated burglary); s 12 (taking motor vehicle or other conveyance without authority); s 12A (aggravated vehicle taking); s 15 (obtaining property by deception); s 25 (going equipped for stealing). The following offences under the Misuse of Drugs Act 1971 are also trigger offences, if committed in respect of a specified Class A drug: s 4 (restriction on production and supply of controlled drug); s 5(2) (possession of a controlled drug); s 5(3) (possession of a controlled drug with intent to supply).

2.48   The new s 63B and s 63C of PACE 1984 contain various consequential provisions relating to what warning a person to whom a request is being made must be given, the recording of the authorisation and the grounds for the reasonable suspicion. Section 63C(3) also will amend s 38 of PACE 1984 to authorise a custody officer to continue the detention of a person where he has reasonable grounds for believing that the detention of the person is necessary to enable a sample to be taken from him under s 63B. That detention cannot extend after the end of the period of six hours beginning when he was charged with the offence.

Fingerprints

2.49   The position with respect to the taking of the fingerprints of a juvenile is, in principle, no different from that in respect of an adult. Except where the provisions of s 61(3) to (7) of PACE 1984 are satisfied, fingerprints may not be taken without consent. In that context, that consent will, in the case of a juvenile aged under 14, be that of his parent or guardian.[1] In respect of a juvenile aged at least 14, although he or she can give consent, the consent of the parent or guardian will, in addition, be required.[2] Such consent, if given, must be in writing if it is given at a time when the person is at a police station.[3]

---

1   See para **2.39**.
2   Code D, para 1.11.
3   PACE 1984, s 61(2).

2.50   Section 61(3) of PACE 1984 provides that the fingerprints of a person detained at a police station may be taken without consent:

'(a) if an officer of at least the rank of superintendent authorises them to be taken; or

(b) if—

    (i) he has been charged with a recordable offence[1] or informed that he will be prosecuted for such an offence; and

    (ii) he has not had his fingerprints taken in the course of the investigation of the offence by the police.'

Such an authorisation as stated in para (a) above may be given only if the officer has reasonable grounds to suspect the involvement of the person whose fingerprints are to be taken, and has reasonable grounds to believe that his fingerprints will tend to confirm or disprove his involvement. Such an authorisation must be either given or reduced to writing, on the same basis (PACE 1984, s 61(7)), and recorded on the custody sheet if the fingerprints are taken without consent (PACE 1984, s 61(8)).

---

1   'Recordable offence' means any offence to which regulations under s 27 of PACE apply.

2.51 A person's fingerprints may also be taken if he or she is convicted of a recordable offence (PACE 1984, s 61(6)).[1] Again the necessary reason must be given to the individual in writing (PACE 1984, s 61(8)).

---

1   For recordable offences, see note 1 to para **2.50**.

2.52 A further power to take fingerprints arises by virtue of s 27 of PACE 1984. By s 27(1), if a person:

'(a) has been convicted of a recordable offence;

(b) has not at any time been in police detention for the offence; and

(c) has not had his fingerprints taken –

    (i) in the course of the investigation of the offence by the police; or

    (ii) since the conviction,

any constable may at any time not later than one month after the date of the conviction require him to attend a police station in order that his fingerprints may be taken.'

Such a requirement must give the person at least seven days within which he must attend, and may direct him to so attend at a specified time of day or between specified times of day (PACE 1984, s 27(2)). A power of arrest exists in respect of a person who fails to comply (PACE 1984, s 27(3)). Clearly in this context care should be taken in making any such demand of a juvenile. A requirement that failed to have regard to the age or welfare of the juvenile will be challengeable. Such a requirement might also impact on a parent or guardian. Any such requirement should therefore involve consultation, or at any rate, communication with that parent or guardian.

Identification

2.53 The detailed rules as to how suspects are to be identified are set out in Code D, and interpreted through the substantial quantity of case-law that has arisen. That mass of authority is beyond the scope of this book. The principles of identification in Code D are applicable to juveniles as much as to adults, but, as noted earlier, the consent of, and presence of, the appropriate adult will be necessary either in addition to or, in the case of a suspect under 14 years of age, in substitution for that of the juvenile.[1] Thus the appropriate adult will need to consent to participation in an identification parade under Code D, para 2.3. There is no guidance in Code D as to the contrary situation: the holding of a parade at the request of the juvenile. Logically, such a request should be by suspect and appropriate adult, or, in the case of a juvenile under the age of 14, by the appropriate adult. Disputes between the two might theoretically arise, and since the whole purpose of Code D is to provide fair means of identification, there are clearly advantages in the holding of a parade provided it can be held fairly in terms of the composition of the parade. Care will need to be taken to ensure that if a parade is held the composition fully complies with Annex A to Code D.

---

1   See para **2.39**.

2.54   The Notes of Guidance provide a more detailed framework in respect of the operation of Code D. A person, including a parent or guardian, should not be the appropriate adult if he is suspected of involvement in the offence, is the victim, is a witness, is involved in the investigation or has received admissions prior to attending to act as the appropriate adult. If the parent of a juvenile is estranged from the juvenile, he should not be asked to be the appropriate adult if the juvenile expressly and specifically objects to his presence. If a juvenile admits an offence to, or in the presence of, a social worker other than during the time that the social worker is acting as the appropriate adult for that juvenile, another social worker should be the appropriate adult in the interests of fairness. A solicitor acting as such is not to be regarded as an 'appropriate adult'.

Detention

2.55   A juvenile should not be placed in a police cell unless there is no other way of guaranteeing his security or the cell is considered to be more comfortable than alternative secure accommodation within the police station (Code C, para 8.8). If a juvenile is placed in a cell, the reason must be recorded and he must not be kept there with an adult suspect (para 8.8). Indeed, to place a juvenile with an adult would be inappropriate and potentially be a breach of the Convention under Art 3 (inhuman or degrading treatment or torture) or Art 8 (respect for private and family life, etc). Whenever possible, juveniles and other persons at risk should be visited more frequently (Note 8A).

It is the duty of the custody officer to decide whether sufficient evidence exists to charge the person with the offence for which the arrest was made. During the period of detention, various reviews must occur (PACE 1984, ss 42–44).

First review	Not later than 6 hours after detention
Second review	Not later than 9 hours after first review
Third and subsequent reviews	Not later than 9 hours after previous review
	In addition, where the investigating officer considers there is sufficient evidence to charge, he must take the suspect before the custody officer

If there is insufficient evidence to charge at the end of 24 hours, the suspect must be released, unless that 24-hour period has been extended by an officer of the rank of superintendent or above. That officer must have reasonable grounds to believe that detention is necessary to secure or preserve evidence relating to the offence for which the arrest was made, or to obtain such evidence by questioning, and that the offence is a serious arrestable offence, and that the offence is being investigated diligently and expeditiously. Any further extension beyond that 36-hour period can only be subject to a warrant of further detention obtained from a magistrates' court, for a period not exceeding 36 hours, which may, in turn, be extended by one further period of 36 hours. Thus the maximum period of detention in total amounts to 96 hours.

In reaching a decision, the officer must provide an opportunity to the detained person himself to make representations (unless he is unfit to do so because of his condition or behaviour) or to his solicitor or the appropriate adult if available at the time. Other people having an interest in the person's welfare may make representations at the review officer's discretion.

After hearing any representations, the review officer or officer determining whether further detention should be authorised must note any comment the person may make if the decision is to keep him in detention. The officer must not put specific questions to the suspect regarding his involvement in any offence, nor in respect of any comments he may make in response to the decision to keep him in detention. Such an exchange is likely to constitute an interview as defined by para 11.1A[1] and would require the associated safeguards which protect and govern the conduct of interviews.

---

1   See para **2.26**.

2.56   Before conducting a review the review officer must ensure that the detained person is reminded of his entitlement to free legal advice (see Code C, para 6.5). It is the responsibility of the review officer to ensure that all such reminders are noted in the custody record (Code C, para 15.3). If the detained person is likely to be asleep at the latest time when a review of detention or an authorisation of continued detention may take place, the appropriate officer should bring it forward so that the detained person may make representations without being woken up. An application for a warrant of further detention or its extension should be made between 10 am and 9 pm, and if possible during normal court hours. It will not be practicable to arrange for a court to sit specially outside the hours of 10 am to 9 pm. If it appears possible that a special sitting may be needed (either at a weekend, Bank/Public Holiday or on a weekday outside normal court hours but between 10 am and 9 pm), the clerk to the justices should be given notice and informed of this possibility, while the court is sitting if possible.

If in the circumstances the only practicable way of conducting a review is over the telephone then this is permissible, provided that the requirements of s 40 of PACE 1984 or of Sch 3 to the Prevention of Terrorism (Temporary Provisions) Act 1989 are observed. However, a review to decide whether to authorise a person's continued detention under s 42 of PACE 1984 must be done in person rather than over the telephone (Code C, para 16.4). If at any time after a person has been charged with or informed that he may be prosecuted for an offence, a police officer wishes to bring to the notice of that person any written statement made by another person or the content of an interview with another person, he shall hand to that person a true copy of any such written statement or bring to his attention the content of the interview record, but shall say or do nothing to invite any reply or comment save to warn him that he does not have to say anything but that anything he does say may be given in evidence and to remind him of his right to legal advice. If the person cannot read then the officer may read it to him. If the person is a juvenile or mentally disordered or mentally handicapped, the copy shall also be given to, or the interview record brought to the attention of, the appropriate adult.

2.57   Questions relating to an offence may not be put to a person after he has been charged with that offence, or informed that he may be prosecuted for it, unless they are necessary for the purpose of preventing or minimising harm or loss to some other person or to the public or for clearing up an ambiguity in a previous answer or statement, or where it is in the interests of justice that the person should have put to him and have an opportunity to comment on information concerning the offence which has come to light since he was charged or informed that he might be prosecuted. Before any such questions are put to him, he must be warned that he does not have to say anything but that anything he does say may be given in evidence and reminded of his right to legal advice. A record must be made of anything a detained person says when charged.

Detention after charge and bail

2.58   Section 38(1) of PACE 1984 provides that where a person arrested for an offence otherwise than under a warrant endorsed for bail is charged with an offence, the custody officer must, subject to s 25 of the Criminal Justice and Public Order Act 1994, order his release from police detention, either on bail or without bail,[1] unless:

'(a) if the person arrested is not an arrested juvenile –

    (i) his name or address cannot be ascertained or the custody officer has reasonable grounds for doubting whether a name or address furnished by him as his name or address is his real name or address;

    (ii) the custody officer has reasonable grounds for believing that the person arrested will fail to appear in court to answer to bail;

    (iii) in the case of a person arrested for an imprisonable offence, the custody officer has reasonable grounds for believing that the detention of the person arrested is necessary to prevent him from committing an offence;

    [(iiia) in the case of a person who has attained the age of 18, the custody officer has reasonable grounds for believing that the detention of the person is necessary to enable a sample to be taken from him under section 63B below;[2]

    (iv) in the case of a person arrested for an offence which is not an imprisonable offence, the custody officer has reasonable grounds for believing that the detention of the person arrested is necessary to prevent him from causing physical injury to any other person or from causing loss or damage to property;

    (v) the custody officer has reasonable grounds for believing that the detention of the person arrested is necessary to prevent him from interfering with the administration of justice or with the investigation of offences or of a particular offence; or

    (vi) the custody officer has reasonable grounds for believing that the detention of the person arrested is necessary for his own protection;

(b) if he is an arrested juvenile –

    (i) any of the requirements of paragraph (a) above is satisfied; or

    (ii) the custody officer has reasonable grounds for believing that he ought to be detained in his own interests.'

If release is not required by s 38(1), the arrested juvenile may be detained. However, in such a case, unless the custody officer certifies (s 38(6)):

'(a) that, by reason of such circumstances as are specified in the certificate, it is impracticable for him to do so; or

(b) in the case of an arrested juvenile who has attained the age of 12 years that no secure accommodation is available and that keeping him in other local authority accommodation would not be adequate to protect the public from serious harm from him',

he must secure that the arrested juvenile is moved to local authority accommodation.[3] Where an arrested juvenile is moved to such accommodation under s 38(6), it is lawful for any person acting on behalf of the authority to detain him (PACE 1984, s 38(6B)). Once the juvenile is in detention, the custody officer ceases to have, in respect of that juvenile, the responsibilities in relation to persons detained imposed under s 39(1). A certificate which has been issued under s 38(6) must be produced to the court before which he is first brought (s 38(7)).

---

1   In which case, if the juvenile has been arrested under the authority of a warrant, the parent
     or guardian must enter into a recognisance as may be determined by the custody officer as
     sufficient to secure the attendance of the juvenile at the hearing: Children and Young
     Persons Act 1969, s 29(1). The recognisance may be conditional on the parent or guardian
     attending as well as the juvenile.
2   Added by the Criminal Justice and Courts Act 2000, s 57 which introduces a new
     s 38(1)(a)(iiia), which related to the changes in respect of drug testing outlined at para
     2.46.
3   'Local authority accommodation' means accommodation provided by or on behalf of a
     local authority (within the meaning of the Children Act 1989 (PACE 1984, s 38(6A)).

2.59   If it is not practicable to make arrangements for the transfer of a juvenile
into local authority care, the custody officer must record the reasons and make
out a certificate to be produced before the court together with the juvenile.
Neither a juvenile's behaviour nor the nature of the offence with which he is
charged provides grounds for the custody officer to decide that it is
impracticable to seek to arrange for his transfer to the care of the local
authority. Similarly, the lack of secure local authority accommodation must not
make it impracticable for the custody officer to transfer him. The availability of
secure accommodation is only a factor in relation to a juvenile aged 12 or over
when the local authority accommodation would not be adequate to protect the
public from serious harm from the juvenile. The obligation to transfer a
juvenile to local authority accommodation applies as much to a juvenile
charged during the daytime as it does to a juvenile to be held overnight, subject
to a requirement to bring the juvenile before a court under s 46 of PACE 1984.

As noted in para **2.58** above, the provisions in s 38 of PACE 1984 are subject to
those of s 25 of the Criminal Justice and Public Order Act 1994. Section 25, as
originally enacted, restricted the power of a court, or detention officer, to grant
bail in cases of murder, or attempted murder, manslaughter, rape or attempted
rape. In the light of objections to the blanket nature of the prohibition, which
potentially infringed Art 5 of the European Convention on Human Rights,[1] it
was amended by s 56 of the Crime and Disorder Act 1998. As amended, it
provides that a person who in any proceedings has been charged with or
convicted of an offence to which the section applies in circumstances to which
it applies shall be granted bail in those proceedings only if the court or, as the
case may be, the constable considering the grant of bail is satisfied that there
are exceptional circumstances which justify it (s 25(1)). The specified offences
are those set out above. The circumstances to which s 25(1) applies are
specified by s 25(3): it applies to a person charged with or convicted of any such
offence only if he has been previously convicted by or before a court in any part
of the United Kingdom of any such offence or of culpable homicide, and in the
case of a previous conviction of manslaughter or of culpable homicide, if he
were then sentenced to imprisonment or, if he were a child or young person, to
long term detention under any of the relevant enactments. The section does
not apply whilst an appeal against conviction or sentence is pending (s 25(4)).

The term 'conviction' is defined by s 25(5) to include:

'(a) a finding that a person is not guilty by reason of insanity;

(b) a finding under section 4A(3) of the Criminal Procedure (Insanity) Act 1964 (cases of unfitness to plead) that a person did the act or made the omission charged against him; and

(c) a conviction of an offence for which an order is made placing the offender on probation or discharging him absolutely or conditionally.'

---

1   No one shall be deprived of his liberty except in accordance with certain specified cases and in accordance with a procedure prescribed by law. See in particular Art 5(1)(c) which permits such detention for the purpose of bringing the person before the competent legal authority on reasonable suspicion of having committed an offence or when it is reasonably considered necessary to prevent his committing an offence or fleeing after having done so. The potential for infringement has since been confirmed by rulings of the Commission on Human Rights in *CC v United Kingdom* [1999] Crim LR 229 (see para **2.60**, below) and *Caballero v United Kingdom* [2000] Crim LR 587.

2.60   The term 'exceptional circumstances' is not defined by s 25. Despite the view of the Government that a court should have regard to the matters set out in Sch 1 to the Bail Act 1976[1] that would not either give the term 'exceptional circumstances' any meaning (for it is those matters that are relevant on any bail application irrespective of the terms of s 25) or deal with the question as to whether the amended provision was Convention compliant. In *CC v United Kingdom*[2] the Commission on Human Rights found, by a majority of 19 to 12, that the original s 25 infringed Art 5(3) and Art 5(5).[3] In so deciding, it stated that judicial control of interference by the executive of the individual's right to liberty is an essential feature of the guarantee embodied in Art 5(3). Thus, an accused must be brought promptly before a judge who, having heard the accused, must examine all the facts arguing for and against the existence of a genuine requirement of public interest justifying, with due regard to the presumption of innocence, a departure from the rule of respect for the accused's liberty. As far as the danger of reoffending is concerned, a reference to the person's antecedents cannot suffice to justify refusing release. Section 25(3) prohibited that consideration, and there was thus a breach of Art 5(3). Since there was no possibility in English law for the applicant to apply for compensation for the violation of Art 5(3) there had also been a breach of Art 5(5).[4]

The Court of Human Rights in *Caballero v United Kingdom* did not adjudicate upon the correctness of the analysis of the Commission in *CC v United Kingdom* (because violation of Art 5(3) was conceded by the UK Government), but there is no reason to doubt the correctness of that analysis, which is consistent with other case-law from the Court. On that basis, the question remains as to whether the amended s 25(3) complies with Art 5(3). There is significant doubt that it does.[5] The Law Commission suggest that a court may simply give particular weight to the nature of these particular offences when considering, on the facts, whether to grant bail, a view that it considers to be on the borderlines of compatibility. An alternative approach would be for courts to give a wide meaning to the term 'exceptional circumstances' in a way that would permit a court to take an individual view on the facts of the case. That would, arguably, not fly in the face of the words of the statute, in that, as noted above, the 1994 Act was amended by the 1998 Act precisely because of doubts about Convention compatibility. Whatever the interpretations, the Law Commission recommend the repeal of s 25.

1   See Card and Ward, *Crime and Disorder Act 1998* (Jordans, 1998), at para 9.23.
2   See para **2.59**.
3   Article 5(5) provides: 'Everyone who has been the victim of arrest or detention in contravention with the provisions of this Article shall have an enforceable right to compensation'.
4   For analysis of *CC v United Kingdom*, see Leach, 'Automatic Denial of Bail and the European Convention' [1999] Crim LR 300.
5   See Law Commission Working Paper 137, *Bail and the Human Rights Act 1998*.

2.61   Wider issues apply in respect of the criteria set out in s 38(1)(a) of the 1976 Act. These matters are discussed later, in the same context as court decisions relating to bail.[1] However, note should also be taken of the fact that the custody officer is required to have regard to the matters set out in para 2 of Part 1 to Sch 1 to the Bail Act 1976 (PACE 1984, s 38(2A)). Paragraph 2 states that a defendant need not be granted bail if the court is satisfied that there are substantial grounds for believing that the defendant, if released on bail (whether subject to conditions or not) would:

'(a)   fail to surrender to custody; or
(b)   commit an offence while on bail; or
(c)   interfere with witnesses or otherwise obstruct the administration of justice, whether in relation to himself or to any other person.'

No obligation is imposed on the custody officer to consider whether to grant bail subject to conditions can prevent, or is an appropriate means of preventing, a refusal of bail. It is submitted that that is implicit: the power to impose conditions when granting bail implies that consideration should be given as to whether such a step should be taken to do so. A failure to so consider would, arguably, be a breach not only of pre-existing domestic law but also potentially breach Art 5(3) of the European Convention on Human Rights.

1   See para **2.62** and **3.40**.

2.62   By s 47(3A) of PACE 1984, where a custody officer releases an arrested person on bail, he must appoint for the appearance of that person:

'(a)   a date which is no later than the first sitting of the court after the person is charged with the offence; or
(b)   where he is informed by the clerk to the justices for the relevant petty sessions area that the appearance cannot be accommodated until a later date, that later date.'

The term 'cannot be accommodated' is not in any way defined, and within limits would appear to be within the judgment of the relevant clerk, subject to challenge on normal judicial review grounds. The intention is to speed up processes to enable 'simple' guilty pleas to be dealt with at the next court hearing.[1]

---

1   *Review of Delay in the Criminal Justice System: A Report* (the Narey Report), p 28.

2.63   A security (money or some other item of value) may be required by a custody officer to secure his surrender to custody (Bail Act 1976, s 3(5)). The pre-condition is that it must be necessary to prevent absconding.

Cautioning, reprimands and final warnings

2.64   Diversion from the criminal justice system is an important strategy in respect of young offenders. The practice of formally cautioning, rather than prosecuting, offenders can be traced back to 1929, but until the Crime and Disorder Act 1998 came into force the formal caution never had a statutory basis, and was often used in an unsatisfactory and inconsistent way. The Royal Commission on Criminal Justice recommended an extension of the practice to more petty offences, a recommendation leading to a new Home Office Circular which encouraged the use of formal cautioning to keep young offenders out of the youth justice system for as long as possible.[1] For a person to be cautioned, there needs to be evidence of the suspect's guilt sufficient to give a reasonable prospect of a conviction; the suspect should admit guilt and be willing to be cautioned.

---

1   See, generally, Wilkinson and Evans, 'Police Cautioning of Juveniles: The Impact of the Home Office Circular 14/1985' [1990] Crim LR 165; Westwood, 'The Effects of Home Office Guidelines on the Cautioning of Offenders' [1991] Crim LR 591; Evans, 'Police Cautioning and the Young Adult Offender' [1991] Crim LR 598.

2.65   The Circular indicated that the cautioning power should be used as follows:

(a)   in deciding whether to charge or summons an offender, no account will be taken of any previous convictions or of any earlier cautions;

(b)   the seriousness of the accused's action will determine whether a prosecution should take place, the police having regard to any aggravating features, such as the use of violence;

(c)   the views of the victim should be borne in mind;

(d)   there is a presumption in favour of a caution for a juveniles;

(e)   if a caution is appropriate, regard will then be had to the previous cautions or pending prosecutions of the offender.

2.66   Section 65 of the Crime and Disorder Act 1998 introduced a system of reprimands and warnings for young offenders, replacing the pre-existing system of police cautions for young offenders. The rationale for the change was two-fold. First, research shows that those children who show signs of criminal behaviour at an early age are most likely to end up as serious or persistent offenders.[1] Early intervention may prevent this occurring. The Government believes that 'many young people can be successfully diverted from crime without recourse to court proceedings, provided the response is clear, firm and constructive'.[2] Secondly, where the juvenile does not respond to having been dealt with outside the formal court system, and offends again, there must be swift and appropriate action. In this context, a warning by the police is often the most effective way of preventing further crime. Around 68% of offenders who are cautioned for the first time are not cautioned again or re-convicted within two years. However, cautions grow less effective as they are repeated. The Audit Commission in 1996 pointed to evidence suggesting that, after three occasions, prosecution is more effective than cautioning in preventing re-offending.[3] The White Paper which preceded the 1998 Act characterised the existing system as too haphazard, with too often the caution failing to result in follow-up action, the opportunity for early intervention to turn young offenders against crime being lost.[4] It stated that 'inconsistent, repeated and ineffective cautioning has allowed some children and young people to feel that they can offend with impunity'. Reforms in the cautioning system have not been successful in the past in achieving greater consistency in practice between forces. It is with the intent of achieving a more consistent and effective scheme that the 1998 Act introduced a new scheme of reprimands and final warnings.

1   Graham and Bowling, Home Office Research Study No 145 *Young People and Crime* (HMSO, 1996).
2   *Tackling Youth Crime: A Consultation Paper* (Home Office, 1997), at para 54.
3   Ibid, White Paper, paras 5, 9.
4   White Paper, paras 5, 10.

2.67   The features of the scheme introduced by the 1998 Act are as follows:

–   a first offence might meet the response of a police reprimand, provided it is not serious;
–   any further offence would have to result in a final warning or prosecution;
–   in no circumstances should an offender receive two reprimands;
–   if a first offence results in a final warning, any subsequent offence should normally lead to prosecution;
–   only where two years have elapsed since a final warning and the subsequent offence is minor should prosecution not follow for an offence subsequent to a final warning;
–   the police can always decide to prosecute for any offence.

Reprimand and final warnings are recorded by the police, and may be taken into account subsequently by a sentencing court.

2.68   Following the commencement of s 65, no caution is to be given to any child or young person (s 65(8)).[1] Any caution given prior to commencement is to be regarded as a reprimand or warning (s 65(8)). A first caution is to be treated as a reprimand, a second or subsequent caution as a warning (s 120(1) and Sch 9, para 5).

By s 65(1), the powers relating to reprimand and warning in s 65(2) to (5) apply where:

(a) a police officer has evidence that a child or young person ('the offender') has committed an offence;
(b) the police officer considers that the evidence is such that, if the offender were prosecuted for the offence, there would be a realistic prospect of his being convicted;
(c) the offender admits to the police officer that he committed the offence;
(d) the offender has not previously been convicted of an offence; and
(e) the police oficer is satisfied that it would not be in the public interest for the offender to be prosecuted.

---

1   White Paper, op cit, para 10.6.

The power to reprimand

2.69   The police officer may reprimand the offender if the offender has not previously been reprimanded or warned (s 65(2)). He must warn rather than reprimand if he considers the offence to be so serious as to require a warning (s 65(4)). The Home Secretary intends to publish guidance as to the circumstances in which it is appropriate to give reprimands or warnings, including criteria as to levels of seriousness for the purposes of deciding whether a charge, or a warning, is appropriate, the category of police officers by whom reprimands and warnings may be given, and their form (s 65(6)). Such guidance will be important in ensuring that the decisions taken by the police (whose responsibility it will be for deciding whether to reprimand, warn or charge a young offender[1] are consistent and fair).

---

1   Consultation Paper, op cit, para 59.

The power to warn

2.70   By s 65(3), the police officer may warn the offender if:

'(a)   the offender has not previously been warned; or
(b)   where the offender has previously been warned, the offence was committed more than two years after the date of the previous warning and the constable considers the offence to be not so serious as to require a charge to be brought …;'

No person may be warned under para (b) above more than once.

The giving of the reprimand or warning

2.71   By s 65(5), the police officer shall:

'(a)   give any reprimand or warning, where the offender is under the age of 17, in the presence of an appropriate adult;[1] and

(b) explain to the offender and, where he is under that age, the appropriate adult in ordinary language –

    (i) in the case of a reprimand, the effect of subsection (5)(a) of section 66 ... [that a reprimand may be cited in criminal proceedings in the same way as a conviction];

    (ii) in the case of a warning, the effect of subsections (1), (2), (4) and (5)(b) and (c) of that section [reference to youth offending team,[2] participation in rehabilitation scheme, non-availability of conditional discharge power and citation in like circumstances as criminal conviction], and any guidance issued under subsection (3) of that section.'

As originally enacted the reprimand or warning was to be given at the police station. However, the inflexibility of that approach, and the need to deal with these matters quickly and expeditiously, avoiding delays, led to amendment of s 65(5) by s 56 of the Criminal Justice and Courts Services Act 2000. Experience showed that the effect of the reprimand or warning could be enhanced by delivering it as part of a restorative process involving the young offender, his or her parents, and, if appropriate, the victim. The reprimand or warning may now be given anywhere, provided it is given in the presence of an appropriate adult.[1] That section is not yet in force: until it is the reprimand or warning will continue to be given at the police station. This change is accompanied by a power vested in the police to release on bail until such time as the reprimand or warning can be administered.

---

1   For the meaning of 'appropriate adult', see para **2.12**.

2.72   A reprimand may be cited in criminal proceedings in the same way as a conviction (s 66(5)). Where a warning is given, the police officer must refer the person to a youth offending team (s 66(1)); the effect of that is that usually the offender will be placed on a programme of interventions prepared by the team, the purpose of which will be to help the offender (and his or her family) to change the attitudes and behaviour which led to the offending so as to prevent any further offending.[1] The team is under a duty to assess the person referred and, unless considered inappropriate to do so, that team shall arrange for that person to participate in a rehabilitation programme (s 66(2)). A 'rehabilitation programme' is defined by s 66(6) as a programme the purpose of which is to rehabilitate participants and prevent them from re-offending. There appears to be no limits as to what can be included in a plan for this purpose. That programme might include an assessment of the young person to establish the reasons for offending behaviour including any problems requiring attention, and may include work with parents to help them to become more effective in supervising their child, short-term counselling or group work with the young offender to bring about behavioural change, reparation to victims, supervised community or youth activities, or work to improve attendance and achievement at school. Care should, however, be taken to ensure that the requirements of the plan do not become disproportionate and give rise to possible challenge under Art 8 of the European Convention.

2.73   Although there is a duty on the part of the police to refer the offender to the YOT, there is no obligation to delay the administration of the final warning until the YOT has determined whether an intervention programme is appropriate and, if so, what form it should take. Although such a requirement would have provided the police with more information on which to base their decision as to whether to issue a final warning, it would have introduced delay into the process and broken the direct link between offence and consequences of offending.

2.74   If a programme of interventions is proposed by the YOT, an offender cannot be prosecuted for failure to participate in that action plan, or to co-operate with it or to complete it fully or successfully. However, a report of a failure by a person to participate in a rehabilitation programme arranged for him may be cited in criminal proceedings in the same circumstances as a conviction of his might be (s 66(5)). The meaning of this provision is far from clear. The Consultation Paper stated that 'any unreasonable non-compliance would be recorded on the individual's criminal record'.[1] Leaving on one side the fact that s 66(5) does not contain the qualifying word 'unreasonable', the term used by s 66(5) is 'failure by a person to participate', not 'non-compliance'. Although total failure to participate is clearly with s 62(5), anything which falls short of that, arguably, should not. After all, 'non-compliance' involves a qualitative assessment, with no opportunity for any disputes about that assessment to be determined or tested. It is submitted that 'failure to participate' should be construed narrowly. In cases where there is unsatisfactory levels of participation, the appropriate course of action is for the youth offending team to modify its programme of interventions.

1   Op cit, para 68.

2.75   The original intention of the Government was that a conditional discharge should not be available in respect of a person aged between 10 and 19 in respect of a further offence for which he is convicted within two years of a final warning. This lack of any discretion was intended to provide a further incentive for the offender to remain out of trouble.[1] The absolute nature of that prohibition met resistance during the consultation period, and s 66 now permits such an order to be made, but only in exceptional circumstances. If the person is convicted of an offence within two years of the warning, the sentencing court cannot make a conditional discharge order under s 12 of the Powers of Criminal Courts (Sentencing) Act 2000 unless it is of the opinion that there are exceptional circumstances which justify its doing so (s 66(4)). There is no prohibition or limitation on the granting of an absolute discharge, which would be appropriate in cases where the offence is a technical one and there are overwhelming mitigating circumstances,[2] but the normal expectation is that, in the majority of cases, a person who commits a further offence after receiving a final warning will know that they face significant punishment.

1   Consultation Paper, op cit, para 69.
2   Ibid, para 70.

2.76   In *R v Chief Constable of Lancashire, ex parte Atkinson*,[1] the court considered the legality of police action in administering a caution. Although decided on the old law relating to cautions, its statements are instructive as to the attitude the courts should take generally on these matters. The court stated that to be validly administered a caution can be given only where there is sufficient evidence of an offender's guilt to give a realistic prospect of conviction, the offender admits the offence and the offender gives informed consent to being cautioned. However, provided it is clear that there has been an admission, it is not necessary that the admission was obtained in circumstances which satisfied PACE codes, although in many cases it would be wise to satisfy those requirements. In *R v Commissioner of Police for the Metropolis, ex parte K*,[2] the Divisional Court held that a clear breach of cautioning guidelines meant that it could, but not necessarily would, intervene. That case concerned a 12-year-old boy, and the court was satisfied that in reality there had not been an admission of the offence. It is not proper to seek an admission of guilt as part of the cautioning process itself, although it is perfectly proper to acknowledge on the record of caution that the offence has been admitted.[3]

1   (1998) 162 JP 275, DC.
2   [1995] TLR 305.
3   *R v Commissioner of Police for the Metropolis, ex parte Thompson* [1997] 1 WLR 1519.

DISCRETION TO PROSECUTE

2.77   The Code for Crown Prosecutors[1] is applied in determining whether an offence is sufficiently serious in order to warrant prosecution of a juvenile, as opposed to the administration of a reprimand or final warning. Amongst the factors that are to be taken into account, besides the offence itself, will be the likely penalty or sentence, the age of the offender and the victim.

The decision whether to prosecute may be the subject of judicial review. In *R v Chief Constable of Kent, ex parte L*,[2] the court stated, that where a policy exists in respect of the cautioning of juveniles, the decision to commence or discontinue proceedings is subject to judicial review where it could be shown that the decision to prosecute was made regardless of, or contrary to, that policy. This was applied in *R v Commissioner of Police for the Metropolis, ex parte P*[3] where the cautioning of a juvenile improperly, and in contravention of the Code for Crown prosecutors, was judicially reviewable.

When the decision to prosecute a juvenile is taken, s 5(8) of the Children and Young Persons Act 1969 applies. This provides that when a person has decided to lay an information in respect of an offence, where he has reason to believe that the alleged offender is a young person,[4] he must notify the appropriate local authority, unless he himself is that authority. For this purpose, the 'appropriate local authority' will be the local authority for the area where the young person resides, or, if he does not appear to reside in any local authority area, that for the area where the offence, or, in the case of multiple offences, one of them, was committed (1969 Act, s 5(9)).

Notice does not have to be in writing, and must be given as soon as reasonably practicable after the decision to institute a prosecution has been taken.[5] Furthermore, failure to comply with s 5(8) does not render the subsequent prosecution, and any conviction, a nullity, the Court of Appeal deciding in *R v Marsh (Dwayne Douglas)*[6] that the requirement in s 5(8) was directory, not mandatory.

---

1 Issued by the Director of Public Prosecutions pursuant to Prosecution of Offences Act 1985.
2 [1993] 1 All ER 756, DC.
3 (1996) 5 Admin LR 6, DC.
4 Which for this purpose includes a child of 10 or over: Children and Young Persons Act 1969 (Transitional Modifications of Part I) Order 1970, SI 1970/1882, art 4.
5 *DPP v Cottier* [1996] 1 WLR 826, DC.
6 [1997] 1 WLR 649, CA.

DETENTION TIME-LIMITS

2.78 By s 2 of the Prosecution of Offences Act 1985 (the 1985 Act), and regulations made thereunder,[1] time-limits determine how long the prosecution have to complete the 'preliminary state' of proceedings (the 'overall time-limit') and the length of time during which the accused may, during that period, be kept in custody (the 'custody time-limit').[2] No regulations governing the preliminary stage have ever been made. That will in the future change as part of the general attempt to reduce delays in the criminal justice system. By contrast, custody time-limits exist by virtue of the Prosecution of Offences (Custody Time-Limits) Regulations 1987.[3] These apply to indictable offences, whether tried on indictment or summary offences as either way offences. For this purpose, they define the preliminary stage as the period from first appearance in court and the start of summary trial or the decision as to whether to send for trial, and in the Crown Court as the period between sending for trial and the start of the trial.

---

1 Prosecution of Offences (Custody Time-Limits) Regulations 1987, SI 1987/299.
2 If a prosecutor appeals against the grant of bail by a youth court to the Crown Court, and the appeal succeeds, the Crown Court judge will need to specify the date from which the relevant period of detention is calculated.
2 SI 1987/299.

2.79 The applicability of the Regulations to youth court proceedings was considered in *R v Stratford Youth Court, ex parte S*[1]: a youth aged 14 appeared before a youth court charged with robbery. The court of trial had decided that the times on limits in custody contained in Prosecution of Offences (Custody Time-Limits) Regulations 1987 did not apply because of the nature of the offence and age of the defendant. The court also committed the juvenile to secure accommodation relying on hearsay evidence admitted under the Children (Admissibility of Hearsay Evidence) Order 1993.[2] The Divisional Court held that the custody time-limits did apply: robbery is an either-way offence included within reg 4(3). An either-way offence is not defined in regulations, but the court referred to s 17 of the Magistrates' Courts Act 1980 and Sch 1. Robbery in the case of a child is either-way. Whether it is triable summarily or on indictment depends on the application of s 24 of the Magistrates' Courts Act 1980. Further, an application for a remand to secure accommodation is a family proceeding and the evidence given did relate to the 'upbringing, maintenance or welfare of a child'; and was within the terms of the 1993 Order, which permits hearsay evidence in such a case relating to the upbringing, maintenance or welfare of a child. In any event, it is well recognised that hearsay evidence is admissible in bail proceedings.

---

1   (1998) 162 JP 552, DC; see also *In re Moles* [1981] Crim LR 170.
2   SI 1993/621.

2.80   Section 22 of the 1985 Act provides that, where an overall time-limit has expired, the appropriate court must stay the proceedings. The appropriate court is, in the case of a case committed or sent for trial, the Crown Court, and, in any other case, the magistrates' court specified in the summons or warrant in question, or where the accused has already appeared or been brought before a magistrates' court, a magistrates' court for the same area. If the accused escapes from lawful custody or fails to surrender to bail, the effect of s 22 of the 1985 Act is to suspend the operation of the time-limits during the period when the accused is unlawfully at large, and such additional period, if any, as the appropriate court may direct, having regard to the disruption occasioned by the person's escape or failure to surrender and the length of the period during which the accused was unlawfully at large. A right of appeal against such an order by a magistrates' court lies to the Crown Court (1985 Act, s 22(7)). The appropriate court may also at any time before the expiry of the time-limit extend, or further extend, the overall custody time-limit (s 22(3)). It may do so if it is satisfied (s 22(3)):

'(a)   that the need for the extension is due to:

  (i)   the illness or absence of the accused, a necessary witness, a judge or a magistrate;
  (ii) a postponement which is occasioned by the ordering of the court of separate trials in the case of two or more accused or two or more offences; or
  (iii) some other good and sufficient cause; and

(b)   that the prosecution has acted with all due diligence and expedition.'

In the case of an offence triable either-way, the maximum period of custody between the accused's first appearance and the start of the summary trial, or, the date of deciding to commit for trial at the Crown Court, is 70 days.[1] If, however, the court decides prior to the expiration of 56 days to proceed to summary trial the relevant period is 56 days.[2] The equivalent period in cases in the Crown Court is 112 days from committal to trial.[3] Applications can be made for extension of the time-limit in accordance with reg 7.

---

1   Prosecution of Offences (Custody Time-Limits) Regulations 1987, r 4(2).
2   Ibid, r 4(3).
3   Ibid, r 5(2).

2.81   When brought into effect, s 22A of the 1985 Act will permit the Home Secretary to make regulations specifying additional time-limits in respect of those under 18 years of age. These time-limits may be:

(a) in respect of maximum period between arrest and the ending of the date fixed for first appearance in court (the 'initial stage limit'); and
(b) in respect of maximum period between the time of conviction and the time of sentence.

These regulations, when made, will interact with the general regulations made under s 22. A magistrates' court may extend, or further extend, the initial stage time-limit, but only if it is satisfied:

(a) that the need for the extension of time is due to some good and sufficient cause; and
(b) the investigation has been conducted and where applicable the prosecution has acted with all due diligence and expedition (s 22A(3)). An appeal against such a decision lies to the Crown Court.

Where the initial stage time-limit expires before the person arrested is charged with the offence, he must not be charged with it unless further evidence relating to it is obtained, and

(a) if he is then under arrest, he must be released;
(b) if he is then on police bail, his bail (and any duty on conditions to which it is subject) must be discharged s 22A(4)).

Chapter 3

TRIAL

Court of Trial – International Dimension – Mode of Trial – Composition of Court – Publicity

COURT OF TRIAL

3.1   Children and young persons must generally be tried summarily, in the youth court. This has various consequences, one of which is that the sentencing power of the court is limited. A youth court cannot impose a sentence of detention on a young offender, aged 15 or over, of longer than 24 months. If the court wishes to keep open the possibility of a longer custodial sentence being imposed it must send the case for trial on indictment at the Crown Court, which will have open to it the power to impose a sentence under s 53(2) of the Children and Young Persons Act 1933. It can only do that if one of the exceptions set out below applies.

If a person under the age of 18 appears or is brought before a court charged with an indictable offence other than homicide,[1] he must be tried summarily unless one of the exceptions apply (Magistrates' Courts Act 1980, s 24(1)). The exceptions to that are contained in s 24(1)(a), (b) and (1A)):

'(a)   where the juvenile has attained the age of 14 and the offence is one to which section 53(2) of the Children and Young Persons Act 1933,[2] applies, and the court considers that if the juvenile is found guilty of the offence it ought to be possible to sentence him to such a term as permitted by section 53(2);

(b)   if the juvenile is charged jointly with a person who has attained the age of 18 and the court considers it necessary in the interests of justice to commit them both for trial;

(1A) where the juvenile is charged with an offence which falls under section 24(1)(a), and is committed for it, the court may also commit him for trial for any other indictable offence with which he is charged at the same time (whether jointly with a person who has attained that age or not) if that other offence could be joined in the same indictment.'

In such cases the juvenile will be tried in the adult Crown Court, a position that was condemned by the European Court of Human Rights in *T v United Kingdom; V v United Kingdom.*[3]

---

1   Which includes murder, manslaughter, causing death by reckless driving, killing in pursuance of a suicide pact and infanticide.

2   The offences to which s 53(2) of the 1933 Act apply are offences which, if committed by an adult, are punishable with a term of imprisonment of 14 years or more, or an indecent assault on a woman, contrary to the Sexual Offences Act 1956, s 24(1)(a), in either case not

being an offence for which the sentence is fixed by law, or (in the case of those aged 14 to 17 inclusive) causing death by dangerous driving contrary to the Road Traffic Act 1988, s 1, or causing death by careless driving whilst under the influence of drink or drugs contrary to s 3A of the 1988 Act.

3   (1999) *The Times*, 17 December.

3.2   The applicable age for the purposes of s 24 is the age as at when the court makes its decision as to the mode of trial. In *R v Islington North Juvenile Court, ex parte Daley*[1] the House of Lords ruled that that was so, irrespective of the fact that the accused was under 18[2] when he first appeared or was brought before the court to answer the information, and thus was entitled to elect trial by jury pursuant to s 18 of the 1980 Act, in respect of an 'either-way' offence.[3]

If it appears to the court that the accused is under 18, then, unless the exceptions set out above apply, the defendant will be tried summarily. If, however, during the hearing the court finds the accused in fact to be over the age of 18, it may none the less continue dealing with the accused as if he or she were a juvenile, although it is not obliged to do so (Children and Young Persons Act 1933, s 48).

---

1   [1983] 1 AC 347, sub nom *Re Daley* [1982] 2 All ER 974.
2   At the date of the decision the relevant age was 17, but was raised to 18 by the Criminal Justice Act 1991, Sch 8, para 6.
3   Approving *R v St Albans Juvenile Court, ex parte Godman* [1981] 2 All ER 311, and disapproving *R v Amersham Juvenile Court, ex parte Wilson*, which had suggested otherwise.

3.3   In determining whether to commit a juvenile for trial in respect of a grave offence, the court should not consider what sentence should be imposed on the juvenile but, rather, whether the court which sentences the accused should have the option available to it to impose a longer term of detention than that generally available.[1] The correct approach is illustrated by the decision of a Divisional Court in *R v Devizes Youth Court, ex parte M*,[2] where a ground of challenge to a decision to commit under s 24(1) of the 1980 Act was that it was wrong to commit under s 24(1)(a) when a non-custodial sentence was more likely than detention. In this case, the charge was one of arson. The Divisional Court concluded that it was for the justices to make an appropriate judgment as to whether, if the applicant contested the charge and it went to trial, it ought to be possible for the sentencing court to impose a term of detention under s 53 of the Children and Young Persons Act 1933. Arson was a difficult crime in respect of which to sentence and the Divisional Court was not prepared to intervene to quash the decision of the court which had committed under s 24(1). Article 6 of the European Convention on Human Rights was not, at the time of the decision, part of English law, and, in any event, was a matter for the Crown Court to consider. For that reason, it could not affect the functions exercisable uner s 24(1). It should be considered whether this remains true now that the Human Rights Act 1998 is in force, in the light of the decisions in *Thompson and Venables*,[3] and in the context that it is preferable that a young defendant should stand trial alone.[4]

In *R v Fareham Youth Court, ex parte M; R v Fareham Youth Court, ex parte Crown Prosecution Service*[5] the Divisional Court indicated that a juvenile charged with rape should always be committed to the Crown Court for trial. The youth court had accepted jurisdiction, but then later sought to change its mind. The Divisional Court, in upholding the challenge made to that subsequent change of mind by the youth court, indicated that where a youth court has accepted jurisdiction and a guilty plea has been entered, that court could not later change its mind and decline to accept jurisdiction.[6] Nor could the prosecution achieve the same result by issuing a notice of transfer: that power cannot be used to reverse a court's decision to proceed by way of summary trial.

---

1   See para **3.1**.
2   27 January 2000.
3   See para **3.12**.
4   See para **3.13**.
5   (1999) 163 JP 812, QBD.
6   See para **3.4**.

3.4   The decision to accept summary jurisdiction may be changed. By s 25(6) of the 1980 Act, if a youth court has accepted jurisdiction on the basis that s 24(1)(a) or (b) did not apply, then, if at any time before the conclusion of the evidence for the prosecution the court considers that the case is one which, after all, ought not to be tried summarily by virtue of s 24(1), it may discontinue the summary trial and proceed to inquire into the information. It may for that purpose adjourn the hearing without remanding the accused. The converse situation equally applies: if the court has concluded that s 24(1) does apply, it may at any time before the case is transferred for trial, deal with the case itself and proceed to summary trial (1980 Act, s 25(7)).

3.5   Section 24 concerns the procedure in magistrates' courts only, and does not deprive the Crown Court of jurisdiction to join counts to an indictment.[1] In *R v S (Paul John)*[2], the appellant had been brought before a youth court charged with two offences of assault occasioning actual bodily harm, and three of indecent assault. The indecent assaults were not considered suitable for summary trial. In order to avoid problems relating to the length of adjournments, the youth court did not accept a guilty plea to the charges of assault, but indicated that such a plea would be accepted at a later date. As a result, when the case came before the Crown Court no plea on these offences had been accepted by the court; the charges of actual bodily harm were withdrawn by the Crown Prosecution Service, who indicated that those charges would be added to the indictment at the Crown Court. This was possible because of the terms of s 2(2) of the Administration of Justice (Miscellaneous Provisions) Act 1933, which permits an indictment to include any counts founded on facts disclosed to the magistrates' court, and also counts founded on material of which notice had been given to the defendant. The Court of Appeal, in dismissing an appeal against conviction on those counts of actual bodily harm, concluded that the Crown Court had the power in law to do what it had done, the joinder of offences being a matter for the Crown Court in accordance with the normal rules of evidence and procedure. It noted also that the matter was one of exercise of discretion by the court: the Crown Court equally has a discretion to refuse to add counts to an indictment, and might do so where to add them would be an abuse of process.

---

1   The normal rule is that offences may be joined together on indictment if they arise out of circumstances which are the same as or connected with those giving rise to the offence for which he is being committed.
2   [1999] 1 Cr App R 1, CA.

Trial in adult magistrates' court

3.6   Section 46 of the 1933 Act provides that no charge against a child or young person, or any relevant application (other than for bail or for a remand), can be heard by a court of summary jurisdiction which is not a youth court. There are exceptions to this general rule, which are as follows (s 46(1)(a), (b), (c)):

'(a)   a charge made jointly against a child or young person and a person who has attained the age of 18, must be heard in the adult magistrates' court;

(b)   where a child or young person is charged with an offence, the charge may be heard by the adult magistrates' court if a person who has attained the age of 18 is charged at the same time with aiding, abetting, causing, procuring, allowing or permitting that offence;

(c)   where in the course of any proceedings before any court of summary jurisdiction other than a youth court it appears that the person to whom the proceedings relate is a child or young person, the court, if it thinks fit to do so, may proceed with the hearing and determine those proceedings.'

If a notification is received that the accused desires to plead guilty without appearing, then if the court has no reason to believe that the accused is a child or young person, the accused must be deemed to have attained the age of 18 for the purposes of the application of s 46(1) (1933 Act, s 46(1A)).

Power to remit case to youth court

3.7   By s 29 of the 1980 Act, where a juvenile appears or is brought before a magistrates' court other than a youth court on an information jointly charging him and one or more other persons with an offence, and that person, or one of those persons, has attained the age of 18, subs (2) of s 29 applies.

Section 29(2) states that if:

'(a)   the court proceeds to the summary trial of the information in the case of both or all the accused, and the adult accused or each of them pleads guilty; or

(b)   the court –

(i)   in the case of the adult accused, or each of them, proceeds to inquire into the information as examining justices and either sends the case to the Crown Court for trial or discharges him; and

(ii)   in the case of the juvenile, proceeds to the summary trial of the information, then if in either situation the juvenile pleads not guilty, the court may, before any evidence is called in his case remit him for trial to a youth court acting for the same place as the remitting court or for the place where he habitually resides.'

It should be carefully noted, however, that the power to remit is a power to remit for trial, not to remit for the mode of trial to be determined.[1] Thus if a juvenile and adult are jointly charged, and the court concludes that there is insufficient evidence on which to send the adult to the Crown Court for trial, the court must then proceed to decide whether the case against the juvenile should be sent for trial to the Crown Court pursuant to s 24(1) of the 1980 Act. Only when it has decided not to do so should it remit to the youth court for trial.[1] Where a magistrates' court decides to make a remission, there is no right of appeal against that order, and the remitting court may give such directions as appear to be necessary with respect to his custody or for his release on bail until he can be brought before the youth court (1980 Act, s 29(4)).

---

1   *R v Tottenham Youth Court, ex parte Fawzy* [1998] 1 All ER 365, DC.

3.8   A more general power to remit for sentence is contained in s 56(1) of the 2000 Act.[1] This provides that, subject to the exceptions described at para **3.6**, any court by or before which a child or young person is found guilty of an offence other than homicide may, and if it is not a youth court, must (unless satisfied that it would be undesirable to do so), remit the case to a youth court acting for the place where the offender was committed or sent for trial at the Crown Court. If the offender was not committed or sent for trial to the Crown Court, then the offender will be remitted to a youth court acting either for the same place as the remitting court or for the place where the offender habitually resides.

Where such case is so remitted the offender must be brought before a youth court accordingly, and that court may deal with him in any way in which it might have dealt with him if it had been tried and found guilty by that court.

There is no power of appeal against such a remission. Any appeal will be against any order made by the court to which the case has been remitted (s 8(5)). The remitting court may, subject to s 25 of the Criminal Justice and Public Order Act 1994, give such directions as appear to be necessary with respect to the custody of the offender or for his release on bail until he can be brought before the youth court. The remitting court must cause to be transmitted to the clerk to the youth court a certificate setting out the nature of the offence and stating that the offender has been found guilty, and that the case has been remitted pursuant to s 8.

Before remitting the case to the youth court, the offender, and his parent or guardian if present, must be informed as to how the court proposes to deal with the case and allow them to make representations (Magistrates' Courts (Children and Young Persons) Rules 1992, r 224(1)[2]). The offender need not be so informed if the court considers it undesirable to do so. When making any order, the court must explain to the child or young person the general nature and effect of the order unless, in the case of an order requiring the parent or guardian to enter into a recognizanace, it appears undesirable to do so (r 11(2)).

The question remains as to how that phrase 'undesirable to do so' should be applied. It is a question of fact in each case, and the discretion of the court is not limited. However, some guidance was given, in the context of the predecessor provisions,[3] in *R v Lewis*[4] where factors that a court was entitled to take into account included the fact that the judge who presided over the trial might be better informed about the case, if remitting the case would lead to disparity in sentencing two or more defendants, or whether duplication of proceedings might result.

---

1   Formerly s 56(1) of the 1933 Act.
2   SI 1992/2071.
3   1933 Act, s 56(1).
4   (1984) 6 Cr App R(S) 44.

3.9   It was noted above that exceptions exist to the general duty to remit. A magistrates' court is not obliged (although may choose to do so) to remit if the court, were it not to remit, would be obliged to refer the case to a youth offender panel.[1] In addition, no duty to remit exists if a magistrates' court is of the opinion that the case is one that can properly be dealt with by means of:

> '(a)   an order discharging the offender absolutely or conditionally; or
> (b)   an order for the payment of a fine, or
> (c)   an order requiring the offender's parent or guardian to enter into a recognizance to take proper care of him and exercise proper control over him,
>
> with or without any other order that the court has power to make when absolutely or conditionally discharging an offender.[2]'

---

1   2000 Act, s 8(7).
2   2000 Act, s 8(8).

The international dimension

3.10   As noted earlier, at para **1.27**, one of the most important contexts within which the youth justice system has to operate is that provided by the various international provisions relating to the rights of juveniles. The European Convention on Human Rights is, of course, at the forefront of these, but there are other relevant provisions. Amongst these are the United Nations Standard Minimum Rules for the Administration of Juvenile Justice (the Beijing Rules), the United Nations Conventions on the Rights of the Child and Art 14 of the International Covenant on Civil and Political Rights 1966. All of these provisions focus on the essential principle that processes and rules governing the treatment of young defendants must have due regard to the age and welfare of the child or young person.

3.11   These wider international provisions are recognised by the Court of Human Rights and have been taken into account in determining matters under the various provisions of the Convention.[1] They were also considered relevant by the Divisional Court in *McKerry v Teesdale and Wear Valley Justices*.[2]

---

1   *T v United Kingdom; V v United Kingdom* (1999) *The Times*, 17 December.
2   (2000) *The Times*, 29 February.

3.12   The key provisions in the European Convention relating to youth justice are Art 3, Art 5, Art 6, Art 8 and Art 10. In *T v United Kingdom; V v United Kingdom*[1] the Court of Human Rights made findings adverse to the UK Government which have, or will have, significant implications for the treatment of juveniles within the criminal justice system, and, in particular, the mode of trial. In these two cases, T and V each complained that their trial for murder in an adult court contravened the provisions of the Convention. As noted earlier, the main grounds of challenge were as follows:

–   that the cumulative effect of the age of criminal responsibility, the accusatorial nature of the trial, the adult proceedings in a public court room, the length of the trial, the jury of 12 adult strangers, the physical lay-out of the courtroom, the presence of the media and public, the attacks by the public on the prison van which occurred and the disclosure of their identities together gave rise to a breach of Art 3 (inhuman or degrading treatment);

–   that there was a breach of Art 6 (the 'fair trial' provision) in that the accused could not participate effectively in the conduct of their cases;

–   that the age of criminal responsibility was contratry to the Convention;

–   that the sentence of detention during Her Majesty's Pleasure contravened Art 3 and Art 5 (no deprivation of liberty except by due process);

–   that the fixing of the tariff by the Home Secretary amounted to a breach of Art 6, in that it was not by an independent judicial authority; and

–   that there was no opportunity to have the continued lawfulness of the detention determined by a judicial body, contrary to Art 5.

The Court of Human Rights upheld the complaints of T and V, although not on all the grounds submitted. In particular, the court concluded that the nature of the proceedings against each of the accused was a breach of Art 6, in that the applicants were, in the context of a public hearing in the Crown Court, unable to participate effectively in the criminal proceedings. It also was of the view that the procedure for determining and reviewing the tariff for the length of the indeterminate sentence was unfair, and infringed both Art 5 and Art 6.

Although a challenge to the age of criminal responsibility failed, age, coupled with issues relating to the fairness of the trial, may give rise to wider issues. The procedures, substantive law and orders of the court must be appropriate to the age of the child or young person. In particular, the application of adult modes of trial, or adult procedures, in respect of offences which should be tried on indictment in the Crown Court might lead to a breach of Art 6 of the Convention. It is in that context that a Practice Direction has been issued by the Lord Chief Justice.

3.13   It is clear that courts have to have regard to the welfare of the juvenile. This principle is enshrined into English law by s 44 of the Children and Young Persons Act 1933. Every court, in dealing with a child or young person brought before it, must have regard to the welfare of that child. However, note should also be taken of the terms of s 37 of the Crime and Disorder Act 1998 which states that the principal aim of the youth justice system is to prevent offending by children and young persons. The purpose of introducing this broad statement of the youth justice system was to put beyond doubt the fact that the welfare of the child or young person is not the first consideration of the youth justice system, although the achievement of the aim set out in s 37 of the 1998 Act may well have the effect of promoting the welfare of the child or young person. The international context set out above suggests, however, that the new overall duty stated by s 37 cannot be achieved by disregarding the basic rights of the young defendant to be treated in a way appropriate to his age and maturity.

3.14   The Court of Human Rights in *T v United Kingdom; V v United Kingdom* did not conclude that the trial of a very young accused of itself contravenes the fair trial provisions of Art 6. However, it did consider that it is essential that a child charged with an offence is dealt with in a manner which takes full account of his age, level of maturity and intellectual and emotional capacities, and that steps are taken to promote his ability to understand and participate in the proceedings. In the case of a young child charged with a grave offence attracting high levels of media and public interest, the hearing should be conducted in a way so as to reduce the child's feelings of intimidation and inhibition. In these cases, despite the special measures taken, the formality and ritual of Crown Court trial must have seemed incomprehensible and intimidating. The accused were, on the particular facts, unable to participate effectively, and thus denied a fair hearing.

One of the central arguments of the applicants was that the mode of trial, and the conduct of that trial was in breach of the provisions of Art 6 of the Convention which entitle any accused to a fair trial. It was noted above that it is essential that a child charged with an offence is dealt with in a manner which takes full account of his age, level of maturity and intellectual and emotional capacities. It follows from that that it is necessary to conduct the hearing in such a way as to reduce, as far as possible, the feelings of the juvenile of inhibition or intimidation. The usual procedure in respect of juveniles accused of the lesser criminal offences is that they are tried in the Youth Court, from which the general public is excluded and in relation to which there are automatic reporting restrictions on the media. Presumptively, that should be the procedure to be followed, with departures from it only where unavoidable, and, even then, in accordance with procedures modified to reflect the lack of age or maturity.

At the trial of T, special measures were taken at the Crown Court in the light of the applicant's young age and to promote his understanding of the nature of the proceedings: he had had the trial procedure explained to him and was taken to see the court room in advance; the hearing times were shortened so as not to tire the defendants excessively. Despite this, the Court of Human Rights concluded that the formality and ritual of the Crown Court must have at times seemed incomprehensible and intimidating to a child aged 11. In the view of the Court, there was evidence that certain of the modifications to the courtroom, in particular the raised dock, which was designed to enable the defendants to see what was going on, had the unfortunate effect of increasing the applicant's sense of discomfort during the trial, since he felt exposed to the scrutiny of the press and public. The trial generated high levels of press and public interest, both inside and outside the courtroom, to the extent that the judge in his summing-up referred to the problems caused to witnesses by the blaze of publicity and asked the jury to take this into account when assessing their evidence. There was also expert psychiatric evidence that the applicant T suffered from post-traumatic stress disorder, which, combined with the lack of any therapeutic work since the date of the offence, had limited his ability to instruct his lawyers and adequately testify in his own defence.

In these circumstances, the court did not consider it was sufficient for the purposes of Art 6 that the applicant was represented by skilled and experienced lawyers. Although the applicant's lawyers were within 'whispering distance', it was considered unlikely that the applicant would have felt sufficiently uninhibited, in the tense courtroom and under public scrutiny, to have consulted with them during the trial. Nor, given his immaturity and his disturbed emotional state, would the appellant have been capable of co-operating with his lawyers and giving them information for the purposes of his defence, even outside the courtroom.

For those reasons, the court considered that the applicant was unable to participate effectively in the criminal proceedings against him. He was therefore denied a fair trial within the meaning of Art 6.

3.15 It is in this context that the *Practice Direction (Crown Court: Trial of Children and Young Persons)* was issued.[1] It applies to trials of children and young persons in the Crown Court ('young defendants'). The essential features identified by this Practice Direction are as follows.

– It applies to 'young defendants' in the Crown Court.
– The steps taken to comply with it should be judged in the light of the age, maturity and development (intellectually and emotionally) of the young defendant on trial.
– The trial process should not expose the young defendant to avoidable intimidation, humiliation or distress.
– All possible steps should be taken to assist the young defendant to understand and participate in the proceedings.
– The welfare of the young defendant must be considered (s 44 of the 1933 Act).

–   The court should consider at a plea and directions hearing whether a young defendant jointly accused with an adult should stand trial separately, and should ordinarily so order unless of the opinion that a joint trial would be in the interests of justice and would not be unduly prejudicial to the welfare of the young defendant.

–   A pre-trial familiarisation visit to the court might be appropriate.

–   In cases involving widespread public or media interest, the assistance of the police should be enlisted to try and ensure that a young defendant was not exposed to vilification, intimidation or abuse.

–   Relevant publicity orders should be made.

–   Trial should, so far as possible, be conducted in a courtroom where all participants are on the same, or almost the same, level.

–   A young defendant should normally be free to sit with family, and in a way that allows easy, informal access to legal representatives.

–   Explanations in understandable language should be given at each stage of proceedings, and the trial conducted, so far as practicable, in language which the young defendant can understand.

–   The timetable for the trial should take into account the inability of young defendants to concentrate for long periods.

–   Generally, no wigs and robes should be worn.

–   The court should be prepared to restrict attendance at the trial to a small number, perhaps those with an immediate and direct interest in the outcome. The number of those attending from the media might be restricted to such number as was judged practicable and desirable.

It is clear from this Practice Direction that separate trial should be the preferred option, in cases where the young defendant is accused jointly with an adult. That will enable a court to take a view as to whether trial in the youth court, rather than in the Crown Court, is appropriate means of trial.[2]

---

1   [2000] 2 All ER 205.
2   See para **3.3**.

Composition and sittings of the court

3.16   These have been dealt with at paras **1.3–1.16**.

Persons entitled to be present

3.17   Section 47 of the Children and Young Persons Act 1933 states that the only persons who may be present at any sitting of a youth court are:

(a) members and officers of the court;
(b) parties to the case before the court, their solicitors and counsel, and witnesses and other persons directly concerned in that case;
(c) bona fide representatives of newspapers or news agencies;
(d) such other persons as the court may specifically authorise to be present.

In *R v Southwark Juvenile Court ex parte NJ*,[1] a social worker, who had the supervision of a child under the direction of a local authority, was held to have the right to be present at a sitting of a juvenile court, pursuant to s 47(2)(b). Although s 47(2) was a directory, and not mandatory, requirement, the failure to comply with which did not go to the very jurisdiction of the case, certiorari issued to quash the decision of the juvenile court because, in the circumstances, justice had not been seen to be done. She had desired to seek an adjournment on behalf of the accused, and a fair-minded observer might have concluded that justice had not been seen to have been done.

---

1   [1973] 3 All ER 383.

3.18   No child, other than an infant in arms, may be present in court during the trial of any other person charged with an offence or during the preliminary proceedings, except where his presence is required as a witness or otherwise for the purposes of justice (1933 Act, s 36).

3.19   The court may, and, in the case of a child or young person under the age of 16, must, require his parent or guardian to attend at the court during all the stages of the proceedings, unless the court is satisfied that it would be unreasonable to require such attendance having regard to all the circumstances of the case (1933 Act, s 34A). This includes, where appropriate, the local authority, if the child is in care or in local authority accommodation. Attendance of the parent or guardian can be enforced by the issue of a summons or warrant.

Publicity pre-proceedings

3.20   The law severely restricts the extent to which details of an offence involving a person under the age of 18 can be reported. This basic restriction on the right to report fully such proceedings is justified on the grounds of the protection of the young defendant, notwithstanding the basic right of freedom of expression contained in Art 10 of the Convention. Indeed, adverse or excessive publicity may contribute to issues of fairness highlighted by *T v United Kingdom; V v United Kingdom*.[1] These basic protections have been extended by the 1999 Act, so as to prevent unnecessary and harmful publicity which might identify the young defendant not only at the trial, but also in the pre-trial period, particularly in causes célèbres. This international dimension is discussed further at para **3.38**.

Section 44 of the Youth Justice and Criminal Evidence Act 1999, when in force, will restrict the extent to which details can be published. It will apply where a criminal investigation[2] has begun in respect of:

(a)   an alleged offence against the law of England and Wales, or Northern Ireland;

(b)   an alleged civil offence[3] (other than one that falls under para (a)) which is committed by a person subject to service law.[4]

Where it applies, no matter relating to any person involved in the offence may, while he is under the age of 18, be included in any publication if it is likely to lead members of the public to identify him as a person involved in the offence (1999 Act, s 44(2)). The phrase 'person involved in the offence' is a reference to:

(a) a person by whom the offence is alleged to have been committed; or
(b) or, in certain circumstances, set out below:

    (i) a person against or in respect of whom the offence is alleged to have been committed;[5] or
    (ii) a person who is alleged to have been a witness to the commission of the offence.

The circumstances referred to above in the context of para (b) of s 44(4) if a relevant programme is transmitted, or a publication published on or after a date specified by the Home Secretary (1999 Act, s 44(5)).

---

1   (1999) *The Times*, 17 December.
2   'Criminal investigation', in relation to an alleged offence, is a reference to an investigation conducted by police officers, or other persons charged with the duty of investigating offences, with it being ascertained whether a person would be charged with an offence (1999 Act, s 44(13)(b).
3   'Civil offence' means an act or omission which, if committed in England and Wales, would be an offence against the law of England and Wales.
4   A person is subject to service law if he is subject to military law, air force law or the Naval Discipline Act 1957, or a person to whom Part II of the Army Act 1955 or of the Air Force Act 1955 applies, or to whom Parts I and II of the Naval Discipline Act 1957 apply.
5   Unless the provisions of Sexual Offences (Amendment) Act 1992, s 1, apply (anonymity of victims of certain sexual offences).

3.21   The restrictions contained in s 44(2) cease to apply once there are proceedings in a court in respect of the offence (1999 Act, s 44(3)). In such circumstances, the rules relating to restrictions on reporting, set out below, apply.

3.22   Where s 44(2) applies, the details that may not be published include the name and address of any person, the identity of any school or other educational establishment attended by him, the identity of any place of work, and any still or moving picture of him (1999 Act, s 44(6)). The restriction may be dispensed with by an 'appropriate criminal court', to the extent specified in the order, if it is satisfied that it is necessary in the interests of justice to do so (1999 Act, s 44(8)). This power may be exercised by a single justice (1999 Act, s 44(10)). In deciding whether to make such an order, dispensing, to any extent, with the restrictions imposed by s 44, the court must have regard to the welfare of that person (s 44(8)). That appears to be a matter to which the court must have regard, but does not negate the wider duty, discussed at para **1.9**, to prevent re-offending.

The term 'appropriate criminal court' is defined by s 44(9). It means:

(a) in a case involving an alleged criminal offence, any court in England and Wales (or, where appropriate, Northern Ireland) which has jurisdiction in or in relation to any criminal proceedings (but not a service court, unless the offence was alleged to have been committed by a person subject to service law);

(b) in relation to a civil offence committed by a person subject to service law, any court set out in (a) above, or a service court.

3.23 If a magistrates' or youth court makes, or refuses to make, an order under s 44(7), a right of appeal exists, and is to the Crown Court (s 44(11)). That right of appeal is available to any party to the original application, but also, with leave of the Crown Court, to any other person (s 44(11)). On such an appeal, the Crown Court:

(a) may make such order as is necesary to give effect to its determination of the appeal; and

(b) may also make such incidental or consequential orders as appear to it to be just (s 44(12)).

Publicity restrictions in court proceedings

3.24 The statutory rules relating to the welfare of juveniles involved in legal proceedings and to the imposition of and dispensing with reporting restrictions are contained in the Children and Young Persons Act 1933[1] restrictions on reports of proceedings in which children or young persons are concerned. By s 49(1), the following restrictions apply in relation to which the section applies:

'(a) no report shall be published which reveals the name, address or school of any child or young person concerned[2] in the proceedings or includes any particulars likely to lead to the identification of any child or young person concerned in the proceedings; and

(b) No picture shall be published or included in a programme service as being or including a picture of any child or young person concerned in the proceedings.'

The proceedings to which s 49 applies are proceedings in a youth court, proceedings on appeal from a youth court, proceedings to vary or revoke a supervision order under Sch 7 of the 2000 Act, and proceedings on appeal from such proceedings to vary or revoke (s 49(2)).

---

1 Extensively amended by the Youth Justice and Criminal Evidence Act 1999. These amendments are not yet in force, with a new s 49(3).

2 A person is 'concerned' if they are the person against whom the proceedings are brought or who are witness in those proceedings (1933 Act, s 49(4)).

3.25 The power to lift the restrictions is contained in s 49(4A). If a court is satisfied that it is in the public interest to do so, it may lift the restrictions, in relation to any child or young person who has been convicted of an offence. This is by order, to any specified extent with the requirements of the section, in relation to any proceedings before it to which s 49(4A) applies by virtue of subs 2(a) or (b) (proceedings in or appeals from youth courts), being proceedings relating to:

(a) the prosecution or conviction of the offender for the offence;
(b) the manner in which he, or his parent or guardian, should be dealt with in an aspect of the offence;
(c) the enforcement, amendment, variation, revocation or discharge of any order made in respect of the offence;
(d) where an attendance centre order is made in respect of the offence, the enforcement of any rules governing such an order,[1]
(e) the enforcement of any requirements in respect of a drug treatment and testing order.[2]

Before an order is made under s 49(4A), the parties must be given an opportunity to be heard, and take into account any representations that are made (1933 Act, s 49(4N)).

---

1   See para **5.37**.
2   See para **5.100**.

3.26   The requirements of s 29 may be dispensed with by a court in relation to a child or young person if it is satisfied:

(a) that it is appropriate to do so for the purpose of avoiding injustice to the child or young person; or
(b) that, in respect of a child or young person to whom s 49(5) applies who is unlawfully at large, it is necessary to dispense with its requirements for the purposes of apprehending him and bringing him before a court or returning him to the place in which he was in custody.[1]

This last provision applies to any child or young person convicted of a violent or sexual offence,[2] or an offence punishable in respect of an adult by a term of imprisonment of 14 years or more (s 49(5)).

---

1   Subject to the consent of the Director of Public Prosecutions (s 49(7)), after notice given to the legal representative of the child or young person.
2   See para **3.36**.

3.27   The right to freedom of expression is of course a fundamental one, recognised both by Art 10 of the European Convention on Human Rights and by s 10 of the Human Rights Act 1998. The restrictions imposed by s 49 are extensive, and intended to strike a balance between reporting and protecting the child or young person, who has internationally protected rights. These rules, in s 49, must now be read in the light of international protections set out earlier, at para **1.27**. In *McKerry v Teesdale and Wear Valley Justices*[1], the Divisional Court noted those international protections, and Recommendation No R(87) 20 of the Committee of Ministers of the Council of Europe on Social

Reactions to Juvenile Delinquency, which emphasised the need for privacy in proceedings against a juvenile. The court noted that the principle of privacy inherent in Art 8 had to be balanced against the principle of freedom of expression contained in Art 10, with some tensions existing between these two principles. It was a hallowed principle that justice was administered in public, open to full and fair reporting of court proceedings, but that was limited in the case of juveniles where great weight had to be given to their welfare. Section 49(4A) of the Children and Young Persons Act 1933 permits a court, in certain circumstances, to dispense with anonymity. That power had to be exercised with great care, caution and circumspection: it would be wholly wrong to use that power as an additional punishment. The court also said that it saw no place for 'naming and shaming'. It would rarely be the case that the criteria set out in s 49(4A) ('in the public interest to dispense with the reporting restriction') were met. However, in deciding that, it was entirely appropriate for the court to permit a reporter to address them on the issue, and it was likely they would wish that to occur.

---

1   (2000) 164 JP 355, DC.

3.28   Assuming the restriction has not been lifted, breach of it is an offence. By s 49(9), if a report or picture is published or included in a programme service in contravention of s 49(1), the following persons are liable on summary conviction to a fine not exceeding Level 5 on the standard scale:

'(a)   in the case of a publication or written report of a picture as part of a newspaper, any proprietor, editor or publisher of the newspaper;

(b)   in the case of the inclusion of the report or picture in a programme service, any body corporate which provides the service and any person having functions in relation to the programme corresponding to those of an editor of a newspaper.'

3.29   Further relevant provisions are to be found in s 39 of the 1933 Act, which confers power to prohibit publication of certain matters. In any proceedings, a court may direct that:

'(a)   no newspaper report of the proceedings shall reveal the name, address or school, or include any particulars calculated to lead to the identification of any child or young person concerned in the proceedings, either as being the person by or against or in respect of whom the proceedings are taken, as being a witness therein;

(b)   no picture shall be published in any newspaper as being or including a picture of any child or young person so concerned in the proceedings as aforesaid;

except insofar (if at all) as may be permitted by the direction of the court.'

This provision will, when the Youth Justice and Criminal Evidence Act 1999, s 48, comes into force, be amended, and no longer apply to criminal proceedings. Publication in contravention of any such direction is punishable on summary conviction with a fine not exceeding Level 5 on the standard scale.

BAIL AND REMANDS

3.30   The normal rules relating to bail apply equally to juveniles as they do to adult accused. However, for this purpose a juvenile is a person aged under 17 years (1969 Act, s 12). A defendant aged 17 is, for this purpose, to be treated as an adult. It will already be apparent, however, from the human rights context identified in the context of *T v United Kingdom; V v United Kingdom*[1] that any decisions to grant or refuse bail must have regard to the age and maturity of the defendant and to the proportionality of any deprivation of liberty relative to the risk sought to be prevented by the withholding of bail. So, too, with the imposition of conditions.

---

1   See para **3.15**.

3.31   A court which remands a juvenile must, unless it releases him on bail, remand the juvenile to local authority accommodation,[1] unless the provisions of s 23(4) and (5) of the 1969 Act relating to violent or sexual offences apply.[2]

Such a remand to local authority accommodation does not confer parental responsibility on the local authority.[3] If the juvenile is looked after by a local authority, the remand will be to that local authority.[4] If not, the relevant local authority, is that for the area in which in which it appears to the court that the juvenile resides, or the local authority for the area in which the offence, or one of them, was committed.

---

1   Children and Young Persons Act 1969, s 23(1).
2   See para **3.43**.
3   *North Yorkshire County Council v Selby Youth Court Justices* [1994] 1 All ER 991, DC.
4   1969 Act, s 23(2).

3.32   The court which remands the juvenile to local authority accommodation may impose such conditions which could have been imposed if the court was granting bail, but must first consult the authority (1969 Act, s 23(7)). Thus, the general law relating to bail conditions applies, and should be borne in mind in the context of age and maturity, and whether conditions may obviate the need for more stringent provisions, such as a security requirements. They should be practicable, understandable and enforceable. The power to require a parent to act as surety should also be noted. If a parent or guardian of a defendant under the age of 17 (and still under 17 at the date of his return to court) agrees to act as surety, the court can impose a requirement on that parent or guardian to secure compliance with that condition (Bail Act 1976, s 3(7)). This can only be done with agreement. The parent or guardian who so agrees cannot be liable for a sum greater than £50.

One such possible condition, for example, might be a curfew.[1] Such conditions should be explained to the juvenile in ordinary language in open court, as should the reasons for their imposition. A court may also impose requirements on the local authority with the objective of securing compliance with the conditions imposed on the juvenile, or to prohibit the placing of the juvenile with any named individual (1969 Act, s 23(9)). Such conditions can also be imposed on an application by the local authority (1969 Act, s 23(10)), and requirements imposed on that local authority to ensure compliance with the conditions imposed.

Once again, the general human rights context should be borne in mind. Whilst bail conditions are valid if proportionate and appropriate, they must in fact be so. Restriction on liberty, such as a curfew, amounts to an interference with the right to private and family life, under Art 8 of the Convention. That may be justified, for the prevention of crime or the administration of justice, under Art 8(2), but the limitation must go not further than is justified by those aims.

---

1   For the purposes of the Criminal Justice Act 1967, s 67(1), remand on such a basis to a
     local authority or registered children's home does not count toward the period of custodial
     sentence to be served, unless the accommodation had been provided for the purpose of
     restricting liberty: see *R v Secretary of State for the Home Department, ex parte C* [2000] 1 All ER
     651, HL.

Security requirements

3.33   Powers to impose security requirements are contained in s 23(4) of the 1969 Act, and apply in respect of children aged 12 or above. There is no power to commit a 10- or 11-year-old to secure accommodation (1969 Act, s 24(5)). A child aged under 13 should not be placed in secure accommodation in a children's home without the approval of the Secretary of State.[1]

The relevant provisions of the 1969 Act provision were amended by s 60(1) of the 1991 Act and by s 20 of the 1994 Act, to permit remand directly to secure local authority accommodation, in certain circumstances. These amendments were not implemented, owing to the lack of local authority secure accommodation. The growth in numbers of places in such accommodation has in recent years been a high priority. Gradual, but only partial, improvement in the position led in 1998 to the government introducing, in the 1998 Act, provisions that would permit the introduction of remands to local authority secure accommodation on a partial, and incremental, basis.[2] As noted above, the changes in the 1991 and 1994 Acts were never brought into force, and were repealed by the 1998 Act. The result is that, although the provisions of the 1969 Act remain in force, they do so in an amended form, as provided by complex provisions contained in the 1998 Act. The 1969 Act provisions, whilst they remain in force, permit, in certain circumstances, a male of at least 15 years who is charged with, of convicted of, a violent or sexual offence, to be committed to a remand centre or to prison. This power has been repealed prospectively, from a date to be set. Remand of a juvenile to prison service establishments is regarded as wrong in principle; young defendants should ideally be remanded to institutions appropriate to their age. Indeed, the potential for challenge under the European Convention on Human Rights clearly exists. However, the shortage of secure accommodation has led to this power remaining in being, albeit being replaced by the provisions contained in the Crime and Disorder Act 1998.

---

1   Children (Secure Accommodation) Regulations 1991, SI 1991/1505 (the 1991 Regulations).
2   See Card and Ward *The Crime and Disorder Act 1998* (Jordans, 1998), para 9.38.

3.34   The position can be summarised as follows.

10 or 11-year-old child	No security requirement possible	1969 Act, s 23(5)	para **3.32**
12 or 13-year-old child	Security requirement on local authority	1969 Act, s 23(4), (5)	para **3.33**
Young person aged 14	Security requirement on local authority	1969 Act, s 23(4), (5)	para **3.33**
Female aged 15 or 16	Security requirement on local authority	1969 Act, s 23(4), (5)	para **3.34**
Male aged at least 15 who satisfies conditions	Commit to remand centre or prison	1969 Act, s 23(4), (5) (1991 Act amendments)	para **3.36**
Male aged 15 or 16 who satisfies conditions	Remand to local authority security accommodation, remand centre or prison	1969 Act, s 23(4) (5) (1998 Act not yet in force)	para **3.38**

3.35   A security requirement is a requirement that the person in question is kept in secure accommodation. It is the duty of every local authority to ensure that it is in a position to comply with a security requirement (1991 Act, s 61). It may do so either by providing secure accommodation itself, or by reaching arrangements with other local authorities to secure such services (1991 Act, s 61(2)). Without a security requirement, a local authority will be governed by s 25 of the Children Act 1989.[1] This provides that a child who is being looked after by a local authority may not be placed, and, if placed, must not be kept, in accommodation provided for the purpose of restricting liberty (ie secure accommodation) unless it appears:

'(a)   that –

    (i)   he has a history of absconding and is likely to abscond from any other description of accommodation; and

    (ii)   if he absconds, he is likely to suffer significant harm, or

(b)   that if he is kept in any other description of accommodation he is likely to injure himself or other persons.'

Section 25 permits the Secretary of State to make Regulations; these are the Regulations.

---

1   Section 25 does not apply to a child who is detained under what was s 53 of the 1933 Act or uner any provision of the Mental Health Act 1983. It does apply to detained children under PACE 1984, s 38(6); 1991 Regulations, regs 5, 6.

3.36   There is no power to remand a child aged 10 or 11 to local authority secure accommodation. In respect of a child who has attained the age of 12, or a young person, a security requirement may be imposed only if:

(a) he is charged with, or been convicted of, a violent or sexual offence,[1] or an offence punishable, in the case of an adult, with imprisonment for a term of 14 years or more; or

(b) he has a recent history of absconding while remanded to local authority accommodation, and is charged with or is convicted of an imprisonable offence[2] alleged or found to have been committed while he was so remanded,

and, in either case the court is of the opinion that only such a requirement would be adequate to protect the public from serious harm from him.

In respect of remanded children, s 25 of the 1989 Act applies only if:

(i)   the child is charged with or has been convicted of violent or sexual offences, or an act punishable in the case of an adult with imprisonment for a term of 14 years or more, or

(ii) the child has a recent history of absconding while remanded in local authority accommodation, and is charged with or has been convicted of an imprisonable offence alleged or found to have been committed whilst he was so remanded (1991 Regulations, reg 6(1)).

The effect of the application of s 25 is that the child cannot be kept in secure accommodation without the authority of a court for an aggregate of 72 hours (whether or not consecutive) in any period of 28 consecutive days. Those remanded under s 23 of the 1969 Act may not be subject to a remand in secure accommodation in excess of 28 days; this means that further court authorisation is required (1991 Regulations, reg 13).

3.37   A security requirement must not be imposed on a child or young person who is not legally represented unless he applied for legal aid and his application was refused on the ground that it did not appear that his means were such as he required assistance, or, having been informed of his right to apply for public funding, he refused or failed to apply (s 23(5A)).

The reasons for the imposition of the security requirement must be explained to the child or young person in open court, and be specified in the warrant of commitment (s 23(5A)).

---

1   Within the meaning of Part I of the Criminal Justice Act 1991. See now the 2000 Act, s 161:

' "sexual offence" means any of the following –
   (a)   an offence under the Sexual Offences Act 1956, other than an offence under section 30, 31 or 33 to 36 of that Act;
   (b)   an offence under section 128 of the Mental Health Act 1959;
   (c)   an offence under the Indecency with Children Act 1960;
   (d)   an offence under section 9 of the Theft Act of burglary with intent to commit rape;
   (e)   an offence under section 54 of the Criminal Law Act 1977;
   (f)   an offence under the Protection of Children Act 1978;
   (g)   an offence under section 1 of the Criminal Law Act 1977 of conspiracy to commit any of the offences in paragraphs (a) to (f) above;
   (h)   an offence under section 1 of the Criminal Attempts Act 1981 of attempting to commit any of these offences;
   (i)   an offence of inciting another to commit any of those offences; ...
"violent offence" means an offence which leads, or is intended or likely to lead, to a person's death or to physical injury to a person, and includes an offence which is required to be charged as arson (whether or not it would otherwise fall within this definition).'
2   'Imprisonable offence' means an offence punishable in the case of an adult with imprisonment (1969 Act, s 23(12)).

3.38   The 1998 Act introduced one alternative amendment to the provisions of s 23(4) and (5) to the 1969 Act, and applies to children or young persons who fall within the prescribed description. Section 23(12) of the 1969 Act gives the Home Secretary the power to prescribe, by reference to age or sex, the categories of person to which the provisions apply. An order has been made: the Secure Remands and Committals (Prescribed Description of Children and Young Persons) Order 1999.[1] Under this Order, the following have been prescribed:

(1)   any child who is of the age of 12 or 13;
(2)   any person who is of the age of 14;
(3)   any female person who is of the age of 15 or 16.

In respect of any such person, where the prescribed security conditions are satisfied, the power to remand to secure local authority accommodation exists. Thus, males aged 15 or 16 do not fall within the terms of s 23(4), and fall to be dealt with in the context of the alternative provisions introduced by s 98 of the 1998 Act.

---

1   SI 1999/1265.

3.39   By virtue of s 23(4) of the 1969 Act, if a young person who is male and has attained the age of 15:

(1)   is charged with, or convicted of a violent or sexual offence, or an offence punishable in the case of an adult with imprisonment for a term of imprisonment for a term of imprisonment of 14 years or more; or

(2) has a recent history of absconding whilst remanded to local authority accommodation and is charged with or has been convicted of an imprisonable offence alleged to have been committed whilst he was so remanded;

and, in either case, the court is of the opinion that only remand would be adequate to protect the public from serious harm from him, the court must commit him to a remand centre or to prison. The court must state in open court that it is of that opinion, and the reasons for that opinion explained to the young person in ordinary language.

The trial

3.40   The trial will follow normal procedures, within the context of the trial of a juvenile discussed earlier. Care must be taken to ensure that the proceedings are conducted in a manner which reflects the age and maturity of the defendant.[1]

The power to proceed in the absence of a child or young person is contained in the 1933 Act. By s 42, where in any proceedings for an offence specified in Sch 1 to that Act, the court is satisfied that the attendance before the court of a child or young person in respect of whom the offence is alleged to have been committed is not essential to the just hearing of the case; the case may be proceeded with in the absence of the child or young person. That, however, should be read in the context of the fair trial provisions contained in Art 6 of the European Convention on Human Rights.

---

1   See para **3.15**.

3.41   Evidence may be given through an interpreter. The relevant principles to be applied were stated in *R v West London Youth Court, ex parte N.*[1] The accused should be provided with an interpreter fluent in the language of the accused, or in another language with which the accused is fluent. This right is rooted in fairness and the right of an accused to be present at his own trial.[2]

---

1   [2000] 1 All ER 823.
2   *R v Begum* (1985) 93 Cr App R 96.

3.42   In *R v West London Youth Court, ex parte N,* the court stated that a fair trial is impossible unless two conditions are satisfied. These are that the accused comprehends the case against him, including the nature of the proceedings, and that, secondly, the defendant is capable of advancing his own case by communicating with those who advise him. There is a duty on the court itself to be satisfied that the interpreter and accused properly understand each other. The understanding must be sufficiently full to achieve the essential object of a fair trial. Any interpreter must be impartial.[1] In *R v Begum,*[2] the accused, a woman from rural Pakistan whose native tongue was Punjabi, entered a plea of guilty to a charge of murder. The interpreter provided had a native tongue of Gujurati. Each had a limited knowledge of Urdu. In allowing the appeal, and substituting a conviction for manslaughter, the Court of Appeal concluded that her plea to the charge of murder had been entered without the respective offences (and, in particular, the possible defence of provocation) being explained to her in language she could understand. Watkins LJ said:

> 'There are many languages on our streets. A number of them contain overtones of the dialects in which those languages are spoken ... No one should minimise the difficulties which sometimes occur in obtaining the services of an interpreter who is fluent not only in the language of the person who has to be interrogated but who also has knowledge of the dialect in which that language is spoken ...'

---

1   *R v Imrie* (1917) 12 Cr App R 282; *R v Mitchell* [1970] Crim LR 153.
2   (1985) 93 Cr App R 96.

3.43   The problem arose in an acute form in *R v West London Youth Court, ex parte N*.[1] An 11-year-old defendant in the youth court could speak only Bosnian Romany, a dialect of classical Romany, in respect of which there were, in the United Kingdom, no competent interpreters. At the trial of a co-accused, an attempt had been made to use a process of 'double interpretation', which amounted to the translation of the one language into a second, and then the translation of that second language into a third. The stipendiary magistrate in the instant case heard evidence from a linguist who stated that he had an 80 per cent mutual knowledge of N's language in court-room language. The magistrate ruled that double interpretation could never be lawful, but that K, the linguist, was competent to act as N's interpreter. This conclusion was overturned on an application for judicial review. The Divisonal Court held that, although double interpretation was neither ideal or convenient, it was justified in cases where it proved impossible to find an interpreter who spoke fluently both English and the native tongue of the defendant. Where the defendant was fluent in another language other than his own, it was open to a translator to translate into that language. Where double interpretation was used, both interpreters had to have sufficient skills for the interpretation of their part of the processes. Ideally, each should be a qualified interpreter and each should be independent and impartial. Thus, it was never proper to utilise the 'appropriate adult' or anyone else partial to the defendant. Each interpreter had to be fluent in their common language as well as the language into which they had to translate, whether English or the language of the defendant. These principles applied at both the investigative and trial stages. The interviewing officer, or court, should ensure that there was proper mutual understanding between the defendant and the interpreter who was to interpret into the defendant's language, and in respect of the two interpreters who were to translate in the common language. The second interpreter should also be fluent in English. This question of double interpretation is one which had never arisen for decision in *R v Begum*. Such a conclusion was in accordance with Art 6(3) of the European Convention. That states, inter alia, that:

> 'Everyone charged with a criminal offence has the following minimum rights
>
> (a) to be informed promptly, in a language which he understands and in detail, of the nature and cause of the accusation against him ...
>
> (e) to have the free assistance of an interpreter if he cannot understand or speak the language used in court.'

Simon Brown LJ relied on the decision of the Court of Human Rights in *Kamasinski v Austria* where the Court stated:

> 'The right ... to the free assistance of an interpreter applies not only to oral statements made at the trial hearing but also to documentary material and the pre-trial proceedings. Paragraph 3(e) signifies that a person "charged with a criminal offence" who cannot understand or speak the language used in court has the right to the free use of an interpreter for the translation or interpretation of all those documents or statements in the proceedings instituted against him which it is necessary for him to understand or to have rendered into the court's language in order to have the benefit of a fair trial ... However, paragraph 3(e) does not go so far as to require a written translation of all terms of written evidence or official documents in the procedure. The imperative assistance provided should be such as to enable the defendant to understand the case against him and to defend himself, notably by being able to put before the court his version of events. In view of the need for the right guaranteed by paragraph (3)(e) to be practical and effective, the obligation of the competent authorities is not limited to the appointment of an interpreter, but, if they are put on notice in the particular circumstances, may also extend to a degree of subsequent control over the adequacy of the interpretation provided.'

The court then concluded that Art 6(3)(e) did not dictate that the interpretation should necessarily be simultaneous nor that every word had to be interpreted if a summary would suffice. Accordingly, in the view of Simon Brown LJ, the Convention permitted double translation provided adequate safeguards were in place. The ultimate imperative is to achieve a fair and properly understood trial in which the defendant is able to do justice to his own particular cause.

---

1   [2000] 1 All ER 823, DC.
2   (1989) 13 EHRR 36.

3.44   The normal rules of evidence apply equally to trials in the youth court as they do in respect of adults. An exposition of those rules is outside the scope of this book, but particular evidential issues in respect of the competence of witnesses may arise in the context of the trial of young defendants.

3.45   Generally speaking, the rule in criminal cases is that witnesses are both competent and compellable to give evidence. Issues of competence and compellability are questions of law: in deciding such matters the court may receive expert testimony (Youth Justice and Criminal Evidence Act 1999, s 53(4)(5)). The burden of proof of demonstrating competence or compellability is on the party seeking to call that witness (1999 Act, s 53(2)). Where that burden is on the accused, it will be satisfied on the civil standard of the balance of probabilities.

The rules governing competence of children have in the recent past caused the courts some difficulty, with case-law suggesting that the testimony of very young children should not be considered at all. Attempts by Parliament to change this approach have not always achieved their desired aims. The only issue of understanding that a court now has to explore is whether the potential witness can understand the questions put to him. The latest parliamentary intervention is s 53 of the Youth Justice and Criminal Evidence Act 1999. It sets out a basic rule of competence which applies to all witnesses, and draws no distinctions between adults, children, those suffering mental handicap or illness, and those suffering temporary incapacity.

Section 53 states that, at every stage in criminal proceedings, all persons are (whatever their age) competent to give evidence, subject only to the terms of s 53(3) and (4) (1999 Act, s 53(1), (2)). An accused person is always a competent witness in his or her own defence. Section 53(3) provides one of two exceptions to the general rule of competence. It states:

> 'A person is not competent to give evidence in criminal proceedings if it appears to the court that he is not a person who is able to –
>
> (a)   understand questions put to him as a witness, and
> (b)   give answers to them that can be understood.'

The meaning of the phrase 'understand questions put to him as a witness' is quite clear. Age is not a determinant of competence, although this is a further clarification of the law rather than a change. Section 33A(2A) of the Criminal Justice Act 1988 states that a child's evidence shall be received unless it appears to the court that the child is incapable of giving intelligible testimony. Nevertheless, although age is not a determinant of competence, it is relevant in the sense that an advocate must be expected to put questions in a form, and in language, appropraite to the age of the child. A failure to do so in the context of a young defendant might result in an infringement of the defendant's right to a fair trial within the meaning of Art 6 of the European Convention.

3.46   A witness who is aged 14 years or over testifies on oath, provided that that witness has a sufficient appreciation of the solemnity of the occasion and of the particular responsibility to tell the truth which is involved in taking an oath (1999 Act, s 55(2)). A witness is, if able to give intelligible testimony, to be presumed to have a sufficient knowledge of those matters if no evidence tending to show the contrary is adduced by any party (1999 Act, s 55(3))). If it is, then the burden of proof is on the party seeking to have the witness sworn that, on the balance of probabilities, the witness is 14 or more and has that sufficient appreciation of the solemnity of the occasion (1999 Act, s 54(4)). It will be for the judge, in absence of the jury, to determine the matter, if necessary with the aid of expert testimony (1999 Act, s 55(1), (5), (6)).

If the criteria for being sworn are not met by a witness who is none the less competent, that witness must testify unsworn (1999 Act, s 55(1)).

Chapter 4

YOUTH OFFENDER CONTRACTS

*Introduction – Referral to the Youth Offender Panel – The Pre-conditions – Compulsory Referral –
Discretionary Referral – The Making of a Referral Order – Connected Offences – Multiple Offences
– Deferral for sEntence – The Contents of the Order – The Establishment of a Panel – Meetings of a
Panel – The First Meeting: Agreement of Contract with Offender – The Management of the Contract
– How is the Reference to be Made – The Powers of the Court*

INTRODUCTION

4.1   Part I of the Youth Justice and Criminal Evidence Act 1999 introduced a
new order available to be used in respect of young people convicted for the first
time. Those provisions have been repealed and re-enacted in Part III of the
consolidating Act, the Powers of Criminal Courts (Sentencing) Act 2000 (the
2000 Act). That Act came into force on 24 August 2000. References in this
Chapter are, unless otherwise indicated, to the relevant provisions of the 2000
Act.

Where the pre-conditions contained in s 1 are satisfied, a youth court or
magistrates' court may, and in some circumstances must, refer the offender to a
youth offender panel. A youth offender panel (created by virtue of s 21 of the
2000 Act) will agree a contract with the young offender, which will involve
reparation to the victim and measures to tackle the causes of offending. The
sentencing court will set the contract's duration. If a contract cannot be agreed
or is broken, the young offender will be returned to the sentencing court to be
sentenced for the original offence.

This power which came into force on 1 April 2000, marks a significant
departure from other provisions that have been adopted hitherto, in that in
some cases the youth court has no choice but to make the referral order. It thus
is a restriction on the sentencing powers of the court, assuming the
pre-conditions to be satisfied. The power is being piloted in schemes which will
run from March 2000 until 31 December 2001. The aim is to introduce the
order generally by early 2002.[1]

4.2   During the passage of the 1999 Act through Parliament, the rationale
underpinning the changes was explained by Lord Williams of Mostyn, Minister
of State, Home Office[2] as follows:

> 'We are committed to the reduction of crime and the fear of crime. If we are to
> achieve that ambitious goal ... we must take effective action to deal with young
> offenders. Our primary aim is to prevent offending by children and young people.

However, when they break the law, meaningful punishment is necessary to help young people to take responsibility for their actions, to make amends for their crimes and reparation to their victims and to return to the law-abiding community ... If we can stop today's delinquents becoming tomorrow's recidivists, we will have done a good job for society, for prospective victims, and in terms of preventing the endless waste of human life and resource which is seen by anyone who regularly visits prisons ... We believe that the young offender panel is an imaginative tool for the criminal justice system. It can step in at the time which virtually all criminologists and penologists know is so critically important, right in the early stages; in other words, it can put first-time offenders back on the right track.'

It remains to be seen whether this aim is in fact met by these provisions.

---

1   The pilots will operate in Blackburn with Darwen; Cardiff; London (Hammersmith & Fulham, Kensington and Chelsea and the City of Westminster); Oxfordshire; Nottingham and Nottinghamshire; Suffolk; Swindon and Wiltshire. They will be independently evalauted by a team from Goldsmiths College, University of Kent and University of Leeds with a view to making the provisions available across England and Wales from early 2002.
2   HL Committee 2nd Reading, 15 December 1998.

4.3   This order is a sentence of the court, but is not to be regarded as of the same nature as other 'sentences'.[1] However it might be perceived by the offender,[2] its intended purpose is to ensure that the conviction of the young offender will trigger an inquiry into the reasons for that offending behaviour, imposing on the young offender who pleads guilty the principle of restorative justice[3] through the intervention of a youth offending panel.[2] It is for that reason that the mandatory referral process was introduced, notwithstanding the oft-expressed objections to sentencing provisions that remove discretion from a sentencing court.[4]

---

1   Lord Williams of Mostyn, HL Committee 2nd Reading, 15 December 1998, cols 375, 386.
2   See the comments of Lord Cope of Berkeley, ibid, col 377, who considered that referral would be perceived by the offender as a punishment.
3   Lord Williams, ibid, cols 375–376. For the concept of restorative justice, see para **1.7**. See Lord Cope, ibid, cols 373–374.
4   See para **1.8**.

4.4   A Crown Court does not have the power to make a referral to a youth offender panel. At first sight, this might seem slightly odd, given that a young offender might have been convicted following trial on indictment jointly with an adult, or that a Crown Court might be dealing with an appeal from a youth court. In relation to the former, no power to make an order under s 16 of the 2000 Act exists, a position for which no real explanation was forthcoming during the passage of the 1999 Act. However, in relation to the Crown Court, the referral order power is available to the Crown Court by virtue of the operation of s 48(4) of the Supreme Court Act 1981, which provides that the Crown Court may award any punishment available to the youth court.

REFERRAL TO THE YOUTH OFFENDER PANEL

The pre-conditions

4.5   The power to make a referral to a Youth Offender Panel arises only where the conditions contained in s 16(1) of the 2000 Act are satisfied. Section 16 applies only where a youth court or other magistrates' court is dealing with a person under the age of 18 at the date of sentence[1] for an offence, and the pre-conditions stated in s 16(1)(a), (b) and (c) are each satisfied. These are as follows:

> '(a)   neither the offence nor any connected offence is one for which the sentence is fixed by law;
>
> (b)   the court is not, in respect of the offence or any connected offence, proposing to impose a custodial sentence on the offender or make a hospital order . . . in his case; and
>
> (c)   the court is not proposing to discharge him absolutely in respect of the offence.'

A court therefore has the power to make a referral only where it is proposing to impose a non-custodial sentence. A 'custodial sentence' is defined for this purpose by s 76(1), and means:

(a)   a sentence of imprisonment (as to which, see s 89(1)(a) of the 2000 Act);[2]

(b)   a sentence of detention under s 90 or s 91 of the 2000 Act;[3]

(c)   a sentence for custody for life, under s 93 or s 94 of the 2000 Act;[4]

(d)   a sentence of detention in a young offender institution (under s 96 of the 2000 Act or otherwise);[5]

(e)   a detention and training order (under s 100 of the 2000 Act).[6]

A sentence of imprisonment does not include a committal for contempt of court or any kindred offence (2000 Act, s 76(2)).

A 'hospital order' has the meaning given to it by s 37 of the Mental Health Act 1983.[7]

---

1   Not the date of commission of the offence: see Lord Williams of Mostyn, Minister of State, op cit, cols 371–372. Any attempt by a prosecutor to avoid the operation of the mandatory requirement by delaying the date of hearing would amount to an abuse of process. See *R v Derby Crown Court, ex parte Brooks* (1984) 80 Cr App R 164, HL; *R v Schlesinger* [1995] Crim LR 137, CA.

2   Section 89(1)(a) of the 2000 Act prohibits a court from passing a sentence of imprisonment on a person for an offence if he is aged under 21 when convicted of the offence.

3   Section 90 imposes a duty on a court to impose on a person convicted of murder and who appears to the court to have been aged under 18 at the time the offence was committed a sentence detaining him during Her Majesty's pleasure. Section 91 provides for the detention for a specific period of an offender under 18 who is convicted of certain serious offences.

4   Section 93 and 94 deal with the duty, and in some cases power, to impose a sentence of custody for life on a person aged at least 18 but under 21.

5   Section 96 provides for detention in a young offender institution for certain offenders aged at least 18 but under 21.

6   Section 100 permits a court to make a detention and training order in respect of certain
      offenders aged under 18.
7   By the Mental Health Act 1983, s 37(1), a hospital order is an order authorising the
      admission and detention of a person convicted of an offence punishable with
      imprisonment in such hospital as may be specified, or placing him under the guardianship
      of a local social services authority, or of such other person approved by the local social
      services authority as may be specified.

4.6   Where s 16 applies, s 19 imposes further restrictions, by prohibiting a
court from dealing with an offender in certain ways, either for the offence itself
or for a connected offence. The 'prohibited ways' (2000 Act, s 19(2)) are
defined by s 19(4) and prohibit the combination of a referral with a community
sentence,[1] with a fine, with a reparation order or with a conditional discharge.
In addition, a referral may not be combined with a binding over order, or with
orders made under s 150 of the 2000 Act[2] or s 8 of the Crime and Disorder Act
1998[3] (2000 Act, s 19(2), (4), (5)). Further, if an offender is made the subject of
a reference in respect of an offence, then the powers of a court in respect of any
connected offence are further limited: not only is the court bound by the
'prohibited ways': it is under an obligation in respect of the connected offence
either to make a referral, or, alternatively, discharge the offender absolutely;
there are no other alternatives (2000 Act, s 19(3)).

The purpose of the mandatory provision is to concentrate this disposal on
first-time offenders in order to attempt to break the cycle of offending.[4]
However, there is no restriction on combining referral with absolute discharge
for another offence.[5] Note should also be taken of the fact that a person cannot
be deferred for sentence (s 19(7)). However, nothing in these provisions
prevents a magistrates' court from remitting a case to the youth court for
sentence, under s 8 of the 2000 Act, from adjourning for inquiries under
s 10(3) of the Magistrates' Courts Act 1980, or from using the powers in ss 35,
38, 43 or 44 of the Mental Health Act 1958 (remands for reports, interim
hospital orders and committal to the Crown Court for a restriction order (2000
Act, s 19(7)).

1   Within the meaning of Part IV of the 2000 Act; see Chapter 5.
2   Binding over of parent or guardian.
3   Parenting order: see para **1.26**.
4   Lord Williams of Mostyn, op cit, col 386.
5   Lord Williams of Mostyn, ibid, col 407.

4.7   The permitted sentence combinations are summarised in Table 1 below.

Table 1

Referral	Custody	No
Referral	Suspended sentence	No
Referral	Community sentence	No
Referral	Fine	No
Referral	Reparation order	No
Referral	Conditional discharge	No
Referral	Absolute discharge	Yes
Referral	Bind over order of offender or parent	No
Referral	Parenting order	No

4.8   In each case, the power to make a referral must be available to the court, in the sense that the court must have been notified by the Home Secretary that arrangements for the implementation of referral orders are available in the area in which it appears to the court that the offender resides or will reside, that notice not having been withdrawn (2000 Act, s 16(5)). These provisions were initially introduced on a pilot basis.[1] A court must therefore determine the place of residence (or intended residence) of the young offender before determining whether it can, or must, make an order. It is not open to a court to make an order, and then indicate that the offender should reside in the area in which the power to make an order is available. By contrast, if the power to make an order exists, and subsequently the offender moves to an area where no such arrangements for such orders are in place, the powers contained in s 11 will apply[2]; and enable the panel to refer the question back to the appropriate court.

---

1   See para **4.1**.
2   See para **4.35**.

Compulsory referral

4.9   Section 17(1) of the 2000 Act *requires* a youth court or magistrates' court to make a referral if the pre-conditions stated in s 17(1)(a), (b) and (c) are satisfied. These are as follows:

> '... the offender –
>
> (a)   pleaded guilty to the offence and to any connected offence;
> (b)   has never been convicted by or before a court in the United Kingdom of any offence other than the offence and any connected offence; and
> (c)   has never been bound over in criminal proceedings in England and Wales or Northern Ireland to keep the peace or to be of good behaviour.'

There is thus no *obligation* to refer if the offender pleads not guilty to an connected offence, although the *power* to refer may exist. Nor does an obligation arise if the offender has been the subject of a caution, reprimand or final warning,[1] or been convicted of an offence outside the UK. For the purposes of s 17(1), an offender who has been conditionally discharged for an offence is to be deemed to have been convicted of that offence, despite the terms of s 14 of the 2000 Act, or its Northern Irish equivalent (s 17(5)).[2]

---

1   See paras **2.64**.
2   Section 14 of the 2000 Act states that, subject to certain exceptions, an absolute or conditional discharge is deemed not to be a conviction for most purposes.

Discretionary referral

4.10   Where a court is not bound to make a referral by virtue of s 17(1), it may nevertheless make a discretionary referral if the pre-conditions in s 17(2) (the 'discretionary referral conditions') are satisfied. These are as follows:

'(a)   the offender is being dealt with by the court for the offence and one or more connected offences;
(b)   although he pleaded guilty to at least one of the offences mentioned in paragraph (a) ..., he also pleaded not guilty to at least one of them;
(c)   he has never been convicted by or before a court in the United Kingdom of any offence other than the offences mentioned in paragraph (a) ...; and
(d)   he has never been bound over in criminal proceedings in England and Wales or Northern Ireland to keep the peace or to be of good behaviour.'

Thus the essential difference between the compulsory and discretionary referral conditions is the question of denial of one or more offences. Again, for the purposes of s 17(2), an offender who has been conditionally discharged for an offence is to be deemed to have been convicted of that offence, despite the terms of s 14 of the 2000 Act,[1] or its Northern Irish equivalent (s 17(5)).

The Home Secretary has the power to amend these pre-conditions, by regulation, in any way he considers appropriate (2000 Act, s 17(3)). If he does so, any description of the offender may be framed by reference to such matters as the Home Secretary considers appropriate, including (in particular) one or more of the following (2000 Act, s 17(4)):

'(a)   the offender's age;
(b)   how the offender has pleaded;
(c)   the offence (or offences) of which the offender has been convicted;
(d)   the offender's previous convictions (if any);
(e)   how (if at all) the offender has been previously punished or otherwise dealt with by any court; and
(f)   any characteristics or behaviour of, or circumstances relating to, any person who has at any time been charged in the same proceedings as the offender (whether or not in respect of the same offence).'

Thus the potential exists for the procedure to be made available to those who have previous convictions. That is not, however, the current position.

---

1   See para **4.9**.

The making of a referral order

4.11 The 2000 Act does not make provision for a pre-sentence report (PSR) to have been considered prior to the making of a referral order, and, indeed, at first sight, a PSR might seem unnecessary if the compulsory referral conditions are applicable. Nevertheless, the general rules apply.[1] Clearly, a PSR will be important in assisting the court to determine whether such a referral is necessary or appropriate. There is no requirement that the parents or guardian of an offender be present when the offender is sentenced.

---

1   See para **3.65**.

Connected offences

4.12 An offender may be being sentenced for more than one offence. In such cases then, provided the offences are connected, a court may make a referral order in respect of each of the offences (s 18(4)), whether concurrently or wholly or partly consecutive (s 18(6)). The only limit is that the total length of the period of the youth offender contract that results must not exceed 12 months. For these purposes, the term 'connected offence' means that the offence is one for which the offender falls to be dealt with at the same time as he is dealt with for the other offence (s 16(4)). It does not require either the date or the court of conviction to be the same in respect of each offence (s 16(4)). If these criteria are satisfied, the resulting orders are to be regarded as associated with each other (ss 16(4), 18(4)).

Multiple offences

4.13 Obviously, as noted above, an offender may be being sentenced for one or more offences or connected offences. If that is the case, a referral is made in respect of each offence or connected offence for which the offender is being sentenced (unless, in the case of a connected offence, an absolute discharge is made (2000 Act, s 19(3)(a)), and, in such cases, the orders are 'connected' with each other (s 18(7)). The court does not in these circumstances make one single order, but, rather, must make one order in respect of each offence.[1] Where more than one such order is made, they must refer the offender to the same youth offender panel (s 18(5)), and the detailed provisions of the referral orders must be the same, although the length of the referrals may be different.

The court may direct that the periods specified in the orders be concurrent, or be additional to each other, but are subject to the overall restriction that the total period for which such a contract is to have effect does not exceed 12 months (s 18(6)).

---

1   Lord Williams of Mostyn, op cit, col 407.

Deferral for sentence

4.14   Where the compulsory referral conditions apply, a court may not defer sentence under s 1 of the 2000 Act.[1] This is because the Government was concerned to 'connect punishment or disposal with rapid court appearances and sentence'.[2] There is no point in delaying sentence to reflect the changing circumstances of the young offender: all such matters will be taken into account by the panel. Obviously, this does not prevent the adjourning for reports, because the court is obliged to make a reference only if a custodial sentence is inappropriate. However, a magistrates' court may remit the offender for sentence to the youth court, under s 8 of the 2000 Act.

---

1   Section 1 of the 2000 Act provides: 'Subject to the provisions of this section the Crown Court or a magistrates' court may defer passing sentence on an offender for enabling the court or any other court to which it falls to deal with him to have regard, in dealing with him, to his conduct after conviction (including, where appropriate, the making by him of reparation for his offence or to any other change in his possession)'.
2   Lord Williams of Mostyn, op cit, col 409.

4.15   By s 18(3), on making a referral, the court must explain to the offender in ordinary language:

'(a)   the effect of the order; and
(b)   the consequences which may follow –

   (i)   if no youth offender contract takes effect between the offender and the panel under section 23 . . . ; or
   (ii)   if the offender breaches any of the terms of any such contract.'

The consent of the offender is not necessary for an order to be made.

4.16   The fact of conviction and of disposal by way of the making of a referral is, of course, part of the criminal record of the offender. However, the Rehabilitation of Offenders Act 1974 (as amended by the 1999 Act) (Sch 4, para 6) provided that the rehabilitation period in respect of an offender who is made the subject of a referral order will take effect as follows:

(a)   if a youth offender contract takes effect under s 8,[1] the rehabilitation period is the period beginning with the date of conviction, and ending on the date when (in accordance with s 9) that contract ceases to have effect (1974 Act, s 5(4B)(a));
(b)   if no contract takes effect under s 8,[1] the rehabilitation period is the period beginning with the date of conviction and having the same length as the period for which a contract would have had had one taken effect (ignoring the provisions of Sch 1, paras 11 or 12 (1974 Act, s 5(4B)(b);[2]
(c)   if a contract is extended by virtue of paras 11 or 12 of Sch 1,[2] the rehabilitation period runs from the date of conviction until the date when the extended contract ceases to have effect, or (if no such extended contract takes effect) would have ceased to have effect (1974 Act, s 5(4C)).

Thus, the effect of these provisions is that when the offender satisfactorily completes the contract, the referral order is spent.

1   See para **4.25**.
2   See para **4.40**.

The contents of the order

4.17   Section 18(1) of the 1999 Act provides that the referral order must:

(a)   specify the youth offending team[1] responsible for implementing the order. This will be the team having the function of implementing referral orders in the area in which it appears to the court that the offender resides or will reside. If a court makes an order in respect of more than one offence, the orders will refer the offender to a single youth offender panel (s 18(5));
(b)   require the offender to attend each of the meetings of a youth offender panel to be established by the team for the offender; and
(c)   specify the period during which any youth offender contract taking effect between the offender and the panel under s 23 of the 1999 Act is to have effect. That period must not be less than 3 months nor more than 12 months in length (s 18(1)(c)).

In addition, a court may make an order requiring:

(a)   the 'appropriate person';[2] or
(b)   in a case where there are two or more appropriate persons, any one of them, to attend the meetings of the youth offender panel (s 20(1)).

This power must be exercised, in the case of an offender under the age of 16 years at the date when the court makes a referral order in his case, so as to require at least one appropriate person to attend meetings of the youth offender panel (s 20(2)(a)) and, if the offender is a child who is being looked after by a local authority (within the meaning of the Children Act 1989),[3] the person required to attend those meetings must be, or include, a representative of the local authority (s 20(2)(b) and (6)). However, a court must not make such an order requiring attendance of the appropriate person if it is satisfied that it would be unreasonable to do so (s 20(3)(a)). Similarly, the scope of the requirement to attend should not go beyond what the court is satisfied is reasonable (s 20(3)(b)). It is open to a court to require the attendance of more than one appropriate person: thus, both parents could, if appropriate, be required to attend, thus avoiding the situation where one parent is less of a controlling influence than another on the offender. In some cases, however, that may not be practicable or even desirable.

1   See para **1.18**.
2   See para **4.18**.
3   By the Children Act 1989, s 105(1) 'Local authority' means, in relation to England and Wales, the council of any county, a metropolitan district, a London Borough or the Common Council of the City of London, and in relation to Scotland, a local authority within the meaning of s 1(2) of the Social Work (Scotland) Act 1968.

4.18   The question of who amounts to an 'appropriate person' for those purposes is dealt with by s 20(4) and (5). Each of the following is an 'appropriate person':

(a)   each parent or guardian (s 20(4))[1]; and
(b)   any representative of a local authority which looks after a person aged under 16 (s 20(5)(a) and (6)).

Where an order is made requiring the attendance of an appropriate person, then by s 20(1), the referral order must:

(a)   specify the youth offending team responsible for implementing the order. This will be the team having the function of implementing referral orders in the area in which it appears to the court that the offender resides or will reside. If a court makes an order in respect of more than one offence, the orders will refer the offender to a single youth offender panel (s 20(5));
(b)   require the offender to attend each of the meetings of a youth offender panel to be established by the team for the offender; and
(c)   specify the period for which any youth offender contract taking effect between the offender and the panel under s 23 of the 2000 Act is to have effect.[2] That period must not be less than 3 months nor more than 12 months in length (s 18(1)(c)).

The court must send him (or the authority) a copy of the order forthwith (s 5(8)).

Legal representation is not forbidden by the 1999 Act, but it is not anticipated that this should occur. The very purpose of the meeting is to address the needs of the young offender, prompting the Minister of State to observe that legal representation 'is the very last thing one wants'.[3]

---

1   By s 107(1) of the Children and Young Persons Act 1933, '"guardian", in relation to a child or young person, includes any person who, in the opinion of the court having cognisance of any case in relation to the child or young person or in which the child or young person is concerned, has for the time being the care of the child or young person.' A local authority is not for this purpose a guardian: see *Leeds County Council v West Yorkshire Metropolitan Police* [1982] 1 All ER 274.
2   See para **4.24**.
3   Lord Williams of Mostyn, op cit, col 426.

The establishment of a panel

4.19   Where a referral order is made in respect of an offender (or two or more associated orders) the YOT must:

(a)   establish a youth offender panel for the offender;
(b)   arrange for the first meeting of the panel to be held for the purpose of seeking to reach agreement with the offender as to a programme of behaviour under s 23 of the 2000 Act;[1]

(c) subsequently arrange for the holding of any further meetings of the panel
     needed under s 25 in the light of a failure to agree a contract of behaviour
     at the first meeting (s 21(1)).[2]

The composition of, conduct of and discharge of functions by, the youth
offender panel must be in accordance with guidance issued by the Home
Secretary (s 21(2)). Further, the qualifications of, or criteria for service as,
members may be regulated by Regulations (s 21(4)). The minimum composition is, however, set out by s 21(4): one member appointed by the YOT from
amongst its members, and two members who are not members of that team.

---

1   See para **4.24**.
2   See para **4.28**.

4.20   It may be that the YOT specified in the order does not, or will not, have
the function of implementing referral orders in the area where the offender
resides, or proposes to reside, because of a change, actual or prospective, in the
offender's place of residence. In that case, s 21(5) grants a power to the court
which made the referral order to vary that order, so as to specify the youth
offending team for the area in which the offender does, or will, reside. No court
other than the sentencing court has this power of variation. Although the 2000
Act is silent on the point, no doubt an application for variation will be made by
the youth offending team referred to in the order; there is no reason why,
however, such an application cannot be made by any interested party, the only
pre-condition in s 21(5) being that it must 'appear to the court'. The court will
not, of course, have to be identically constituted.

Where such a variation order is made, s 21(6) applies. The effect of this is that
the new team will have to constitute a panel, arrange for the first meeting (if
that has not already occurred) and take over a contract of behaviour if that has
been agreed. Of course, if that contract is regarded as unsuitable in all or any
respects, then the appropriate action by the new team is to vary it in accordance
with the terms of s 26. If no such contract is in existence, then the new team will
negotiate one.

Meetings of a panel

4.21   Section 21(2) requires a panel to be constituted, conduct its proceedings and discharge its functions in accordance with guidance given from time
to time by the Home Secretary. That guidance will incorporate national
standards and set out advice on specific issues, for example about how a victim
is to be approached in respect of reparation.

The 2000 Act envisages:

–   a first meeting (s 23);
–   such further meetings as are needed where there is failure to agree a
     programme of behaviour (s 25);

- a 'progress meeting' (s 26);
- 'the final meeting' (s 27).

In respect of each of these meetings (s 22(1)), it is the obligation of the YOT to notify the offender and any appropriate person of the time and place at which he is required to attend that meeting. The Act does not specify how such notification is to be given, but both fairness and commonsense suggest that such notification should be in writing.

Speed is regarded as important. It is envisaged that the initial meeting be held quickly. One of the problems with this is that some contact with the victim of the crime will be needed to inform the panel's discussions. There will therefore need to be a certain amount of preparatory work.[1] In this context, a three-day target may be too short, but, conversely, 14 days too long.[1] Home Office Guidance issued during 2000 puts some flesh on the legislative scheme. Contact is to be made with the offender within five working days. The panel may not have a PSR, for it is unlikely that any such report will have been prepared, but it will often have a previous record of the young person, including a risk assessment and progress report, carried out in relation to a final warning. Information about past and current offending behaviour, relevant family circumstances and education and health needs will be essential if the programme of activity is to be targeted effectively to prevent re-offending. In this regard, the powers contained in s 115 of the Crime and Disorder Act 1998 enable information to be shared between public authorities, although not, seemingly, between the statutory and voluntary sectors. Initial contact with the victim should be made within five working days of the making of the order. The initial contact will explore whether or not the victim wishes to attend the initial meeting of the youth offender panel and whether he or she wishes to accept direct reparation.

---

1   Lord Williams of Mostyn, op cit, col 416.

4.22   Failure to attend a meeting by the offender is not a criminal offence. Nor is it inevitably a breach of the contract of behaviour, although there is no reason why a requirement to attend such meetings should not be made a term of the agreement made under s 23. However, s 22(2) provides that if the offender fails to attend any part of such a meeting, the panel may:

'(a) adjourn the meeting to such time and place as it may specify; or
(b) end the meeting and refer the offender back to the appropriate court.'

These are alternatives, but no great significance from this arises. Adjourning the panel does not lose the ability to refer the matter back to the appropriate court; s 22(2) will operate in respect of the adjourned meeting, and therefore a likely pattern is that a panel might refer back to the appropriate court only after an earlier adjournment. What happens if an offender is referred back to the appropriate court is dealt with by Sch 1 to the 2000 Act, discussed at paras **4.37** *et seq*. Because consequences follow from failure to attend, it is clearly important that it should be capable of proof that the offender was aware that the meeting is being held. This is the reason why the offender should be notified in writing.[1]

---

1   See para **4.26**.

4.23   At any meeting, the offender may be accompanied by one person aged 18 or over chosen by the offender (who need not be the same person for each meeting). This is stated by s 22(3) to be an entitlement, but is subject to the agreement of the panel. There is no such entitlement to have present a person aged under 18 years. Thus a young person may be aged 17, married to a young woman of the same age, yet would not be entitled to have her present. On one view of the meaning of s 22(3), she would not (under s 22(3)) be able to attend at all. It can be argued that the words 'One person aged 18 or over chosen by the offender' limit the scope of the panel as to who it may permit to attend; after all, it would have been possible for the words to have read 'One person chosen by the offender, with the agreement of the panel'[1] and, indeed, the proposition that s 22(3) limits the discretion of the panel is supported by the fact that s 22(4) sets out who else the panel may allow to attend. Nevertheless, it is suggested that these difficulties arising owe more to drafting and less to a desire to limit the discretion of the panel. The intention is to give to the panel authority to exclude those who would be unsuitable, because, for example, they are disruptive or have the wrong motivation.[2] Section 22(3) is oddly drafted: it is not easy to reconcile an entitlement with a requirement for agreement; by definition an entitlement does not require the permission or agreement of others. The section perhaps distinguishes between the identify of a peron (which requires agreement) with the subsequent entitlement of that person to attend. Thus the panel may agree several persons as persons whom it will agree may accompany the offender: the offender then has the right to have one of those persons accompany him.

The difficulties in terms of s 22(3) may be more theoretical than real, in the light of s 22(4). This provides that the panel may allow to attend a meeting of the panel:

> '(a)   any person who appears to the panel to be a victim of, or otherwise affected by, the offence, or any of the offences, in respect of which the offender was referred to the panel;
>
> (b)   any person who appears to the panel to be someone capable of having a good influence on the offender.'

There appears to be no right of veto in respect of the offender as to who should not be present. Clearly, there could be no question of an offender having a veto in respect of the presence of a victim, especially in the light of the strategy of making offenders aware of the consequences of their offending behaviour. However, a young offender may be estranged or on bad terms with a parent. These are matters which a panel should have regard to in determining whether an invitation pursuant to s 22(4) should be issued to any individual.

There is no prohibition on a person who is a legal representative attending. Such a person ought not to be present simply because they are a legal representative, but ought not to be excluded if they can be of benefit.[3]

The panel has the discretion to require or permit an individual to attend only for part of a meeting. Meetings may be held in private, for example because the panel wish to withdraw to discuss matters in private. This, like other matters, will be the subject of Home Office guidance. It may be appropriate to see the victim alone, and without the presence of the offender. A key question a panel may need to address is simply this: can the offender's interests be properly safeguarded by consultation?[4]

---

1   See the amendment of Viscount Bridgeman at HL Committee, op cit, col 431.
2   See Lord Williams of Mostyn, op cit, col 431.
3   Lord Williams of Mostyn, ibid.
4   Lord Williams of Mostyn, ibid, col 433.

The first meeting: agreement of contract with offender

4.24   The purpose of the first meeting is (under s 23) to seek to reach agreement with the offender on a programme of behaviour the aim (or principal aim) of which is the prevention of re-offending by the offender.

The terms of the programme are not prescribed by the 2000 Act, and limited only by the matters contained in s 23(3) or by any wider issues arising under concepts of proportionality.[1] Nevertheless, s 23(2) states that they may, in particular, include provision for any of the following:

'(a)   the offender to make financial or other reparation to any person who appears to the panel to be a victim of, or otherwise affected by, the offence, or any of the offences, for which the offender was referred to the panel;
(b)   the offender to attend mediation sessions with any such victim or other person;
(c)   the offender to carry out unpaid work or service in or for the community;
(d)   the offender to be at home at times specified in or determined under the programme;
(e)   attendance by the offender at a school or other educational establishment or at a place of work;
(f)   the offender to participate in specified activities (such as those designed to address offending behaviour, those offering education or training or those assisting with the rehabilitation of persons dependent on, or having a propensity to misuse, alcohol or drugs);
(g)   the offender to present himself to specified persons at times and places specified in or determined under the programme;
(h)   the offender to stay away from specified places or persons (or both);
(i)   enabling the offender's compliance with the programme to be supervised and recorded.'

However, s 23(3) states that the programme may not provide:

'(a)   for the electronic monitoring of the offender's whereabouts; or
(b)   for the offender to have imposed on him any physical restriction on his movements.'

The programme agreed may involve contact with the victim or the involvement in some wider way of the victim of the offence. The terms of s 23(4) are such that the offender may not be required to make financial or other reparation to a victim or other affected person without the consent of that person. Curiously, consent is not required by s 23(4) in respect of any requirement under s 23(1)(b) (mediation sessions with any such victim). This is probably unimportant, because there would be no power to require a victim to attend mediation, and thus by definition it will be consensual. By implication, the terms of s 23(1)(c) are restricted to unpaid work or service in the community not extending to the victim, for otherwise the terms of s 23(1)(a) and s 8(4) make no sense. In this context, various provisions of the European Convention on Human Rights must be borne in mind. First, Art 4 is relevant to questions of reparation. It states, at Art 4(2) that 'No-one shall be required to perform forced or compulsory labour'. This basic right is subject to the exception contained, inter alia, in Art 4(3)(d) ('any work or service which forms part of normal civic obligations'). It is a strained interpretation of the term 'civic obligation' to describe work by way of reparation, yet it can be argued that by agreeing in the negotiated contract to undertake work in the community, or for a specific victim, civic obligations are being assumed. It could, of course, be argued that any work is not 'forced or compulsory' because the offender has in fact agreed to participate in that work. That, however, ignores the realities of the situation: the offender agrees only because of the potential consequences if he does not. However, it would be surprising if indeed a court did not regard such commitments as well within the terms of the Convention. Secondly, the right under Art 8, (respect for private and family life, home and correspondence) should be borne in mind. Again any matters arising under a youth offender contract are agreed. Yet care should be taken to ensure that the requirements being negotiated by the youth offender panel are proportionate and strike a balance between reparation or control on the one hand and the private life of the offender on the other.

---

1   See para **1.37**.

4.25 Reparation is not an essential element of such a programme. In particular, there is no obligation on panels to insist on financial reparation direct to the victim in every case, and the interaction of this provision with that formerly in s 85 of the Crime and Disorder Act 1998 (now s 73 of the 2000 Act) should be noted.[1]

---

1   See para **5.1**.

4.26 Where a programme has been agreed by a panel, the panel must cause a written record of the programme to be produced forthwith (s 23(5)):

> '(a) in language capable of being readily understood by, or explained to, the offender; and
> (b)   for signature by him.'

It is unclear as to what is the precise meaning of s 23(5)(a). The 'or' might at first sight appear to be disjunctive, in the sense of giving the panel the choice, in the light of the personal characteristics of the particular offender. It is submitted that this is not the position, and that the first objective is to cause the written record to be produced in terms that are in fact readily understood by him; only if that is possible should the second limb of s 23(5)(a) come into play. The point is one of importance: the signing-up to the contract by the offender is one that has legal consequences. Failure to comply can result in detention, remand, and referral back to the court of an offender pursuant to the terms of Sch 1 to the 2000 Act. It is therefore crucially important that the offender is, and is seen to be, clearly aware of what is expected of him, and that there is clarity in the terms of the contract. Of course, there is no obligation imposed by s 23(5) to demonstrate that an offender in fact understood the terms of the contract agreed pursuant to s 23.

Once the record has been signed by the offender and by a member of the panel on behalf of the panel, the terms as set out in the record take effect as the terms of a 'youth offender contract' between the offender and the panel, and the panel must cause a copy of the record to be given or sent to the offender (s 23(5)). Clearly, it is to the written record that the offender agrees: the offender is not bound by requirements that may have been imposed in the meeting but not reduced to writing, or by requirements that are inaccurately recorded. The Act does not state that the written record should be sent, or given, within any given timescale, or 'forthwith' or whatever, and, literally read, s 23(5) defines a youth offender contract in terms which assume it comes into being once the written record is produced. It is submitted, however, that a failure to send a copy of the written record to the offender means that it would not be open to the panel to make a reference back to the court under Sch 1. An alternative approach would be to accept that such a reference can be made, but that the court to which a referral is made will not be prepared to take any action if it is not proved that the offender was sent a copy of the contract.

The management of the contract

4.27   A contract takes effect on the first day of the period for which it has effect (s 24(2)). The period for which it has effect will be the period specified in the order being not less than three months or more than 12 months (s 18(1)(c)). It would appear to take effect notwithstanding that a copy of the contract has not been sent to the offender (see above). The length of the period of the contract in circumstances where there is not more than one referral by a court shall be that which results from the court's directions under s 18(6) (s 24(4)). The length of the contract is of course subject to any extensions of the contract ordered by a court under paras 11 or 12 of Sch 1 (s 24(5)(a)),[1] or subject to any revocation under paras 5(2) or 14(2) of Sch 1 (s 24(5)(b) and (6)).[2] In each case, the order expires at the time when the extended period finishes or when the order or orders is or are revoked.

---

1   See para **4.37**.
2   See para **4.38**.

4.28 As noted earlier, a panel at a first meeting will negotiate the contract. Where it appears to a youth offender panel to be appropriate to do so, the panel may:

(a) end that first meeting (or any adjourned meeting) without having reached agreement with the offender on a programme of behaviour of the kind mentioned in s 23(1); and

(b) resume consideration of the offender's case at a further meeting of the panel (s 25(1)).

If, however, it appears to the panel at the first meeting or any further such meeting that there is no prospect of agreement being reached with the offender within a reasonable period after the making of the referral order (or orders), there is no obligation to resume consideration of the offender's behaviour at a further meeting pursuant to s 25(1)(b); instead, the panel must refer the offender back to the appropriate court. The term of s 25(2) should be noted: the panel has no discretion. Once it concludes that there is no prospect of agreement being reached within a reasonable period, it must make that referral back. Likewise, if at a meeting of a panel agreement is reached with the offender but he does not sign the record produced in pursuance of s 23(5), and his failure appears to the panel to be unreasonable, the panel must end the meeting and refer the offender back to the appropriate court (s 25(3)). The wording of s 25(3) is, again, curious: it imposes a requirement of referral back in circumstances where, at a meeting, the offender fails to sign a contract 'produced' to him. Of course, s 23(3) anticipates that a contract might be produced, but also that it might be 'sent': s 25(3) does not create a power, or impose an obligation, to make a reference back where there is a failure to sign a contract which has been sent rather than produced.

4.29 By s 26(1), at any time:

'(a) after a youth offender contract has taken effect under section 23, but

(b) before the end of the period for which the contract has effect',

the specified youth offending team must, if requested by the panel, arrange for the holding of a meeting of the panel (a 'progress meeting') under s 26. The panel is obliged to make such a request in the circumstances set out in s 26(3) and may make such a request in the circumstances in s 26(2). Of course, if neither s 26(2) or (3) apply, the panel may not make such a request.

The *mandatory requirement* under s 26(3) is where:

'(a) the offender has notified the panel that –

   (i) he wishes to seek the panel's agreement to a variation in the terms of the contract, or

   (ii) he wishes the panel to refer him back to the appropriate court with a view to the referral order (or orders) being revoked on account of a significant change in his circumstances (such as his being taken to live abroad) making compliance with any youth offender contract impractical; or

(b) it appears to the panel that the offender is in breach of any of the terms of the contract.'

The *discretionary power* in s 26(2) applies if it appears to the panel to be expedient to review:

'(a) the offender's progress in implementing the programme of behaviour contained in the contract, or
(b) any other matter arising in connection with the contract.'

Where a progress meeting is held, whether under s 26(2) or (3), s 26(4) provides that the panel must do one or more of the following things as it considers appropriate in the circumstances, namely:

'(a) review the offender's progress or any such other matter as is mentioned in subsection (2) ...;
(b) discuss with the offender any breach of the terms of the contract which it appears to the panel that he has committed;
(c) consider any variation in the terms of the contract sought by the offender or which it appears to the panel to be expedient to make in the light of any such review or discussion;
(d) consider whether to accede to any request by the offender that he be referred back to the appropriate court.'

Where the panel has discussed with the offender any breach of the terms of the contract pursuant to s 26(4)(b):

'(a) the panel and the offender may agree that the offender is to continue to be required to comply with the contract (either in its original form or with any agreed variation in its terms) without being referred back to the appropriate court; or
(b) the panel may decide to end the meeting and refer the offender back to that court' (s 26(5)).

4.30 Where a variation in the terms of the contract is agreed between the offender and the panel, the panel must cause a written record of the variation to be produced forthwith:

'(a) in language capable of being readily understood by, or explained to, the offender; and
(b) for signature by him' (s 26(6)).

Any such variation shall take effect once the record has been signed:

'(a) by the offender; and
(b) by a member of the panel on behalf of the panel;'

and the panel must cause a copy of the record to be given or sent to the offender (s 26(7)).

4.31 If at a progress meeting a variation is agreed, but the offender does not sign the record produced and his failure to do so appears to the panel to be unreasonable, the panel may end the meeting and refer the offender back to the appropriate court (s 26(8)). By contrast, if the offender has requested a reference back to the appropriate court under s 26(4)(d), and, after discussion, it is satisfied that there is (or is soon to be) such a change in circumstances as is mentioned in s 26(3)(a)(ii), the panel may decide (but is not obliged) to end the meeting and refer the offender back to the appropriate court.

4.32 The supervisor of the young offender may or may not be the member of the youth offending team who is on the panel. This may, or may not, be appropriate in all the circumstances. A measure of discretion is considered appropriate, and of particular importance will be ethnic and gender representation on the panel. Guidance in support of these provisions will stress the importance of ensuring performance of the duty under s 95 of the Criminal Justice Act 1991 to avoid discrimination on the grounds of race. It is intended to monitor the use of the provisions to ensure fairness of impact on ethnic minorities.

4.33 At the end of the compliance period of the youth offender contract, the specified youth offender team must arrange for the holding of a final meeting between the offender and the panel (s 27(1)). This meeting must occur before the expiration of that period. At that final meeting the panel must (s 27(2)):

'(a)   review the extent of the offender's compliance to date with the terms of the contract; and
(b)   decide, in the light of that review, whether his compliance with those terms has been such as to justify the conclusion that, by the time the compliance period expires, he will have satisfactorily completed the contract;'

and the panel must give to the offender written confirmation of its decision (s 27(2)). The effect of this conclusion is that the panel's decision discharges the referral order (or orders) as from the date of the compliance period (s 27(3)). That decision may be taken in the offender's absence if it appears to the panel to be appropriate to do that instead of exercising the rights under s 22(2) to adjourn or refer back to the court (s 27(4)).

4.34 The question as to what is to happen when a youth offender panel refers an offender back to an appropriate court, or is, whilst subject to a referral order, convicted of further offences is dealt with in accordance with Sch 1 to the 2000 Act (2000 Act, s 28(1)). More specifically, that Schedule applies where a reference is made by a panel under one of the powers or duties described above (Sch 1, para 1(1)).[1] The appropriate court for such a reference is:

'(a)   in the case of an offender under the age of 18 at the time when (in pursuance of the referral back) he first appears before the court, a youth court acting for the petty sessions area in which it appears to the youth offender panel that the offender resides or will reside; and
(b)   otherwise, a magistrates' court and acting for that area (other than a youth court).' (Sch 1, para 1(2))

---

1   See paras **4.28**, **4.29** and **4.32**.

How is the reference to be made?

4.35   A reference is made by the panel sending a report to the appropriate
court explaining why the offender is being referred back to it (Sch 1, para 2).
When that report is received, the court must cause the offender to appear
before it (Sch 1, para 3). To achieve this, a justice acting for the petty sessions
area for which the court acts may:

> '(a)   issue a summons requiring the offender to appear at the place and time
>   specified in it; or
> (b)   if the report is substantiated on oath, issue a warrant for the offender's arrest.'
>   (Sch 1, para 3(2))

Such a summons or warrant must direct the offender to appear or be brought
before the appropriate court (Sch 1, para 3(4)). In respect of those who are in
Scotland, s 4 of the Summary Jurisdiction (Process) Act 1981 (execution of
process of English courts in Scotland) applies in the same way as it applies to
process issued under the Magistrates' Courts Act 1980 (Sch 1, para 3(4)).

4.36   Where the offender is arrested pursuant to a warrant issued under
para 3(2)(b) and cannot be brought immediately before the appropriate court:

(a)   the person in whose custody he is may make arrangements for his
        detention in a place of safety (within the meaning given by s 107(1) of the
        Children and Young Persons Act 1933)[1], for a period of not more than
        72 hours from the time of arrest (Sch 1, para 4), and it is lawful to detain
        him in pursuance of such arrangements; and
(b)   that person must within that period bring him before a youth court (if he is
        under the age of 18 when he is brought before the court) or a magistrates'
        court (if aged 18 or over) (Sch 1, para 4). That court may not be necessarily
        be the 'appropriate court'; if it is not, the provisions of Sch 1, paras 4(3),
        4(4) and 4(5) apply. Paragraph 4(3) empowers the court to direct that
        either the offender is released forthwith or, alternatively, may remand
        him. If such a court does remand him, whether in custody or on bail, s 128
        of the Magistrates' Courts Act 1980[2] applies as if the court referred to in
        s 128(1)(a), (3), (4)(a) and (5) were the appropriate court. However, in
        such cases s 128 is amended by Sch 1, para 5, by the addition in s 128(1) of
        an additional para (d). The effect of this is to empower the remanding
        court to remand an offender under the age of 18 to accommodation
        provided by or on behalf of a local authority, and if it does so it must
        designate as the authority which is to receive him the local authority for the
        area in which it appears to the court that the offender resides or will reside.

1　Section 107(1) of the 1933 Act states that the phrase 'place of safety' means 'a community home, any police station or any hospital, surgery or other suitable place the occupier of which is willing temporarily to receive a child or young person'.

2　The provisions of s 128 referred to enable a magistrates' court –
(a)　to remand in custody (s 128(1)(a);
(b)　to further remand having been brought before a court on remand (s 128(3));
(c)　direct a person remanded on bail to direct him to appear before that court at the end of the period of remand (s 128(4)(a));
(d)　direct a person to appear at a specific time and place to which during the course of the proceedings the hearing may from time to time have been adjourned (s 128(5)).

The powers of the court

4.37　The court has the power to revoke the referral order (or each of the referral orders), provided certain pre-conditions are satisfied (Sch 1, para 5(1), (2)). Where an order is revoked, so too is any related order.

The pre-conditions are specified by Sch 1, para 5(1). It must be proved to the satisfaction of the appropriate court as regards any decision of a panel which results in the offender being referred back to the court:

'(a)　that, so far as the decision relied on any finding of fact by the panel, the panel was entitled to make that finding in the circumstances, and
(b)　that, so far as the decision involved any exercise of discretion by the panel, the panel reasonably exercised that discretion in the circumstances ...'

Schedule 1, para 5(1) is silent as to the burden and standard of proof, and also in respect of the test to be applied in respect of the question of whether discretion was reasonably exercised.

4.38　Having revoked an order, or a related order, the appropriate court may deal with the offender for the offence in respect of which the revoked order was made. More specifically, Sch 1, para 5(5), provides that, in so dealing with the offender for the offence, the appropriate court:

'(a)　may deal with him in any manner in which (assuming section 1 had not applied) he could have been dealt with for that offence by the court which made the order; and
(b)　shall have regard to –

(i)　the circumstances of his referral back to the court; and
(ii)　where a contract has taken effect under section 8 between the offender and the panel, the extent of his compliance with the terms of the contract.'

This power to revoke, or to revoke and re-sentence the offender, cannot be exercised in the absence of the offender, but may be exercised even if the term specified in the contract has expired (whether before or after the referral of the offender back to the court) (Sch 1, para 5(6)). Clearly, the court may commit to the Crown Court for sentence, if the original court had the power to do so. Where it does so, the powers set out in para 5 apply as if the 'appropriate court' were the Crown Court (Sch 1, para 5(7)). A right of appeal against a sentence imposed by a court pursuant to para 5 lies to the Crown Court (para 6). Where a court decides that the pre-conditions have not been satisfied, or (if they are, or would be but for the absence of the offender) the court decides not to exercise the power to re-sentence the offender, para 7 applies. This deals with two alternative situations.

4.39   The first alternative is where no contract has taken effect under s 8, or, the period for which such a contract is to take effect has not expired.

In this situation, the offender continues to remain subject to the referral order (or orders) in all respects as if he had not been referred back to the court (Sch 1, para 7(2)).

If, by contrast, the period for which the contract is to take effect has expired (otherwise than by revocation), the court must make an order declaring that the referral order (or each of them) is discharged (Sch 1, para 7(3)). So, too, in a case where the court decides (contrary to the decision of the panel) that the offender's compliance with the terms of the contract has, or will have, been such as to justify the conclusion that he had satisfactorily completed the contract (Sch 1, para 8).

4.40   The second alternative is where an offender is being dealt with for further convictions during a referral. If that is the case, Part II of Sch 1 applies, provided that the length of the compliance period is less than 12 months (Sch 1, para 10(2)). Although not stated specifically, that period clearly relates to the original length of the compliance period as stated in the contract, not the length of the compliance period which remains unexpired. It should also be noted that para 13(8) empowers the Home Secretary to make such amendments of paras 10 to 12 as he considers appropriate for altering in any way the description of offenders in the case of which an order extending the compliance period may be made.

In this situation, where the further offence, and any associated offences, were committed prior to the referral, and the occasion which led to that referral was the only other occasion on which it has fallen to a court in the UK to deal with the offender for any offence or offences, the relevant court may sentence the offender for the offence by making an order extending his compliance period (Sch 1, para 11). Note should be taken of the fact that para 11 uses the expression 'deal with the offender'. That presupposes a finding or plea of guilt for an offence. The power in para 11 therefore clearly applies in a case where an offender has been before a court on previous occasions but no finding or plea of guilt was made or received. The position where there has been a deferral of sentence is uncertain. In this situation, it has fallen to a court to deal with the offender. Further, an offender is not to be regarded as having been dealt with where the offender was absolutely discharged, but is to be so regarded if he was bound over to keep the peace (Sch 1, para 13(6), (7)).

If, by contrast, the further offence, or associated offence, committed by an offender who has not been dealt with except on the occasion of the referral, was committed after the referral, the court may likewise deal with the offender for that offence, or those offences, by an extension of the period of compliance, but only if the requirements specified in Sch 1, para 12(2) are satisfied. These are that the court must:

> '(a) be satisfied, on the basis of a report made to it by the relevant body that there are exceptional circumstances which indicate that, even though the offender has re-offended since being referred to the panel, extending his compliance period is likely to help prevent further re-offending by him; and
> (b) state in open court that it is so satisfied and why it is.'

The 'relevant body' for this purpose is the panel to which the offender has been referred or, if no contract has yet taken effect between the offender and the panel, the specified youth offending team (Sch 1, para 12(3)).

4.41 Whichever of paras 11 or 12 apply (if they do), the effect of extension must not be such as to extend the offender's compliance period beyond a total period of 12 months (Sch 1, para 13(1)). Further, Part II of Sch 1 imposes certain restrictions. The effect of an extension under paras 11 or 12 is that the court may not also, for that same offence or for an associated offence, make an order binding the offender over to keep the peace or to be of good behaviour, may not make an order under s 150 of the 2000 Act (binding over a parent of guardian), or may not make a parenting order under s 8 of the Crime and Disorder Act 1998 (Sch 1, para 13(5), s 4(5)). Further, the court may not impose a community sentence, a fine, a reparation order under s 73 of the 2000 Act, or a conditional discharge (Sch 1, para 13(3), s 4(4)). In respect of any connected offences, an extension order must be made under paras 11 or 12, or, alternatively, a court may make an absolute discharge. The matters set out above apply equally to connected offences as they do to the original offence (Sch 1, para 13(4)).

4.42 Where an offender is dealt with by a court for an offence, whether committed before or after he was referred to the panel, by making an order other than one extending the compliance period or by discharging the offender absolutely, para 14 applies. The effect of para 14 is that the order of the court revokes the referral order, or orders, and any related orders (s 14(2)). Where this occurs, the court may, if it appears to be in the interests of justice to do so, deal with the offender for the offence in respect of which the revoked order was made in any manner in which (assuming s 1 had not applied) he could have been dealt with for that offence by the court which made the order. In so dealing with the offender under para 14(3), the court must have regard to the extent to which a contract which has taken effect between the offender and any panel has been complied with (para 14(4)). It may, if the original court would have had the power to do so, commit to the Crown Court for sentence. If it does so, the Crown Court may deal with the offender for the offence in any manner in which (assuming s 1 had not applied) he could have been dealt with for that offence by the court which made the revoked order, taking into account the extent of compliance with any contract that had taken effect (Sch 1, para 14(5)). Note should be taken of the provisions of s 4(6): the restrictions on conditional discharges or parenting orders do not apply.

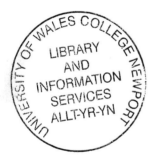

Chapter 5

SENTENCES: COMMUNITY ORDERS

Introduction – The Sentencing Threshold – Community Orders and Custody – Supervision Orders – Attendance Centre Orders – Action Plan Orders – Community Rehabilitation Orders – Community Punishment Orders – Community Protection and Rehabilitation Orders – Curfew Orders – Drug Treatment and Testing Orders.

INTRODUCTION

5.1 Community orders[1] play an important part in the sentencing of young offenders. A sentence which comprises one or more community orders is known as a community sentence (2000 Act, s 33(2)). For this purpose the term 'community order' is defined by s 33(1) of the 2000 Act. The orders listed in that Act are set out below, together with an indication of the original legislative source and the current legislative source within the 2000 Act, where it exists. Discharges, fines and reparation orders are not community orders, and thus the sentencing threshold discussed in Chapter 5 does not apply.

The issue is further complicated, however, by the passage of the Criminal Justice and Courts Services Act 2000 (CJCSA 2000), which is not in force as at the date of going to press. When it is, three of the community orders identified by s 33 of the 2000 Act will undergo a change of name. That change of nomenclature is as follows:

Old Name	New Name	Source
Probation order	Community rehabilitation order	CJCSA 2000, s 43
Community service order	Community punishment order	CJCSA 2000, s 44
Combination order	Community punishment and rehabilitation order	CJCSA 2000, s 45

Those orders are, for simplicity of exposition, referred to in this text by their new names except where the context would make that inappropriate, for example the discussion of earlier case-law.

Still further complications arise in respect of the Criminal Justice and Courts Services Act 2000, which introduces new community orders. These are exclusion orders and drug abstinence orders (CJCSA 2000, ss 46–47). These, again, are not available to courts as at the date of going to press.

Community orders are available in respect of a varying age-range of offenders. Some, such as supervision orders or attendance centre orders are available in respect of young offenders; other orders are available in respect of all offenders irrespective of whether they are young offenders or adult offenders.

		Old	New
Supervision orders	10–17 years	1969 Act	2000 Act, ss 63–68
Attendance centre orders	10–21 years	CJA 1982	2000 Act, ss 60–62
Community rehabilitation order (probation)	16–adult	PCCA 1973	2000 Act, ss 41–45
Community punishment order (community service)	16–adult	PCCA 1973	2000 Act, ss 46–50
Community punishment and rehabilitation order (combination)	16–adult	1991 Act	2000 Act, s 51
Action plan order	10–17	1998 Act	2000 Act, ss 69–72
Curfew order	16–adult	1991 Act	2000 Act, ss 37–40
Drug treatment and testing	16–adult	1998 Act	2000 Act, ss 52–58
Exclusion order	10–adult	N/A	2000 Act, ss 40A–40C (added by CJCSA 2000, s 46)
Drug abstinence order	18 and over	N/A	2000 Act, ss 58A–58C (added by CJCSA 2000, s 47)

---

1   See, generally, Brownlee, *Community Punishment* (Longmans Criminology, 1998).

THE SENTENCING THRESHOLD

5.2   The sentencing scheme created in 1991 placed community sentences in the middle rank of disposals open to a sentencing court, a position that is maintained in the consolidating legislation. The relevant provision, formerly to be found in s 6(1) of the 1991 Act, is now s 35 of the 2000 Act. By s 35, a court must not pass a community sentence on an offender unless it is of the opinion that the offence, or the combination of the offence and one or more offences associated, was serious enough to warrant such a sentence. There is one exception to this principle. As noted earlier, a custodial sentence[1] may be passed only if the court is of the opinion that the offence, together with one or more associated offences,[2] is so serious that only a custodial sentence can be justified, or the offence is a violent or sexual offence, and only such a sentence would be adequate to protect the public from serious harm[3] from the offender (2000 Act, s 79). A custodial sentence can also be imposed where an offender refuses to express his willingness to comply with a requirement which is proposed by the court to be included in:

(a) a community rehabilitation order (probation order) or supervision order and which requires an expression of such willingness; or
(b) a drug treatment and testing order or an order under s 52(4) of the 2000 Act.

The 1991 Act, which introduced this hierarchy of punishments, did not define 'seriousness' for this purpose, and therefore none is found in the 2000 consolidating legislation. Guidance was given by the Court of Appeal in *R v Bradbourn*.[4] In that case, in the context of a similar phrase in the Criminal Justice Act 1982, Lawton LJ observed:

> 'In our judgment the phrase "so serious that a non custodial sentence cannot be justified" comes to this: the kind of offence which when committed by a young person would make right-thinking members of the public, knowing all the facts, feel that justice had not been done by the passing of any sentence other than a custodial one. ...'

In determining whether a community sentence can be imposed, the court will need to be satisfied of the following:

– that the offence, together with associated offences, is sufficiently serious;
– that the offence, together with associated offences, is not so serious that only custody can be justified;
– that the offender will give such consent as may be necessary;
– the fact that the offence was committed whilst on bail is an aggravating factor affecting offence seriousness;[5]
– the fact that the offence was committed during the currency of a community order is not an aggravating factor;[6]
– the court is required to have regard to any mitigating factors about the circumstances of the offence;
– the crossing of the custody threshold does not *require* the court to impose a custodial sentence.[7]

---

1   A 'custodial sentence' is defined by the 2000 Act, s 76.
2   An 'associated offence' is defined by 2000 Act, s 161. An offence is associated with another if:

   (a) the offender is convicted of it in the proceedings in which he is convicted of the other offence, or (although convicted of it in earlier proceedings) is sentenced for it at the same time as he is sentenced for that offence; or
   (b) the offender admits the commission of it in the proceedings in which he is sentenced for the other offence and requests the court to take it into consideration in sentencing him for that offence.

3   'Sexual offence' is defined by the 2000 Act, s 161(2); 'violent offence' by s 161(3); 'protecting the public from serious harm ...' by s 161(4).

4   (1985) 7 Cr App R (S) 180, CA, approved in *R v Cox (David Geoffrey)* [1993] 2 All ER 19, CA.
5   [1993] 2 All ER 32, CA.
6   [1993] 2 All ER 6, CA.
7   *R v Oliver; R v Little* [1993] 2 All ER 6, CA.

COMMUNITY ORDERS AND CUSTODY

5.3   It is wrong in principle to combine a custodial sentence with a community order. Quite apart from the fact that the threshold which has to be reached before a court may impose a custodial sentence is significantly higher than that which would justify the making of a community order, the mixing of sentences of different types is to be discouraged.[1] This remains true even if the term of imprisonment is suspended, for such a term is none the less a custodial sentence. Thus, in *R v Evans (No 3)*[2] the court held that a probation order should never be mixed with a custodial sentence in respect of another offence. In *R v Duporte*,[3] the Court of Appeal quashed an immediate term of imprisonment imposed by a court after the offender had been made the subject of a probation order for another offence after the commission of the offence for which the term of imprisonment had been imposed but before sentence. It was wrong in principle. Again, in *R v Carr Thompson*[4] a court concluded that it was inappropriate to make a probation order on the same occasion as a custodial sentence was imposed. The appellant had appeared before a youth court and admitted three breaches of a community service order imposed by the Crown Court in January 1999. She was committed to the Crown Court for sentence. A few weeks later, she appeared again at the youth court, and pleaded guilty to using threatening words or behaviour. She was sentenced to two months' detention in a young offender institution for that offence. One week later on her appearance in the Crown Court, the Crown Court revoked the community service orders and made probation orders in respect of the offences for which the community service orders had been made. The Crown Court at the same time dismissed the appellant's appeal against the sentence of two months' detention imposed by the youth court. It was submitted that probation orders should not have been made in view of the sentence of two months' detention in a young offender institution imposed in the youth court and maintained in the Crown Court. The court, in quashing the probation orders, applied the principle set out in *R v Evans*: the purposes of a probation order were to be either securing the rehabilitation of offender or protecting the public from harm from him or preventing the commission by him of further offences. In the court's judgment, it was impermissible to combine a probation order with an immediate custodial sentence whether in respect of the same offence or of different offences sentenced on the same occasion.

1   *R v McElhorne* (1983) 5 Cr App R(S) 53, CA.
2   (1959) 43 Cr App R 66, CA.
3   (1989) 11 Cr App R (S) 116, CA.

4   [2000] Crim LR 401, CA.

Combinations of community orders

5.4 Prior to the passage of the Criminal Justice Act 1991, significant restrictions existed on the possible combination of orders. These were in part swept away by the 1991 Act, and that Act overtly prohibited only the making together of probation and community service orders,[1] except in the form of a combination order.[1] The combination order is intended to achieve a mix of these two orders and so, clearly, it is inappropriate to combine them for the same offence in any other way. That position is preserved by s 35(2) of the 2000 Act.

A further limitation is contained in s 69(5) of the 2000 Act. Like its predecessor,[2] s 69(5) prohibits the making of an action plan order in respect of the offender if:

'(a) he is already the subject of such an order; or
 (b) the court proposes to pass on him a custodial sentence or to make in respect of him a probation order, a community service order, a combination order,[1] an attendance centre order, a supervision order or a referral order.'

The prohibition on the combination of custody and an action plan order is clearly a reflection of the basic principle that a sentencing court should not mix custodial and community sentences.[3] Quite apart from these differences in principle, the custody threshold will not have been crossed and thus the court will not generally have the power to impose a custodial sentence. The restriction on the mixing of action plan and the other stated community orders needs more explanation. Community punishment orders[4] and community punishment and rehabilitation orders[5] are targeted at offenders aged 16 and over, and include an element of reparation. Supervision orders and attendance centre orders contain their own regimes designed to work with young offenders, and there is a difference in degree between a supervision order and an action plan order.[6] The overlap between a reparation order and action plan order is clear. However, there appears to be no restriction on combining an action plan order with other community orders, or with a fine or compensation order. An indication of the prohibited combination of orders is contained at the relevant parts of the Chapter dealing with each order.

---

1   See now the renamed community rehabilitation order, community punishment order, community punishment and rehabilitation order.
2   Crime and Disorder Act 1998, s 69(3).
3   See para **5.3**.
4   Ie community service order.
5   Ie combination order.
6   See para **5.46**.

5.5 By s 35(3) of the 2000 Act, subject to the limitations described above, where a court passes a community sentence:

'(a)   the particular order or orders comprising or forming part of the sentence must be such as in the opinion of the court is, or taken together are, the most suitable for the offender, and

(b)   the restrictions on liberty imposed by the order or orders must be such as in the opinion of the court are commensurate with the seriousness of the offence, or the combination of the offence and one or more offences associated with it.'

An exception exists to the rule set out in s 35(3)(b) above, and is contained in s 35(4). Section 35(3)(b) takes effect subject to certain different rules that apply in the context of persistent petty offenders.

In forming the opinion described above, a court must take into account all such information as is available to it about the circumstances of the offence or (as the case may be) of the offence and any associated offences, including any aggravating or mitigating factors (2000 Act, s 36(1)). It will act on the information before it, but that often will not include a Pre-Sentence Report (PSR) unless custody was a real issue. However, the court must obtain and consider a PSR before forming an opinion as to the suitability of the offender for one or more of the following orders, unless it is of the opinion that it is unnecessary to obtain such a report (2000 Act, s 36(4), (5)):

(a)   community rehabilitation order[1] containing additional requirements;
(b)   community punishment order;[2]
(c)   community punishment and rehabilitation order;[3]
(d)   drug treatment and testing order;[4] and
(e)   supervision order including additional requirements.[5]

That right, under s 36(5), to dispense with a report, is subject to a further limitation in respect of an offender under the age of 18, that has already been discussed.

---

1   Ie probation order: see para **5.59**.
2   Ie community service order: see para **5.93**.
3   Ie combination order: see para **5.98**.
4   See para **5.103**.
5   See para **5.13**.

5.6   It does not follow from these requirements that the PSR must have addressed the particular community order that a court might wish to make: a PSR will have been 'considered' even though it does not address the particular order that the court wishes to make, although the clear intent of s 36(5) is that a court should have sufficient information before it to be able to make an assessment of the suitabilty of the offender for the particular order that the court has in mind. Nothing in the Act prevents oral information being given to the court to supplement a PSR. It is for the court[1] to decide whether the information base it has before it is sufficient to enable it to determine the matter, having regard to the overall objectives of the criminal justice system to prevent re-offending[2] and yet to do so with due expedition.[3]

1   *R v Okinikan* [1993] 2 All ER 14.
2   Crime and Disorder Act 1998, s 37(1).
3   See para **1.8**.

SUPERVISION ORDERS

5.7   The provisions of ss 63 to 68 of the 2000 Act re-enact provisions contained in the Children and Young Persons Act 1969 in respect of supervison orders. By s 63(1) of the 2000 Act a supervision order is an order that places an offender aged under 18 years at the date of conviction under the supervision of:

'(a)   a local authority designated by the order;
(b)   a probation officer; or
(c)   a member of a youth offending team.'

A court may not make a supervision order if it is obliged under statute to impose some other sentence. This will be the case where the conviction is one for murder, where the mandatory sentence applies,[1] or where the court is obliged to make a referral to a youth offender panel.[2]

The power to make an order is vested in any youth court, magistrates' court or Crown Court. The effect of the order is to place the offender under the supervision of one of the above for a period not exceeding three years from the date of the making of the order.[3]

The minimum age in respect of an offender who may be subject to a supervision order is 10, the maximum 17.

1   See para **6.1**.
2   See para **4.5**.
3   The form of the order is set out in Form 38, prescribed by the Magistrates' Courts
     (Children and Young Persons) Rules 1992, SI 1992/2071.

5.8   A supervision order is a community order, and thus the normal seriousness threshold must be crossed in respect of that offence and any associated offence. By definition, a custodial sentence and a supervision order are inappropriate in respect of the same offence: the custody threshold will not have been reached. Further, where a court is sentencing for more than one offence, a supervision order should not be combined with a custodial sentence, because the use of sentences of different types in this way is discouraged.[1] Nor, at the other end of the sentencing spectrum, should a supervision order be combined with a discharge. This is because s 12 of the 2000 Act makes discharges available where 'it is inexpedient to inflict punishment'. A community order is a sentence in its own right and thus incompatible with a discharge even though the primary purpose of the supervision order is restorative.

Supervision orders should not be combined with a community rehabilitation order[2] where a 16- or 17-year-old is being sentenced for two or more offences. This would involve the duplication of supervision regimes, involving not only a wasteful duplication of resources but also the possibility for conflict between the supervisory regimes. Such a combination is wrong in principle. Similar reasoning leads to the conclusion that supervision orders cannot be combined with community punishment and rehabilitation orders.[3] No formal legal prohibition against the combining of supervision orders with community punishment orders[4] or curfew orders exists, but such sentence combinations appear to be highly undesirable: given the range of powers to impose requirements in a supervision order, to seek to impose curfew restrictions on a 16 or 17-year-old through a curfew order when a night restriction order could form part of the requirements of a supervision order[5] serves to confirm the correctness of this conclusion.

---

1   *R v McElhorne* (1983) 5 Cr App R (S) 53, CA.
2   Ie probation order.
3   Ie combination order.
4   Ie community service order.
5   See para **5.20**.

5.9   The consent of the offender is not necessary before a supervision order can be made, but up until 1997 consent was necessary in order for certain requirements to be imposed in such an order. Requirements for which consent was needed were requirements of residence (1969 Act, s 12), and, in some circumstances, for mental treatment (s 12B). These requirements for consent were based on a philosophy that the willingness to undergo the supervision, or to comply with the requirement for treatment was a key characteristic of a community order. However, s 38 of the Crime (Sentences) Act 1997 modified these provisions, basing the change on the philosophy that 'it is quite wrong that offenders should be allowed to dictate their sentence to the court'.[1] Section 38 removed the requirement for consent in s 12A(6) and substituted a new s 12A(6). The relevant provision is now to be found in Sch 6 of the 2000 Act. Schedule 6, para 3(4) states that, if the supervised person is under the age of 16, the court must have obtained and considered information about the family circumstances of the offender, and the likely effect of the requirements on those circumstances. Given that the requirements in question in s 12A(3) relate to remaining in a particular place, or refraining from participating in specified activities, and are somewhat analogous to a curfew order, it is not inappropriate that the same requirements be equally applicable. On occasion, the consent of some other person (eg a parent) may be required.

The particular requirements for information or consent are dealt with at the appropriate parts of this Chapter. In determining what requirements can, or should, be imposed, the human rights context should not be ignored. If any provision has the effect of interfering with family life, then the potential exists for a claim, under the Human Rights Act 1998, that there has been a breach of the Art 8 rights of the offender, or, where the requirement has a wider impact on the family of the offender, of a member or members of that family. In such circumstances the onus will be on the public body to show that the requirement was necessary and proportionate in the context of the limitations of the right contained in Art 8(2).[2]

---

1   Baroness Blatch, Minister of State, Home Office, HL Committee, 2nd Reading, 1998, col 974.
2   See para **1.9**.

The making of the order

5.10   Before making an order a court has to be satisfied that the offender resides or will reside[1] in the area of a local authority (2000 Act, s 63(5)). If it is not so satisfied, it can ensure that this is achieved by making a requirement as to residence,[2] under para 1 of Sch 6 to the 2000 Act (2000 Act, s 63(5)).

---

1   The term 'reside' is defined by s 67(1) of the 2000 Act as meaning 'habitually reside'.
2   See para **5.14**.

5.11   The supervision will be conducted by a local authority, probation officer or member of a youth offending team. The supervision arrangements in any case will be in accordance with National Guidance and local protocols, but, as a general proposition, those aged under 16 years are likely to be dealt with through social services supervision, whilst 16- and 17-year-olds will most probably be supervised by probation unless there is already social services involvement.

A local authority must, either itself or in association with other authorities, make arrangements with such persons as it thinks appropriate to ensure the provision of facilities to ensure that directions to supervised persons can be given pursuant to Sch 6, paras 2(1) or 3(2) (2000 Act, s 66(1)). A scheme must be promulgated and available for inspection (s 66(3), (5), (6)).

5.12   As noted earlier, a court may make an order without the consent of the offender, although certain enquiries and consents may on occasion be necessary.[1] The fact that a supervision order is already in force does not preclude the making of a further order. In that case, by s 63(9) of the 2000 Act, a court may revoke that earlier order (although is not obliged to do so). In that circumstance, para 10 of Sch 7 to the 2000 Act applies.[2]

---

1   See para **5.9**.
2   See para **5.31**.

Imposition of requirements in a supervision order

5.13   By s 63(6)(b) of the 2000 Act, a supervision order may contain such provisions as the court considers appropriate for facilitating the performance of the supervisory function. This may include provisions requiring the offender to visit the supervisor. Care must be taken, however, to avoid the use of this general provision to avoid the specific pre-conditions for the imposition of specific requirements. Care must also be taken to ensure that any restrictions on liberty or interferences with home life go no further than are necessary to fulfil the aims of the order and are proportionate.[1]

1　See para **1.37**, for the general human rights position.

Requirements of residence

5.14　A supervision order may require the offender to reside with a named individual (2000 Act, Sch 6, para 1). The agreement of that individual is required. Such a requirement takes effect subject to any requirement imposed paras 2 (requirement to comply with directions), 3 (requirements as to activities, etc), 6 (treatment for mental condition) and 7 (education).

5.15　A court must forthwith serve a copy of the order on the offender and if he or she is aged under 14, to his parent or guardian (2000 Act, s 63(8)). This provision also requires a copy to be sent to the supervisor and the local authority named in the order. In cases where the offender is required to reside with an individual, or to undertake treatment, copies of the order must also be sent to the individual or person in charge of the place specified. A copy of the order should also be sent to the justices' chief executive for the petty sessions area specified in the order, if that is not the area for which the sentencing court acts, and along with such documents and information relating to the case as the court considers likely to be of assistance.

Discretionary intermediate treatment

5.16　This label is used to describe the discretion that the law gives to the supervisor to make directions. By Sch 6, para 2 to the 2000 Act, a supervision order may require the offender to comply with directions given by the supervisor to do all or any of the following:

> '(a)　to live at a place or places specified, or a period or periods specified;
> (b)　to present himself to a person or persons specified in the directions at a place or places specified in the directions and on a specified day or days;
> (c)　to participate in specified activities, on a specified day or days.'

Such requirements are at the discretion of the supervisor (Sch 6, para 2(4)), but must be necessary and proportionate.[1] These requirements are not specified in the order. However, the requirement to require such participation is subject to the fulfilment of any requirement for mental treatment made pursuant to Sch 6, para 6.[2] The total number of days in respect of which a requirement can be imposed under Sch 6, para 2 is not to exceed 90, or such lesser number of days specified by the court for this purpose when making the order (Sch 6, para 2(5)). It is therefore open to a court to specify the number of days it wishes to be subject to this requirement when making the order, and a court should address its mind to that issue. In calculating the number of days in respect of which directions may be given, a supervisor is entitled to disregard any day in respect of which directions were previously given and which were not complied with (Sch 6, para 2(5)). There is no formal procedure to determine any disputes about such matter: any such disputes would be resolved in the context of applications in respect of variation, discharge or non-compliance with directions.

---

1   See para **1.37**, for the general human rights position.
2   See para **5.24**.

Stipulated intermediate treatment

5.17   The powers described above relate to the discretion vested in the supervisor. Paragraph 3 of Sch 6 to the 2000 Act deals with requirements that a court is entitled to insert into an order. If an order contained a requirement to comply with directions under Sch 6, para 2, then this power is not available to the court. If no such order is made by a court, it may require the offender to do one or more of the matters stated in para 3(2). These are:

'(a) to live at a place or places specified in the order, for a period or periods specified;

(b) to present himself to a person or persons specified in the order on a specified day or days;

(c) to participate in activities specified on a day or days specified;

(d) to make reparation specified in the order to a person or persons specified, or to the community at large;

(e) to remain for specified periods betwen 6 pm and 6 am at a specified place, or at one of several specified places (a 'night restriction order');

(f) to refrain from participating in specified activities on a specified day or days during the supervision period, or during the whole of that period, or during a specified portion of it.'

In relation to any of these requirements the court must first:

(a) have consulted the supervisor as to the offender's circumstances, and as to the feasibility of securing compliance with them;

(b) consider, having regard to the circumstances of the case, whether it is necessary to impose such requirements for securing the good conduct of the offender, or for preventing a repetition by him of the same offence or the commission of other offences; and

(c) if the offender is aged under 16, obtain and consider information about his family circumstances and the likely effect of those requirements.

If any requirement requires the co-operation of a person other than the offender and supervisor, that person must consent (Sch 6, para 3(5)). So, too, must any victim of the offence to whom it is proposed to offer reparation.

This emphasis on proper enquiry as to the circumstances and effects of imposing such a requirement is extremely important both to ensure that a workable order is put in place and that the requirements are not disproportionate and are compliant with the requirements of Art 8 of the European Convention. A further context is provided by para 3(6) and 3(7) of Sch 2. These are dealt with below, at para **5.19**.

5.18   It will be noted that an overlap seemingly exists between requirements for reparation in a supervision order and a reparation order: it is for that reason that the provisions of the 2000 Act relating to reparation orders prevent the making of such an order if the court proposes to make a supervision order subject to a reparation requirement. The requirement for reparation is seen as but one strand in the wider work with the offender, and is thus the more appropriate vehicle for such a requirement. National Standards identify the fact that reparation is an important process which participants in supervision orders should engage in.[1]

Note should also be taken of the fact that the reparation requirement in a supervision order is in respect of non-financial reparation. During the passage of the Crime and Disorder Act 1998, the Government made it clear that, in its view, the appropriate vehicle for financial reparation is a compensation order.[2] There is no problem against combining a supervision order subject to a requirement for reparation with a compensation order.

---

1   *National Standards for the Supervision of Offenders in the Community* (Home Office), para 19.
3   See Card and Ward, *The Crime and Disorder Act 1998* (Jordans, 1998), at para 4.8.

5.19   Paragraph 3 of Sch 2 to the 2000 Act contains certain further restrictions on the imposition of a requirement. First, by para 3(6) any requirement imposed by virtue of para 3(2)(b) or (c) must, so far as practicable, be such as to avoid:

'(a)   any conflict with the offender's religious beliefs or with the requirements of any other community order to which he may be subject; and
(b)   any interference with the times, if any, at which he normally works or attends school or any other educational establishment.'

Of course, any failure to comply with this would raise potential issues relating to the right of freedom of religion and right to education, under the European Convention on Human Rights.

Secondly, para 3(7) places a restriction on orders requiring absence from home. An order may not include:

'(a)   any requirement that would involve the offender in absence from home for more than two consecutive nights, or for more than two nights in any one week, or
(b)   if the offender is of compulsory school age, any requirement to participate in activities during normal school hours,

unless the court making the order is satisfied that the facilitates whose use would be involved are specified in a specified scheme for the area in which the offender resides or will reside.'

Night restriction requirements
5.20   The power to make a night restriction requirement fits with a range of measures, such as curfew orders, designed to give the courts power to restrict the movements of an offender at times when he or she may commit further offences. Such a regime could be achieved independently through a curfew order, but can, through a night restriction requirement, form a component element of a longer period of supervision. Where it is proposed to make a night

restriction requirement, the place or one of the places specified must be the place where the offender lives (Sch 6, para 4(1)). It must not require the offender to remain at a place for longer than 10 hours on any one night, and must not be imposed in respect of any day which falls outside a three-month period beginning with the day on which the order is made (para 4(2), (3)). The effect of para 4(5) is that the three-month period is calculated by the time at which a particular restriction begins (para 4(5)). Thus, if the three-month period expires on day X at midnight, but the restriction is a 9 pm to 7 am restriction, no liability for breach of the restriction would arise after midnight of the thirteenth day.

5.21 A night restriction is not absolute. By para 4(6) an offender who is required by a night restriction to remain at a place may leave it if he is accompanied:

'(a) by his parent or guardian;
(b) by his supervisor; or
(c) by some other person specified in the order.'

Requirements of residence with a local authority

5.22 A requirement of residence may be imposed, by virtue of Sch 6, para 5 to the 2000 Act. The pre-conditions are set out in para 5(2) and are that:

'(a) a supervision order has previously been made in respect of the offender;
(b) that the order imposed –

  (i) a requirement under paragraphs 1 [residence], 2 [requirements as to activities etc], 3 [stipulated requirements] or 7 [requirement as to education] ..., or
  (ii) a local authority residence requirement;

(c) the offender fails to comply with that requirement, or is convicted of an offence committed whilst that order was in force; and
(d) the court is satisfied that–

  (i) the failure to comply with the requirement, or the behaviour which constituted the offence, was due to a significant extent to the circumstances in which the offender was living; and
  (ii) the imposition of a local authority residence requirement will assist in his rehabilitation.'

One variation of these pre-conditions is made by para 5(2). If the previous order was a local authority residence requirement, the court does not have to be satisfied in the way specified in para 5(2)(d)(i) above.

These provisions were introduced by s 71(4) of the Crime and Disorder Act 1998. Although removing a person from the home is not a step to be taken lightly, and involves potential issues under Art 8 of the European Convention on Human Rights, it is considered that there are factors associated with the place where an offender lives which may lead to or encourage offending. For that reason it may be in the best interests of the offender to move him or her away from that place for a short period of time. That is what the local authority residence requirement does. No such order may be made unless the offender was legally represented (para 5(7)).[1]

---

1   An exception to this exists where the offender was granted a right to representation funded by the Legal Services Commission as part of the Criminal Defence Service, but the right was withdrawn because of his conduct, or he refused or failed to apply for such representation.

5.23   The requirement must designate the local authority which is to receive the offender, having first consulted them (para 5(4), (5)). The requirement, which cannot exceed six months in length, may stipulate that the offender must not live with a named person (para 5(6)).

Requirements for treatment for mental condition

5.24   Where a court is satisfied, having considered the evidence of a practitioner approved for the purposes of the Mental Health Act 1983, that the mental condition of a supervised person is such as requires and may be susceptible to treatment, but not such as to warrant detention under a hospital order or guardianship order, it may make a requirement that, for a specified period, the offender submit to one of certain specified treatments (Sch 6(1)). These are:

'(a)   treatment as a resident patient in a hospital or mental nursing home, but not a hospital at which high security psychiatric services within the meaning of the Mental Health Act 1983 are provided;

(b)   treatment as a non resident patient at an institution or place specified in the order;

(c)   treatment by or under the direction of a registered medical practitioner specified in the order; or

(b)   treatment by or under the direction of a chartered psychologist specified in the order.'

The court must be satisfied that arrangements can be or have been made for the treatment in question, and that, in the case of a resident patient, for the reception of the patient, and that, in the case of an offender aged at least 14, that that person consents. The requirement cannot continue after the age of 18.

Requirements for education

5.25   A court may require the offender, if of compulsory school age, to comply with such arrangements for his education as may from time to time be made by his parent (being arrangements approved by the local education authority) (2000 Act, Sch 6, para 7). The local education authority must be consulted in advance and has to be satisfied that arrangements exist for that person to receive efficient full-time education suitable to his age, ability and aptitude, and to any special educational needs he may have (para 7(3)). Consultation with the supervisor is required and the court must be satisfied that the requirement is necessary for securing the good conduct of the supervised person or for preventing a repetition of the same offence or the commission of other offences (para 7(5)).

The making of such orders appears uncommon,[1] with a seeming ignorance of the existence of the power to make such an order.

1　See Ball and Connolly *Requiring School Attendance: A Little Used Sentencing Power* [1999] Crim LR 183.

The implementation of the order

5.26　This occurs in accordance with national standards, issued by the Home Secretary. The initial appointment between the supervising officer and offender should, where possible, be made within five working days of the making of the order, the appointment being made before the offender leaves court. The offender should be given written information about what can be expected from the supervisor during the order, what is expected of the offender, the consequences of unacceptable behaviour, including the possibility of breach, and the procedure for the discharge or variation of the order. All this should be explained to the offender. If possible, the offender should be served with a copy of the order and asked to sign it. The supervising order should make the offender aware of what the order will entail, and ensure that the offender is able and willing to co-operate. Similar information should be given to the offender's parents or guardian, and to others who appear to be relevant to the supervision.

Change of address
5.27　Where a person under supervision changes address which involves leaving the area of the supervising authority, an application to vary the order by substituting a new supervising authority can be made by the supervisor to the court (2000 Act, Sch 7).

Variation of order

5.28　A supervision order may be varied in accordance with the 2000 Act, Sch 7. This can include the substitution of a term of reduced length (Sch 7). Variation can be on the application of the supervisor or of the offender. If it appears to the court to be appropriate to do so, the court may vary the order by cancelling any requirement, or by inserting into the order, either in addition or by way of substitution for any of its provisions, any provision which could have been included in the order if the court then had the power to make it and were exercising that power. However, the court cannot insert a requirement for mental treatment more than three months after the date of the making of the original order unless such a requirement is in substitution for one already made, or a night restriction order in respect of any day outside a three-month period from the date of the original order.

The wording of Sch 7 is such that the court has the power only to impose requirements which it has the power to make as at the date of the variation. In determining the power of the court it is, therefore, the age of the order at the date of the variation that matters, not the age as at the date of the making of the original order.

Revocation of supervision order

5.29   A supervision order ceases to have effect on the expiration of a period of three years, or such shorter period as is specified in the order beginning with the date on which the order was made (2000 Act, Sch 7).

An order may be discharged by the youth court where it is appropriate to do so (Sch 7). This power applies to all orders, no matter by which court the order was made. National Standards make clear that early termination of an order should be considered where the offender has made good progress in achieving the objectives set out for the order and where there is not considered to be a significant risk of re-offending, or of serious harm to the public. An application for early termination should normally be considered after the expiration of two-thirds of the term, unless there is good reason for not doing so.

Schedule 7 also entitles a court to vary a supervision order. The terms of Sch 7 are wide enough to include a substitution of a reduced length. Variation can be on the application of the supervisor or the offender. If it appears to the court to be appropriate to do so, the court may vary the order by cancelling any requirement in it or by inserting into the order (either in addition or by way of substitution for any of its provisions) any provision which could have been included in the order if the court then had the power to make it. The court cannot, however, insert requirements for mental treatment more than three months after the making of the original order unless such a requirement is in substitution for one already made, or a night restriction order in respect of any day outside a three-month period from the day of the original order.

5.30   The wording of Sch 7 is such that only requirements which the court has power to make at the date of the variation can be imposed. Therefore, in determining the powers of the court, it is the age of the offender at the time of that variation which is crucial.

Breach

5.31   The power to deal with breach is contained in Sch 7 to the 2000 Act. If the offender is aged under 18 at the date of the breach hearing the appropriate court is the youth court, but, for an offender who has attained that age (even if the offender was aged under 18 at the date proceedings were initiated) the relevant court is the magistrates' court (Sch 7).

The power to deal with a breach of the order exists while the supervision order is in force, but only on the application of the supervising officer. Where the court is satisfied that the offender has failed to comply with any requirement under the order, the court may respond as follows.

(a) Discharge the order, or vary it, if it considers it appropriate to do so (Sch 7). This power to vary is limited by Sch 7. In addition to the discharge or variation, the court may impose a fine not exceeding £1,000, or make an attendance centre order (assumed to have been made under s 60 of the 2000 Act.

(b) If the offender has attained the age of 18 years, the court may discharge the order. If it does that, it may in addition impose any punishment (other than detention in a young offender institution) which it could have imposed on him if it had power now to try him for the offence for which the supervision order was made and had convicted him in the exercise of that power. If the court has no power to try the offender for that offence, the sentence cannot exceed that which the court which could try the offence could have imposed, and the maximum fine must not exceed £5,000.

(c) If the breach action is based on a failure to comply with requirements to undertake specified activities, the power in (b) above applies. This is irrespective of whether the offender has attained the age of 18 (Sch 7). If the court had no power to try the offender for that offence, the sentence it can impose cannot exceed that which the court which could have imposed (in any event, the sentence can be no greater than six months' custody, and the maximum fine must not exceed £5,000). This power exists only where the court which made the order made a statement under s 12D(1).

Schedule 7 requires a court, when dealing with an offender under the above provisions, to take into account the extent to which the offender has complied with the relevant provisions of the supervision order. The statutory provisions do not create a defence of reasonable excuse for failure to comply, and so in this regard differ from the equivalent provisions relating to probation orders. Such matters appear to be relevant to the question of how any breach is to be dealt with.

ATTENDANCE CENTRE ORDERS

5.32 A court may sentence a person aged at least 10 and aged under 21 to an attendance centre order (2000 Act, s 60). Under such an order, the court orders the offender to attend at a centre, run by the police, for a specified number of hours, if it has been notified by the Home Secretary that an attendance centre is available for the reception of persons of that description. The pre-conditions are set out in s 60 of the 2000 Act as follows:

'(a) the offender must be under 21 and convicted of an offence punishable with imprisonment; or

(b) the court would have power but for section 89 of this Act (restrictions on imprisonment of young offenders and defaulters) to commmit the offender to prison for default of payment of any sum of money, or for failing to do or abstain from doing anything required to be done or left undone; or

(c)   the court has power to commit a person aged at least 21 but under 25 in default of payment of any sum of money.'

The original provisions in the Criminal Justice Act 1982 were extended by the Crime (Sentences) Act 1997 to allow an attendance centre order to be made in respect of certain fine defaulters, as part of the draft of measures contained in the 1997 Act to improve fine enforcement and reduce fine default. It is that provision that s 60(1)(c) now re-enacts.

The court must be satisfied that the specified centre is reasonably accessible to the offender having regard to the offender's age, means of access to the centre and to any other circumstances. The court can make an attendance centre order even where the offender has previous custodial experience.

An attendance centre order may also be made against an offender whom the court could commit to prison for default in the payment of a sum of money, failure to comply with an order of the court, or failure to comply with a probation, community service or combination order.

Hours

5.33   The total number of hours at the attendance centre must not be less than 12, except where the offender is aged under 14 and the court considers 12 hours would be excessive having regard to age or other circumstances (2000 Act, s 60(3)). The hours to be served must not exceed 12 except where the court is of the opinion that 12 would be inadequate, in which case the hours must not exceed 24 where the offender is under 16, or 36 where the offender is 16 or over but under 21.

By s 60(5), an order can be imposed irrespective of the fact that an order is still in force with unexpired hours. Such orders should state how the different orders are to take effect. The allocation of individual centres is governed by Home Office Circular 72/1992. Both senior and junior attendance centres exist. Males aged 10 to 15 attend junior centres, as do 16- to 17-year-olds where no senior centre is available. If there is a choice of centre available in respect of such 16- or 17-year-old males, which constitutes the appropriate centre will depend on the number of hours to be served. Orders of up to 24 hours will be served at either type of centre depending on the offender's suitability: the pre-sentence report will, or should, make some assessment of that. For longer orders, the offender will serve the requisite hours at a senior centre, where available. Male offenders aged 18 to 20 serve their sentence at senior attendance centres. Female offenders aged 10 to 17 serve their hours at junior attendance centres. No senior centres for females aged 18 to 20 exist.

Content of order

5.34   An attendance centre order must specify the time at which the offender must first attend (s 60(8)). Subsequent times are fixed by the officer in charge of the centre. Attendance must not be more than once on any one day, or more than three hours on any one occasion. In practice, many attendance centres operate on a fortnightly attendance basis: offenders go for two hours every other Saturday, or, in the case of senior attendance centres, three hours per week.

The usual provisions regarding accessibility, religious and education considerations apply. By s 60(6) the court must not make an order unless it is satisfied that the attendance centre to be specified is reasonably accessible to the person concerned, having regard to his age, the means of access available to him and any other circumstances.

Further, by s 60(7), the times at which the person is required to attend an attendance centre must, so far as practicable, be such as to avoid:

> '(a) any conflict with his religious beliefs or with the requirements of any other community order to which he may be subject; and
>
> (b) any interference with the times, if any, at which he normally works or attends school or any other educational establishment.'

As already noted, this provision is particularly important not only for ensuring the viability of the order, but also ensuring that the Convention rights of the offender are respected.[1]

---

1   See para **1.37** and **5.2**.

Sentence combinations

5.35   An attendance centre order and custody are incompatible, whether for the same or different offences. Attendance centre orders should not be combined with discharges, whether absolute or conditional. However, there appears to be no reason in principle to prevent the combining of an attendance centre order with any other community order where the age of the offender permits.

Making of the order

5.36   Copies of the order must be served by the clerk of the court on the officer in charge of the attendance centre, and served on the offender in person, by registered post or recorded delivery to the last or usual place of abode (s 60(11)). The management of an attendance centre order is in the hands of the officer in charge of the centre. The date and time of first attendance are required to be specified in the order itself (s 60(8)). Subsequent times are fixed by the officer in charge. An offender is not required to be in attendance on more than one occasion in any one day or for more than three hours on more than one day.

The powers in respect of attendance centre orders are contained in the Attendance Centre Rules 1995.[1] In particular, the officer in charge may require an offender to leave the centre if that person is unwell, infested with vermin or suffering from an infectious disease, or fails to behave in an orderly manner or obey orders or instructions given. A failure to comply with such orders or instructions can form the basis of breach action (r 6)).

1   SI 1995/3281.

Variation of the order

5.37   On an application by the offender or officer in charge of the relevant centre, an order can be varied by substitution of an attendance centre which is reasonably accessible to the offender, having regard to age, means of access available to him and any other circumstances (2000 Act, Sch 5(5)). The court may also vary the day or hour specified.

Termination of order

5.38   Clearly, an order terminates when the aggregate number of hours specified in the order under s 60(3) have been served. However, in respect of cases where an order has been made under s 60(1)(b) or (c) in respect of default in the payment of a sum of money, then the special provisions of s 60(12) apply. This provides that where a person ('the defaulter') has been ordered to attend at an attendance centre in such circumstances:

(a)   on payment of the whole sum to any person authorised to receive it, the attendance centre order ceases to have effect;

(b)   on payment of a part of the sum to any such person, the total number of hours for which the defaulter is required to attend at the centre shall be reduced proportionately, that is to say, by such number of complete hours as bears to the total number the proportion most nearly approximating to, without exceeding, the proportion which the part bears to the whole sum.

In short, if, for example, the sum of money has been 50% paid, the hours will be reduced by the number of complete hours which is nearest to, but does not exceed, 50% of the total.

Revocation

5.39   An order can be revoked on an application either by the offender or the officer in charge of the relevant centre, by either:

(a)   the magistrates' court for the petty session division in which the attendance centre is situated; or

(b)   the court which made the order.

A Crown Court order can be revoked by a youth court unless the Crown Court included in the order a direction that the power to discharge is reserved to that court, in which case only the Crown Court can discharge (Sch 5, para 4(2)). The powers of youth courts over Crown Court attendance centre orders are therefore wider than those in respect of Crown Court community rehabilitation, community punishment or community punishment and rehabilitation orders.[1]

Where the order is revoked, the court has the power to deal with the offender for the offence for which the order was made in any manner in which the offender could have been dealt with for that offence by the court which made the order if the order had not been made (Sch 5, para 4(3)). Problems theoretically arise if the order was made for an offence triable only on indictment. No power to commit for sentence is attached to a Sch 5 revocation. However, there is a power to commit in respect of breach (Sch 5, para 2(1)).

---

1   Ie probation, community service or combination orders.

5.40   Where there is breach of an attendance centre order, and an information has been laid that the offender:

(a) has failed to attend in accordance with the order; or
(b) whilst attending has committed a breach of rules which cannot adequately be dealt with under the Attendance Centre Rules 1995,

a summons may be issued requiring the offender to appear at a time and place specified, or if the information is in writing and on oath, may issue a warrant for arrest.

It does not appear from the wording of the section that the order still has to be in force. If an offender has failed, without reasonable excuse, to attend, or has committed such a breach of the rules a court may:

(a) impose a fine not exceeding £1,000; or
(b) in respect of a magistrates' court order, may deal with him for the offence in respect of which the order was made, in any way in which he could have been dealt with for that offence if the order had not been made; or
(c) in respect of a Crown Court order, commit him, either in custody or on bail, to the Crown Court.

The effect of the above is that if the youth court chooses to deal with the offender under Sch 5, para 2(2)(b) above, it can act in the same way as the original sentencing court; the corollary of that is, of course, that any restrictions that applied at that time continue to apply.

In deciding whether, and what way, to deal with the offender under Sch 5, para 2(1)(b), the court must take into account the extent to which the offender has complied with the requirements of the attendance centre order; and, in the case of an offender who has wilfully and persistently failed to comply with those requirements, may impose a custodial sentence despite the restrictions contained in s 79(2) of the 2000 Act. This is an example of custody being available even where the custody threshold has not been reached.

5.41   Where the offender is committed to the Crown Court, the powers in Sch 5, para 3(1) apply: that Court may deal with the offender in any way that it could have done if it had not made the order. Again, the extent of compliance and of wilful and persistent failure (if that in fact was the case) can be used to justify a custodial sentence. Therefore, any restrictions on that court at that time apply equally. The court may commit in custody or on bail to the Crown Court.

Where the defendant fails to appear at an adjourned hearing, the court shall not issue a warrant under this section unless it is satisfied that he has had adequate notice of the time and place of the adjourned hearing.

Appeals

5.42   An offender may appeal to the Crown Court in respect of any order of discharge (or refusal to discharge), variation or failure to comply made by a youth court, other than an order that did not require his presence (Sch 5, para 5(4)). There appears to be no right of appeal against such decisions taken by the Crown Court.

ACTION PLAN ORDERS

5.43   Section 69 of the Crime and Disorder Act 1998 introduced the action plan order, a new community penalty requiring a young offender to comply with an action plan intended to address his offending behaviour. Although there are distinct similarities between the action plan order introduced by s 69, and a supervision order with requirements for intermediate treatment,[1] the intention is that the action plan order should be a new kind of community penalty – one which provides the opportunity for a short but intensive programme of work with the young offender, and his or her parents, to tackle the causes of offending at an early stage.[2] Supervision orders with an intermediate treatment requirement are intended to be less focused and to last longer. The provisions of the 1998 Act are now re-enacted in ss 69 to 71 of the 2000 Act.

The content of the order vary according to the particular offender and his or her offending. It will impose a series of requirements, individually tailored to the young offender and designed to address the specific causes of the offending. It may, for example, require the young offender to comply with educational arrangements, to make reparation to the victim; to observe the terms of a daily or weekly schedule stipulating whereabouts and activities; or to stay away from particular activities.

---

1   See para **5.16**.
2   See *No More Excuses: A New Approach to Tackling Youth Crime in England and Wales* Cm 3809 (1997), para 71, and Alun Michael, MP, Minister of State, Home Office, HC Committee, col 587.

Application of s 69

5.44 The provisions of s 69 apply where an offender aged 10 and above but not more than 17 is convicted of an offence other than one for which the sentence is fixed by law, after the commencement[1] of the section (s 69(1)).

---

1 The provisions are now in general operation, following pilot schemes. Local agreements must be in place: 2000 Act, s 69(7).

Power to make the order

5.45 The action plan order contained in s 69 is a community order and therefore subject to the requirements for, and restriction on, the making of such orders under s 35 of the 2000 Act.[1]

By s 69(1) and (3), the court by or before which the offender is convicted may, if it is of the opinion that it is desirable to do so in the interests of securing his rehabilitation, or of preventing the commission by him of further offences, make an order (an 'action plan order') which:

'(a) requires the offender, for a period of three months beginning with the date of the order, to comply with an action plan, that is to say, a series of requirements with respect to his actions and whereabouts during that period;

(b) places the offender under the supervision for that period of the responsible officer; and

(c) requires the offender to comply with any directions given by that officer with a view to the implementation of that plan.'

The three-month length of the order is intended to provide a short but intensive programme of intervention commensurate with the seriousness of the offending and aimed at tackling the causes of his or her offending.

---

1 See para **5.3**.

Restrictions on the making of an action plan order

5.46 Several restrictions are placed on the making of an order. First, a court must not make an action plan order unless it has been notified by the Home Secretary that arrangements for implementing such orders are available in the area proposed to be named in the order and the notice has not been withdrawn.

Secondly, the court may not make an action plan order in respect of the offender if:

'(a) he is already the subject of such an order; or

(b) the court proposes to pass on him a custodial sentence or a sentence under section 53(1) of the 1933 Act, or to make in respect of him a probation order, a community service order, a combination order, a supervision order or an attendance centre order' (s 69(5)).

The restriction on combining an action plan order with custody is perhaps self-evident, given that, by definition, custodial sentences and community sentences should not be combined.[1] Quite apart from differences in principle, the threshold for a custodial sentence in s 79 of the 2000 Act will not have been crossed. Community punishment orders and community punishment and rehabilitation orders[2] are targeted at offenders aged 16 and over, and include an element of reparation. Supervision orders and attendance centre orders contain their own regimes designed to work with young offenders, and the differences in degree between action plan orders and supervision orders have already been noted.[3] A reparation order may not be combined with an action plan order. There is, however, no obstacle to combining an action plan order with a curfew order, fine or compensation order.

---

1   See para **5.3**.
2   Ie community service orders and combination orders.
3   See para **5.43**.

Procedure when making an order

5.47   By s 69(6), before making an action plan order, a court must obtain and consider:

> '(a) a written report by a probation officer, a social worker of a local authority social services department or a member of a youth offending team,[1] indicating –
>
> > (i)   the requirements proposed by that person to be included in the order;
> > (ii)   the benefits to the offender that the proposed requirements are designed to achieve; and
> > (iii) the attitude of a parent or guardian of the offender to the proposed requirements; and
>
> (b) where the offender is under the age of 16, information about the offender's family circumstances and the likely effect of the order on those circumstances.'

This requirement to consider the family circumstances does not apply in respect of offenders aged 16 or 17 who are being considered for an action plan order. Such persons will often have left home and be living independently. However, the Government intend to issue guidance, which may include asking for sensitivity in cases where offenders aged over 16 have family circumstances or arrangements to which it is appropriate for a court to give greater attention.[2]

It should be borne in mind that, to achieve a report containing the matters set out in s 69, a significant level of contact will have had to have occurred between the reporting officer and the offender, and, where appropriate, his family.

---

1   See para **1.18**.
2   Alun Michael, MP, Minister of State, Home Office, HC Committee, 1998, col 589.

5.48   Before making an action plan order, a court must explain to the offender in ordinary language:

'(a) the effect of the order and of the requirements proposed to be included in it;

(b) the consequences which may follow (under Schedule 5 to this Act)[1] if he fails to comply with any of those requirements; and

(c) that the court has power (under that Schedule) to review the order on the application either of the offender or the responsible officer' (s 69(11)).

---

1   See paras **5.52–5.58**.

Requirements in an action plan order

5.49 By s 70(1), requirements included in an action plan order, or directions given by a responsible officer, may require the offender to do all or any of the following things, namely:

'(a) to participate in activities specified in the requirements or directions at a time or times so specified;

(b) to present himself to a person or persons specified in the requirements or directions at a place or places and at a time or times so specified;

(c) to attend at an attendance centre specified in the requirements or directions for a number of hours so specified [but only if the offence is, in the case of an adult, punishable with imprisonment (s 70(1)];

(d) to stay away from a place or places specified in the requirements or directions;

(e) to comply with any arrangements for his education specified in the requirements or directions;

(f) to make reparation specified in the requirements or directions to a person or persons so specified or to the community at large [provided that that person is a victim of or affected by the offence and consents to reparation (s 70(4)]; and

(g) to attend any hearing fixed by the court under section 70(3) ...'

Such requirements and directions must, so far as practicable, be such as to avoid any conflict with the offender's religious beliefs or with the requirements of any other community order to which he may be subject, and any interference with the times, if any, at which he normally works or attends school or any other educational establishment (s 70(5)). Once again, human rights issues may arise if there is interference with religious beliefs or education.

5.50 The plan should be drawn upon by a member of the YOT, in consultation with the young person and his parents. The question of full parental involvement is not a statutory requirement. National standards are being drawn up by the Home Office, in consultation with the Youth Justice Board.[1]

---

1   See para **1.23**.

Subsequent action by the court

5.51 Immediately after making an action plan order, a court may fix a further hearing for a date not more than 21 days after the making of the order; and direct the responsible officer to make, at that hearing, a report as to the effectiveness of the order and the extent to which it has been implemented (s 71(1)).

At that hearing, the court must consider the responsible officer's report, and:

(i)   may, on the application of the responsible officer or the offender, vary the order, by cancelling any provision included in it; or

(ii) by inserting in it (either in addition to or in substitution for any of its provisions) any provision that the court could originally have included in it (s 71(2)).

A hearing shortly after the making of the order is intended to provide an opportunity for the court, in discussion with the responsible officer, the young offender and his or her parents, to make an early assessment of whether the requirements are effective in practice and an opportunity to amend the order if appropriate.

Discharge, variation and breach

5.52   Schedule 8 to the 2000 Act deals with failure to comply with the requirements of action plan orders, for varying such orders and for discharging them with or without the substitution of other sentences (s 72).

5.53   Schedule 5 to the 2000 Act contains detailed provisions in respect of the variation and discharge of action plan and reparation orders.[1]

The power to discharge or vary a youth court order is vested in the youth court named in the order (Sch 5, para 1). That will be the youth court for the petty sessions area in which the offender resides, or will reside. The power to discharge or vary includes the power to discharge or vary a Crown Court order. The language of Sch 5, para 2 (which deals with discharge or variance) in no way limits the role of the youth court to youth court orders.

If it appears to the appropriate youth court on an application made by the responsible officer or by the offender that it is appropriate to do so, the court may, by Sch 5, para 2(1), discharge the order, or vary it:

'(a) by cancelling any provision included in it; or

(b)   by inserting in it (either in addtion to or in substitution for any of its provisions) any provision that could have been included in the order if the court had then had the power to make the order and were in fact exercising it.'

The court has no power to discharge or vary of its own motion: there must be an application, although clearly a court can, if it wishes to do so, invite an application. If an application for discharge is made and dismissed, no further application for discharge can be made except with the consent of the court (Sch 5, para 2(2)).

5.54   Where the appropriate youth court is satisfied, on an application made by the responsible officer, that the offender has failed to comply with any requirement included in the order, it may (in addition to any order by way of discharge or variation) order the offender to pay a fine not exceeding £1,000, or make an attendance centre order[1] or curfew order in respect of him (Sch 5, para 3(2)(a)). The fine imposed is to be deemed to be a sum adjudged to be paid by a conviction (Sch 5, para 3(6)).

Alternatively, the youth court may discharge the order and deal with the offender for the offence in respect of which the order was made, in any manner in which he could have been dealt with for that offence by the court which made the order if the order had not been made (Sch 5, para 3(2)(b)). Thus, if the youth court wishes to impose a custodial sentence, in the form of a detention and training order,[2] it can only do so if the offence's seriousness is such as to satisfy the custody threshold in s 79 of the 2000 Act.

However, if the court is proposing to deal with the offender for breach of the order, it must take into account the extent to which the offender has complied with the requirements of the order (Sch 5, para 3(7)). If the offender has attained the age of 18 after the date of application, but before the date of hearing, the offender is to be dealt with as if he were still under 18 (Sch 5, para 5(3)). If he had attained the age of 18 prior to the application, he should be dealt with in accordance with that age.

---

1   See para **5.32**.
2   See para **6.3**.

5.55   If the order was a Crown Court order, the youth court, following an application by the responsible officer, may deal with the offender as set out in para **5.54**. Alternatively, it may (although is under no duty to do so) commit the offender in custody or release him on bail until he can be brought or appear before the Crown Court (Sch 5, para 3(2)(c)). Where it follows that course of action it is under a duty (Sch 5, para 3(3)) to supply to the Crown Court a certificate, signed by a justice of the peace, giving:

'(a)   particulars of the offender's failure to comply with the requirement in question, and
(b)   such other particulars of the case as may be desirable.'

Such a certificate purporting to be so signed, is admissible as evidence of the failure of the breach before the Crown Court. That phraseology permits other evidence to be adduced in the Crown Court to prove breach, or no breach, if such evidence exists and is relevant. Schedule 5, para 3(3), does not state that the justices' certificate shall be 'conclusive evidence'. Clearly in all but exceptional cases the certificate is likely to suffice.

5.56   Where failure to comply is proved to the satisfaction of the Crown Court, the order must be revoked, if it is still in force (Sch 5, para 3(5)). The Crown Court may deal with the offender for the offence in respect of which the order was made, in any manner in which it could have dealt with him for that offence, if he had not made the order (Sch 5, para 3(4)). Thus, if it wishes to impose a custodial sentence, in the form of a detention and training order, it can only do so if the offence's seriousness is such as to satisfy the custody threshold in s 79 of the 2000 Act.

Again, the court must take into account the extent to which the offender has complied with the requirements of the order (Sch 5, para 3(7)). If the offender has attained the age of 18 after the date of application, but before the date of hearing, the offender is to be dealt with as if he were still under 18 (Sch 5, para 5(3)). If he had attained the age of 18 prior to the application, he should be dealt with in accordance with that age.

Procedure
5.57 The Act does not specify whether the application by the responsible officer must be in writing. However, no order can be made without the offender being present in court (Sch 5, para 4(1)), unless the order is one of discharge, cancelling a requirement contained in the order, altering the name of any area specified in the order, or changing the responsible officer named in the order (Sch 5, para 4(9)).

The attendance of the offender may be secured by the issue of a summons or warrant (in which circumstances the provisions of the Magistrates' Courts Act 1980, s 55(3) and (4) apply, with some modifications[1] (Sch 5, para 4(2) and (3)).

If the offender is arrested pursuant to a warrant, and cannot immediately be brought before the appropriate court, the person in whose custody he is held may make arrangements for his detention in a place of safety for a period of up to 72 hours from the time of arrest, bringing him before a youth court during that period (Sch 5, para 4(4)). That court may not necessarily be the appropriate youth court: if it is not, the youth court before which the offender is brought may remand to local authority accommodation (provided the offender is aged under 18) or direct his release (Sch 5, para 4(5)). If the offender has attained the age of 18 after the date of application, but before the date of hearing, the offender is to be dealt with as if he were still under 18 (Sch 5, para 5(3)). If he had attained the age of 18 prior to the application, he should be dealt with in accordance with that age.

If the offender is aged 18 or over he should be remanded to a remand centre, if such a centre is available, or, otherwise, to prison. He may, of course, alternatively be released (Sch 5, para 4(6)).

Where an application for discharge or variation is made under Sch 5, para 2(1) the offender may be remanded to local authority accommodation if either his attendance has been secured by warrant, or if the court considers that remand (or further remand) will enable information to be obtained which is likely to assist the court in deciding whether, and if so, how, to exercise its powers (Sch 5, para 4(7)). The relevant local authority must be specified in accordance with the terms of Sch 5, para 4(8).

---

1   As modified (the modifications being italicised) these provide as follows:

    '(3) The court shall not begin to hear the complaint in the absence of the defendant or issue a warrant under this section unless either it is proved to the satisfaction of the court, on oath or in such other manner as may be prescribed, that the summons cannot be served or was served on him within what appears to the court to be a reasonable time before the hearing or adjourned hearing or the defendant has appeared on a previous occasion to answer to the complaint.

(4) Where the defendant fails to appear at an adjourned hearing, the court shall not issue a warrant under this section unless it is satisfied that he has had adequate notice of the time and place of the adjourned hearing.'

Appeals

5.58 An offender may appeal to the Crown Court in respect of any order of discharge (or refusal to discharge), variation or failure to comply made by a youth court, other than an order that did not require his presence (Sch 5, para 5(4)). There appears to be no right of appeal against such decisions taken by the Crown Court.

---

1 See para **5.1**.

COMMUNITY REHABILITATION ORDERS (PROBATION ORDERS)

5.59 Probation orders are one of the most established of community orders. The recent legislative background was established by the Powers of Criminal Courts Act 1973, clearly subject to many amendments made by the multiplicity of criminal justice legislation since, principally, the Criminal Justice Act 1991. The raft of provisions was consolidated by the Powers of Criminal Courts (Sentencing) Act 2000. However, when it comes into force the Criminal Justice and Courts Services Act 2000 makes significant further changes. It reorganises the Probation Service along national lines (the National Probation Service). As noted at para **5.1**, it renames the three orders that lie at the heart of probation work (probation, community service and combination orders). It amends those provisions in matters of detail.

For the purposes of this section the orders are referred to by the acronyms of the new title (viz, community rehabilitation order (CRO), community punishment order (CPO) and community punishment and rehabilitation order (CPRO)) in anticipation of their commencement and for ease of exposition. In matters of detailed law, however, a distinction is drawn between matters in force and those not yet in force.

The order

5.60 A CRO may be made by a court in respect of an offender aged 16 years or over, who is convicted of an offence, where the court by or before he is convicted is of the opinion that his supervision is desirable in the interests of:

(a) securing his rehabilitation; or
(b) protecting the public from harm from him or preventing the commission by him of further offences.

A CRO[1] requires the offender to be under the supervision of a probation order for a period of not less than six months or more than three years (2000 Act, s 41(1)). It may be subject to such requirements as the court, having regard to the circumstances of the case, considers desirable for the purposes (2000 Act, s 42).

---

1   The form of a magistrates' court order is specified by Form 92 or 92A in the Magistrates' Courts (Forms) Rules 1981, SI 1981/553, (as amended).

Sentence combinations

5.61   The general position was stated at para **5.3**: a CRO and custodial sentences should not be combined, irrespective of whether the custodial term is immediate or suspended, because a suspended sentence is to be regarded as a custodial sentence (2000 Act, ss 79 and 118). Quite apart from the fact that the custody threshold is significantly higher than that which would justify the making of a CRO, the mixing of sentences of different types is to be discouraged.[1]

It is beyond doubt that a CRO and CPO cannot be combined for the same offence except in the form of a CPRO, and, also, not for associated offences: the intent of Parliament is that such orders should be combined only in the form of a CPRO. Although the mixture of CRO and CPRO is theoretically available for different offences, and not prohibited by statute, that too appears to be contrary to principle: to accept this is to accept a CRO and CPO together, which is not permitted except in the context of a CPRO. This was confirmed by the court in *Gilding v DPP*.[2]

The other order that is inappropriate to be combined with a CRO is a supervision order, whether for the same or different offences. This would be to contemplate two different supervisory regimes. Which is the appropriate order for a person aged 16 or 17 will depend on the maturity of the offender, in the light of assessments by probation officers, social workers, or by another member of a youth offending team. Who will prepare the report will depend on whether social services have existing contact with the family and the offender's family, and upon local agreements reached between probation and social service juvenile justice units.

There is no sentencing objection in combining a CRO with an attendance centre order or a curfew order, although care needs to be taken to ensure that those do not conflict with any requirements in the probation order.

---

1   See para **5.4**.
2   (1998) *The Times*, 20 May 1998.

5.62   Each CRO must specify the petty sessions area in which the offender resides or will reside, and from which the supervising officer will be drawn

(2000 Act, s 41(3)).[1] Those who are homeless may well have been given probation service assistance in finding temporary accommodation in a probation or voluntary sector hostel, or bed and breakfast. However, homelessness itself is not necessarily a justification for the provision of probation hostel accommodation. Other factors will also be relevant in determining, for example, whether a requirement of residence is appropriate. Such hostel accommodation will be targeted on the more serious offender. In addition, such an order is highly restrictive of the freedom of the offender, and may not be commensurate with the seriousness of the offence. In terms of management, supervision and enforcement of the CRO, it may be impracticable to make an order on nomadic persons, travellers or those with no stable address or no fixed abode. The practicability of supervision seems to be the key factor: a gypsy may be an appropriate subject of an order if living for the time being on a local authority gypsy site, but not if constantly nomadic. The question will need to be addressed by the pre-sentence report with all possible options for the effective supervison of the individual being explored, despite the nomadic lifestyle.

---

1   Problems may arise in respect of those who are resident overseas, in Scotland, Northern Ireland, or who are homeless. Probation orders should not be made with a requirement of residence in another country, eg, that the offender resides in the Republic of Ireland (*R v McCartan* [1958] 1 WLR 933). Quite apart from it being wrong in principle there would be no basis for the supervision of the offender. In relation to those resident in Scotland or Northern Ireland, reciprocal arrangements for the supervision of such orders exist (s 42 and Sch 4). If the offender will be residing in Scotland, a probation order is not to be made unless the court is satisfied that suitable arrangements for the offender's supervision can be made by the regional or islands council for the area in which the offender will reside (Sch 4). Similar requirements exist in respect of those who will be resident in Northern Ireland, the suitable arrangements to be made available by the Probation Board for Northern Ireland (Sch 4).

Requirements

5.63   A CRO may be subject to requirements. By s 41(11) of the 2000 Act, an offender is required to keep in touch with the supervising officer in accordance with such instructions as may be given from time to time, and is also under a duty to notify that supervising officer of any change of address. It may be possible to imply into the duty to report in accordance with instructions an obligation to behave whilst on probation premises or whilst otherwise under the direction of the supervising officer. In that case the unacceptable behaviour may mean that the offender has failed to report in accordance with the instructions of that officer, and that would be the basis of the breach action. Great difficulty would arise in attempting breach proceedings based on such conduct in other circumstances. No legal basis for breach action in such circumstances appears to exist and the extent to which a general requirement can regulate an offender's behaviour is open to doubt. Requirements should be both express and precise. The remedy may be an application for revocation of the order, on the basis that the offender's general conduct and attitude make the objectives of the order unattainable.

5.64   Section 42(1) of the 2000 Act permits the imposition of requirements for the general purpose:

> '(a) securing the rehabilitation of the offender; or
> (b) protecting the public from harm from the offender or preventing the commission by him of further offences.'

Such requirements must meet the criteria the law sets out, and must be part of the order to which the offender consents. In short, they must be drawn to the attention of the offender at the time of making. They must also be necessary and proportionate, in order to comply with the European Convention on Human Rights and the Human Rights Act 1998.[1]

Clarity and sharpness of definition are essential if breach of requirements is to form the basis of breach proceedings.[2] Also, if a statute permits a requirement of attendance at a given place for given periods, these provisions cannot be avoided by the imposition of general requirements under s 42. A court cannot, by a requirement, require the payment of money by way of damages or by compensation: this should be achieved by the making of a separate order, permitted by s 1 of the 2000 Act. The compensation order, if made, is to be regarded as separate from the probation order.[3] This has consequences if the offender is resentenced for the breach of the probation order.

The nature and extent of the requirements imposed will affect the degree of restriction on liberty that the order involved. This will be important in determining whether the order is the appropriate community sentence in the light of the general criteria under s 6 of the 1991 Act. In addition to this general power, s 42 of the 2000 Act and Sch 2 permit the imposition of specific requirements.

---

1   See para **1.34**.
2   See, generally, *Cullen v Rogers* [1982] 1 WLR 729, HL.
3   *R v Wallis* (1979) 1 Cr App R (S) 168; *R v Mathieson (Stephen Kenneth)* (1987) 9 Cr App R (S) 54.

Requirements in respect of residence

5.65   An order may include specific provision in relation to residence (2000 Act, Sch 2, para 1). An order can require residence at an approved hostel or other institution, or at any other place, for a period which should be specified in the order. Arguably, provisions that merely state, for example, a period of residence 'for a period of up to x months' are insufficiently precise. A better approach is to state the period of residence, with an application for amendment of the order if the residence becomes unnecessary or inappropriate. Again, a requirement might permit a requirement of residence with parents, but before imposing any residence requirement the home circumstances of the offender must be considered (Sch 2, para 1(2)). Any requirement of hostel residence should specify the particular hostel. A failure to specify the place might well make the order void for uncertainty. A condition that requires residence at hostel accommodation to be determined by the supervising officer should not be made. Residents of hostels should be made aware that their residence will be regulated by rules. A specific probation requirement stipulating observance of hostel rules is arguably within the literal meaning of the term 'relating to residence' (Sch 2, para 1) although in respect of hostel residence as a condition of bail, s 3(6ZA) of the Bail Act 1976 states that the defendant 'may also be required to comply with the rules of the hostel'. Although the absence of similar provision in the probation legislation might be considered significant, it would be surprising if no such power existed. Some support for such a power is implicit in the decision of *R v Powell (Shane)*[1] where an offender was sentenced to a term of imprisonment for failure to comply with a probation order which included a requirement, amongst others, that the offender should abide by the rules of the hostel. Even if power to include such a requirement exists, however, care should be taken to ensure that the rules are not being used as a means of control which is unrelated to the essential question of residence. If such a requirement can be justified as 'relating to residence', it logically follows that proceedings for breach could be based on that failure to observe hostel rules, although the breadth of the issues on which a court might be called on to adjudicate in any case may cause a court to pause before the imposition of a requirement.

In the absence of such a requirement to comply with the rules of the hostel, such breach of hostel rules can only be the basis of breach action if it makes fulfilment of the residence requirement impossible. Any breach action should be on the basis that the offender's conduct makes his or her continued residence unacceptable to the hostel. That, though, raises the further question of the fairness of the treatment of the offender by the hostel.

---

1   (1992) 13 Cr App R (S) 202.

Requirements regarding activities
5.66   By Sch 2, paras 2 to 4 of the 2000 Act, a CRO order may require the offender:

(a) to report to specified persons at specified places, for no more than 60 days;
(b) to participate in or refrain from participation in specified activities for a period not exceeding 60 days;
(c) to require attendance at a probation centre for not more than 60 days.

The provisions in (a) and (b) are intended to be alternatives, but they are not mutually exclusive. However, since para 2 limits such requirements in either case to periods not exceeding 60 days in the aggregate, it would appear not to be proper to have such requirements exceeding 60 hours in total. The one important exception to this is in respect of an offender who has been convicted of a sexual offence. Any number of days up to the total length of the order may be specified (Sch 2, para 4). This provides important potential for longer-term attendance at group-work facilities, if they exist.

5.67   Before imposing such requirements, the court must consult, in the case of an offender aged under 18, either a probation officer or a member of a youth offending team, and must be satisfied that it is feasible to secure compliance with the requirement, or make the arrangements for securing attendance at the centre (in the case of (c) above (see Sch 2, paras 2(2), 3(2)). If the activity participation in which is required would involve the co-operation of a person other than the offender and the supervising officer, that person must consent to its inclusion (Sch 2, para 3(2)).

In deciding whether such requirements should be imposed, the court should seek to avoid interference with the times which the offender normally works or attends a school or other educational establishment, or the person's religious beliefs (Sch 2, paras 2(7), 3(5)). For example, it should not automatically be assumed that Sunday is the relevant day of worship.

Requirement of treatment by medical practitioner

5.68 Where, following evidence from a qualified medical practitioner (approved for the purposes of s 12 of the Mental Health Act 1983) a court is satisfied that the mental condition of an offender is such as requires, or may be susceptible to, treatment, but is not such as to warrant the making of a hospital order under that Act, a requirement may be imposed that the offender shall, during the whole or part of the order, submit to treatment by or under the direction of a medical practitioner (2000 Act, Sch 2, para 5). The court must be satisfied that arrangements have already been made for the treatment specified in the order. Any requirement which stipulated medical treatment as directed by the supervising officer would be unlawful.

If such treatment is residential then during the period such treatment lasts the legal role of the probation officer is limited to matters necessary for the purpose of revocation or amendment of the order (Sch 2, para 5(5)). This does not prevent liaison and joint work. The medical practitioner, with the agreement of the offender, can arrange for the treatment to be carried out by another medical institution or practitioner, and no amendment of the order will be needed.

5.69 The treatment must be one that may be specified in the order, from one of the following (under Sch 2, para 5(3)):

'(a) treatment as a residential patient in a hospital or mental nursing home within the meaning of the Mental Health Act 1983, but not hospital premises at which high security psychiatric services within the meaning of that Act are provided;

(b) treatment as a non-resident patient at such institution or place as may be specified in the order;

(c) treatment by or under the direction of such registered medical practitioner or chartered psychologist (or both) as may be so specified.'

The nature of the treatment is not to be specified in the order (Sch 2, para 5(3)).

Requirement for treatment for drugs or alcohol dependency

5.70 Where the offender is dependent upon drugs or alcohol, and that dependency caused or contributed to the offence in respect of which the order is proposed to be made, and is or may be susceptible to treatment, then additional requirements are permitted (Sch 2, para 6). The CRO may include a requirement that the offender shall submit, during the whole or any part of the order, to treatment by or under the direction of a person having the necessary qualifications with a view to reducing or eliminating the offender's dependency. The reports to the sentencing court will need to identify the person with the necessary qualifications. The provision does not require this person to be medically qualified: it could, for example, be a suitably qualified probation officer. Although the use of the word 'treatment' is suggestive of medical qualification, it is not likely to be so confined in practice. Similar regulatory provisions as already discussed in relation to psychiatric treatment apply.

5.71 By Sch 2, para 5(4), the treatment must be one of the following:

'(a) treatment as a resident in such institution or place as may be specified in the order;

(b) treatment as a non-resident in or at such institution or place as may be so specified;

(c) treatment by or under the direction of such person having the necessary qualifications or experience as may be specified.'

Appropriate arrangements must be in place and the offender must consent. The overlap between this provision and the drug treatment and testing order should also be noted.[1]

---

1   See para **5.103**.

Curfew requirement
5.72 When in force, s 50 of the Criminal Justice and Courts Act 2000 will incorporate into the Powers of Criminal Courts (Sentencing) Act 2000 a new Sch 2, para 7. It will provide for a new curfew requirement, analogous to that which potentially exists in the case of supervision orders, and to the curfew order in its own right.[1] It reflects the view of the Government that further powers were necessary to keep offenders away from the opportunities to commit crime at times when they are likely to do so. The concept of using the curfew as a crime prevention weapon is not new: the Crime and Disorder Act 1998 introduced a range of measures which potentially operate in respect of children under 10, which have scarcely, if at all, been used,[2] and also the home detention order. The existence of the curfew order and night restriction requirements in supervision orders has already been noted. This new provision will give the choice to the court to combine a curfew for a person aged at least 16 whilst maintaining the supervisory regime inherent in a CRO. It will not be possible to combine a curfew requirement with a curfew order (Sch 2, para 7(6)).

---

1   See para **5.100**.

5.73 A curfew requirement will provide that the offender remain, for periods specified in the requirement, at a place so specified. It may specify different places or different periods for different days, but must not specify:

(a) periods which fall outside the period of six months beginning with the day on which the order is made; or

(b) periods which amount to less than two hours or more than twelve hours in any one day.

5.74 Because of the Human Rights Act 1998 implications of both the offender and those with whom the offender is when subject to the curfew, care will need to be taken to ensure that the requirement is both necessary and proportionate, and that the procedural requirements of Sch 2, para 7 are satisfied. The court must obtain and consider information about the place proposed to be specified in the requirement, including information about the attitude of persons likely to be affected by the enforced presence there of the offender (Sch 2, para 7(7)). In addition the requirement must, as far as practicable, be such as to avoid (Sch 2, para 7(3)):

'(a) any conflict with the offender's religious beliefs or with the requirements of any other community order to which he may be subject; and

(b) any interference with the times, if any, at which he normally works or attends school or any other educational establishment.'

Of course, the appropriate local arrangements for monitoring the curfew must be in place (Sch 2, para 7(5)).

Exclusion requirements

5.75 A second addition to the potential list of available requirements is also incorporated into Sch 2 to the 2000 Act by s 51 of the Criminal Justice and Courts Act 2000. When in force it will provide, through a new Sch 2, para 8, for an exclusion requirement. This provision mirrors the new exclusion order created by the Criminal Justice and Courts Act 2000.[1] A court will thus have a choice between making a free-standing exclusion order, or imposing such a requirement as part of a CRO which provides an on-going supervisory regime. The two may not be combined (Sch 2, para 8(6)).

---

1   See para **1.34**.

5.76 A CRO will, when the new para 8 is in force, be able to provide for a requirement prohibiting the offender from entering a place specified in the requirement for a period of not more than two years. Such a requirement:

(a) may provide for the prohibition to operate only during the periods specified in the order,

(b) may specify different places for different periods or different days.

It may thus be possible to prevent a person from attending particular events, or activities.

5.77 By its nature such an order is inherently restrictive. Although not intended to do so it could theoretically prohibit a violent offender from visiting their home at specified periods. Such a conclusion would have significant human rights implications, and is unlikely to be used in such a way. There is nothing in the provision which prevents such use. Any human rights challenge, will, once again, raise the issue as to whether the interference with the liberty of the individual offender is necessary and proportionate.[1] An exclusion requirement must, so far as practicable, be such as to avoid:

(a) any conflict with the offender's religious beliefs or with the requirements of any other community order to which he may be subject; and
(b) any interference with the times, if any, at which he normally works or attends school or any other educational establishment.

Local arrangements for monitoring must exist (Sch 2, para 8(5)). It is intended to enforce such a requirement through electronic tagging (Criminal Justice and Courts Services Act 2000, introducing a new s 36B into the Powers of Criminal Courts (Sentencing) Act 2000).

Breach, revocation and amendment of a CRO and other orders

5.78   Schedule 3 to the 2000 Act replaces Sch 2 to the Criminal Justice Act 1991 in providing a scheme for breach, revocation and amendment of curfew, probation, community service, combination and drug treatment and testing orders. These provisions are dealt with here, in the context of a CRO, with cross-reference to this section from other parts of this Chapter.

Amendment of order

5.79   An application to amend a requirement in a CRO, CPRO or curfew order is made under para 19 of Sch 3. A magistrates' court for the petty sessions area involved may cancel any requirements in the order, or insert into the order (either in addition to or in substitution for any such requirement) any requirement which the court could include if it were them making the order. This includes a Crown Court order. A court cannot reduce a probation period or increase it beyond three years from the date of the original order (Sch 3, para 19(2)). It can only insert into a probation order, or probation element, a requirement in respect of treatment for mental condition, or dependency on or propensity to misuse drugs or alcohol, if the offender is agreeable, and the amending order is made within three months of the original order. The application can be made by the probation service or offender.

Where a medical practitioner or other person by whom or under whose direction the offender is being treated for his mental condition, or his dependency on drugs or alcohol pursuant to a requirement in a probation order:

(a) is of the opinion –

   (i)   that the treatment of the offender should be continued beyond the period specified in the order, or
   (ii) that the offender needs different treatment, being treatment of a kind to which he could be required to submit in the pursuance of a probation order, or

    (iii) that the offender is not susceptible to treatment, or

    (iv) that the offender does not require further treatment, or

(b) is for any reason unwilling to continue to treat or direct the treatment of the offender,

(he must make a report in writing to that effect to the responsible officer).

That officer is under a duty to apply under Sch 3, para 20 for the variation or cancellation of that requirement. The fact that the responsible officer might disagree is irrelevant: it is in law a matter for the medical practitioner alone.

No such application for variation of an order can be made while an appeal is pending against sentence. Where the order sought is one substituting a new petty sessions area or cancelling a requirement in the order, or reducing the period of any requirement, the offender does not have to be summonsed (Sch 3, para 17). In such case, there is no requirement for notice of the application to be served on the offender, or for consent to be sought. Where the variation goes beyond that, the offender must be summonsed. The 2000 Act does not make provision for the service of notice of an application for variation by an offender, but the point is more theoretical than real, since it is scarcely conceivable that a court would in fact vary without hearing from the probation service. If the offender does not appear, a warrant for arrest may be issued. The offender must express his or her willingness to consent to the order as varied, if that consent is necessary.

The power to vary is in the hands of the magistrates' court, and extends to all orders, even Crown Court orders.

Revocation of probation, community service combination and curfew orders
5.80   The 2000 Act creates a common scheme, in Sch 3. Despite the fact that a combination order is a single order of the court, Sch 3 is not specifically applied to combination orders. Because an order comprises both community service and probation elements, the effect of the 2000 Act is to allow the individual elements of the order to be the subject to an application for revocation.

The powers to revoke orders are drawn widely. They may be used to terminate the order where the offender has made good progress and has satisfactorily responded to supervision. The other major area of use is where other offences have been committed during the currency of the order. Only the Crown Court can revoke, or revoke and re-sentence, without an application being made. Whether such revocation is appropriate will depend on what sentence or penalty the court imposes for the further offence or offences. In particular, an application to revoke the order will usually be appropriate where the court imposes a custodial sentence for a further offence.[1] A community order presupposes by definition that the offender is at liberty to comply with it. For that reason an application should normally be made where an immediate term of imprisonment is imposed. If the court is imposing a custodial sentence, good practice might suggest an application to the supervising court for revocation, so that orders do not remain in force.

If a probation order is not revoked, it continues in force even if it can have no practical effect during the period of imprisonment.[2]

---

1   *R v Rowsell* (1988) 10 Cr App R (S) 411.
2   *R v Havant Justices, ex parte Jacobs* [1957] 1 WLR 365. It should be noted that the problems that arose in that case no longer arise, the legislation having changed.

5.81   The power to amend an order by reason of change of address is, by Sch 3, para 18, vested in the magistrates' court for the petty sessions area responsible for the order. On an application made by the responsible officer, if the court is satisfied that the offender proposes to change, or has changed, his address from one petty sessions area to another it must amend the order. There are limitations contained in para 18(3) and (5) which prevent the court from so amending a probation order containing requirements if in the opinion of the court the order cannot be complied with except if the offender continues to live in the petty sessions area for which the court is responsible, unless it cancels those requirements or substitutes others. Similarly, a CPO or CPRO must not be amended unless arrangements can be made for work to be performed within the new petty sessions area.

Revocation powers: supervising magistrates' court
5.82   The supervising court has jurisdiction to consider applications for revocation (Sch 3, para 10)). This applies to all orders, whether magistrates' court or Crown Court. Except where there are new offences all applications for revocation must be made to the supervising magistrates' court, by the responsible officer or offender. The offender may not make such an application while an appeal against the making of the order is pending (Sch 3, para 10(8)). The court cannot act of its own motion: there must always be an application. This position should be contrasted with that of the Crown Court under para 11(2) which commences with the words 'If it appears to the Crown Court ...'.

5.83   The grounds for revocation are that it appears to the court that it is in the interests of justice:

(a) for the order to be revoked, or
(b) for the offender to be dealt with in some other manner for the offence in respect of which the order was made.

A distinction arises between the powers to revoke a magistrates' court order and the powers in respect of a Crown Court order. An order made by a Crown Court on appeal is to be treated as a magistrates' court order (Sch 3, para 2(3)). In *R v Waltham Forest Magistrates' Court, ex parte Brewer*[1] a magistrates' court sought to commit an offender to the Crown Court under s 8 of the then Powers of Criminal Courts Act 1973 in respect of an offender subject to an order made by a Crown Court on appeal. It was held that the magistrates' court had no power to do so: the power to commit existed only if there were a Crown Court order. In respect of a magistrates' court order, the court may revoke, or revoke and re-sentence in such manner as it could as if the offender had just been convicted. The offender is to be re-sentenced as if he or she were now before the court for the original offence, not on the basis of the original sentencing position (Sch 3, para 10(3)). In dealing with the offender, the court must take into account the extent to which the offender has complied with the requirements of the relevant order (Sch 3, para 10(5)). A person sentenced under these provisions may appeal to the Crown Court against the sentence (Sch 3, para 10(6)).

---

1   (1992) 13 Cr App R (S) 405.

Revocation powers: other magistrates' courts

5.84   A magistrates' court other than that for the petty sessions area named in the order can revoke an order only if the offender is convicted by that court of another offence, and imposes a custodial sentence (Sch 3, para 13(1)). The definition of custodial sentence in s 79 of the 2000 Act 'a sentence of imprisonment' would therefore enable the use of this power where a suspended sentence is imposed.

This power to revoke can be used only where an application is made to it, either by the responsible officer or the offender. The court has no jurisdiction to act without an application, although there is no obligation for that application to be in writing, and an oral application can be made. The court can use this power if it is considered in the interests of justice to do so, having regard to the circumstances that have arisen since the order was made. It can by Sch 3, para 13(3):

(a) if the order was a magistrates' court order, revoke it,
(b) if it was a Crown Court order, commit the offender to the Crown Court, either in custody or on bail, sending such details of the case as are appropriate.

There is now power in either case to revoke and re-sentence. In a case where the other court considers that re-sentencing in respect of a magistrates' court order is appropriate, then that court (ie the non-supervising court) should decline to revoke, because otherwise the supervising court will be deprived of jurisdiction to consider an application for revocation and re-sentencing. The non supervising court has no formal means of requiring the supervising court to consider the matter.

Revocation powers: Crown Court

5.85   The Crown Court has power to revoke an order if an application is made to it by the offender or the responsible officer for the order to be revoked or for the offender to be dealt with in some other way for the offence in respect of which the order was made, or the offender has been convicted of another offence by the Crown Court, or has been committed for sentence to the Crown Court by a magistrates' court (Sch 3, para 11(1)).

No application to the Crown Court is necessary. Nor is the power limited to where the Crown Court intends to impose a term of imprisonment or detention. The Crown Court can revoke even though no application has been made, and even though the offender has complied fully with the order.[1]

Alternatively, in some circumstances the Crown Court has power to revoke the order and re-sentence the offender for the original offence as if that offender had just been convicted by a court of the offence. Again, no application is required. These circumstances are the same as set out above in respect of the revocation power, with one difference: there is no power to revoke and re-sentence where the matter has been committed to the Crown Court by a non-supervising magistrates' court, under Sch 3, para 9(2), in respect of a Crown Court order. In this case the power is one of revocation, not revocation and re-sentence.

Where a community order is revoked on subsequent conviction for an offence, that revocation fails if the conviction is quashed on appeal. In *R v Woodley*[2] a conviction which triggered the revocation of a community service order was quashed. The court indicated that if in those circumstances it was considered inappropriate for the community order to continue an appropriate court for such an application is the supervising magistrates' court.

---

1   *R v Williams* (1979) 1 Cr App R (S) 78.
2   (1991) *The Times*, 27 November.

Breach

5.86   Paragraph 3 of Sch 3 empowers a justice of the peace acting for the responsible court to issue a summons or warrant bringing the offender before a court if it appears that the offender has failed to comply with any of the requirements of the order. In the case of a Crown Court order, including a direction that any failure to comply with requirements be dealt with by the Crown Court, the offender is required to appear before the Crown Court. In other cases, the offender is required to appear before the magistrates' court acting for the petty sessions area in which the offender resides.

5.87   By Sch 3, para 4, if it is proved to the satisfaction of the magistrates' court identified above that the offender has without reasonable excuse failed to comply with any of the requirements of the relevant order, it may deal with him in one of the following ways (para 4(1)):

(a) it may impose a fine not exceeding £1000;
(b) where the offender is aged 16 or over, it may make a community service order;
(c) where the order is a curfew order and the offender is aged under 16, or where the relevant order is a probation order and the offender is under 21, it may make an attendance centre order; or
(d) where the relevant order was a magistrates' court order, it may deal with him, for the offence in respect of which the order was made, in any way in which it could deal with him if he had just been convicted by the court of the offence.

The community service order referred to in para (b) above must not exceed 60 hours in aggregate, and, where imposed for breach of a community service order, the total number of hours of both orders must not exceed the statutory maximum.[1]

---

1   As to which see, para **5.92**.

5.88   In dealing with the offender under para (d) in para **5.87**, the court must revoke the order: it must also take into account the extent to which the offender has complied with the requirements of the order. In the case of an offender who has wilfully failed to comply with the requirements of the order, the court may impose a custodial sentence notwithstanding the fact that the offence seriousness threshold has not been crossed (Sch 3, para 4(2)(b)).

5.89   In the case of a Crown Court order, a magistrates' court is not obliged to deal with it itself: it may commit to the Crown Court (Sch 3, para 4(4)). Where a case is before a Crown Court, either because of the above or because a direction was made as described in Sch 3, para 4(1), the powers of the Crown Court are similar to that outlined above in respect of a magistrates' court, save only that the power to deal with the offender is to the same extent as if the offender had just been convicted by the Crown Court of the offence in respect of which the order was made.

Revocation and breach; the relationship between the two powers

5.90   Potentially, revocation can be used in cases that arise in reality through breach of the order, if there is conduct that justified this. Despite this, care should be taken to avoid using the revocation powers as a means of dealing with breaches of community orders. The powers relating to breach were outlined above, yet if the conduct of the offender is such as to lead a court to the conclusion that the interests of justice demanded that the order be revoked, or that there be revocation and re-sentence, then the pre-conditions for the use of the power are satisfied. Pre-1991 Act case-law served to confirm this.[1] In *R v Jackson (Kimberley Philamena)* the court indicated that where an action had been brought under the then revocation power on facts which, if proved, would have amounted to a breach of the order, evidence should be brought and considered as if proceedings had been brought under the breach provisions. This principle remains valid notwithstanding the enactment of the 1991 Act, and was confirmed as correct in *R v Oliver*.[2] The revocation provisions should not be used as alternative mechanisms for policing community orders. An offender who is the subject of an application for revocation is subject to the risk of re-sentencing. If the grounds for breach exist, Sch 3 sets out the powers available to the court, which include the possibility of being re-sentenced, but include other alternatives. The powers of re-sentence in the revocation provisions are for the original offence, not for the breach: these lesser orders may not be appropriate for the original offence. In addition, inherent in the breach provisions is the legal defence of 'reasonable excuse'. Whilst a court considering revocation powers could consider this, this is not the same thing as having grounds which justify a legal entitlement to dismissal of the charge. The effect of use of revocation rather than breach provisions is to deprive the offender of that escape route. Revocation provisions should not be used where the question before the court is whether the offender has complied with the order. If it is accepted that the offender has complied with the order then revocation is appropriate if there is a change in circumstances. Likewise, if breach provisions have been brought and have failed then further action by way of an application for revocation based on the same facts is generally inappropriate. It can scarcely be in the interest of justice to revoke an order for conduct which is not found to be in breach of the order.

---

1   *R v Goscombe* (1981) 3 Cr App R (S) 61; *R v Jackson (Kimberley Philamena)* (1984) 6 Cr App R (S) 202.
2   [1998] 1 Cr App R (S) 132, CA.

Conditional discharges

5.91   The powers of the court are, in the case of probation orders, increased by para 12 of Sch 3 to the 2000 Act. Where an application is made to the court, a magistrates' court may make a conditional discharge and revoke a CRO, if it considers it in the interests of justice to do so. It may not make such an order in respect of a Crown Court order: only the Crown Court can make a conditional discharge and revoke the original order. The application to revoke and substitute a conditional discharge can be heard in the absence of the offender if the application is made by the responsible officer, and that officer produces a statement to the court from the offender that he understands the effect of the order and consents to the making of the application.

Re-sentencing: principles

5.92   If the court is satisfied that it is in the interests of justice to do so, the court must revoke, and may also re-sentence. If it does re-sentence normal sentencing principles apply.

Where the offender has committed further offences for which the court intends to impose an immediate custodial sentence, revocation will usually be appropriate. In *R v Calvert (Pactice Note)*[1] the court held that where a person subject to a probation order is convicted of a further offence and given a custodial sentence for that, a separate sentence should be passed for the original offence. The general principle is that custodial and non custodial sentences should not be mixed.[2] The offender is not available within the community for supervision. However, there is no absolute rule. In *R v Rowsell,*[3] Ian Kennedy J stated:

> '... the passing of a sentence of imprisonment upon a man who is then subject to a conditional discharge or a probation order is something that happens very frequently. In those cases the question arises what ought to be done about the offence for which the offender is on probation or subject to a conditional discharge. What should be done must depend on the facts of the individual case. In some it may be clear that an offender who has broken a probation order within a matter of days has shown that he has no intention of taking advantage of the help that he has been offered, and it will be right to pass sentence for the original

offence. In other cases where ... the probation order has not had time to have effect, it may be correct to leave the order in being. In other cases it may be that there is so little that will remain of the probation period after the offender's discharge that it would be futile to leave the order in being. Each case will be different, and must be decided on its own facts.'

If it is decided to re-sentence, the offender is dealt with on the basis that he is now before the court for the original offence. Insofar as it is of importance, the relevant date to determine the age of the offender is the date of re-sentencing. The offender is being re-sentenced for the original offence and the sentence of the court must reflect the level of seriousness of the offence.[4] In *R v Garland (Patrick Joseph)*,[5] a case where the re-sentencing was for breach of a 200-hour community service order, the offence justified a term of imprisonment on re-sentencing of 18 months, for taking a conveyance without consent. In *R v Simpson*,[6] a custodial sentence was quashed where the original offence did not justify custody. Where the court is re-sentencing, it is entitled to have regard to the extent to which the offender has complied with the order in respect of which he or she is being re-sentenced. However, unlike the provisions relating to breach proceedings, the revocation provisions do not entitle the court to assume that non compliance means that the offender refuses to give consent to a new community order.

---

1   [1963] 1 WLR 151.
2   *R v Evans* (1959) 43 Cr App R 66.
3   (1988) 10 Cr App R (S) 411.
4   *R v Barresi* [1981] Crim LR 268.
5   (1979) 1 Cr App R (S) 62.
6   [1983] Crim LR 820.

COMMUNITY PUNISHMENT ORDERS (COMMUNITY SERVICE)

5.93   Community punishment orders (CPO) may be made in respect of any offender aged 16 or over who has been convicted of an offence punishable by imprisonment (2000 Act, s 46). Such an order will require the offender to perform unpaid work, for a specific number of hours. The purpose of such an order is to assist in the re-integration of the offender into the community, through positive and demanding unpaid work, keeping to a disciplined standard and making indirect reparation to the community by undertaking socially useful work.

Before an order is made the court is required to consider a pre-sentence report (PSR), which must be in writing. It is also required to be satisfied that projects or tasks are available, and that the offender is a suitable person to perform work under such an order (s 46(4)). This does not mean that the PSR need necessarily have addressed community service, for a verbal indication of the offender's suitabilty for community service will suffice. Theoretically, a community service order can be made even without the consent of the probation service, although such a course of action is unlikely to occur and should be avoided, given that the probation service has responsibility for the overall management and plannning of community service schemes.

No order may be made unless the offence is punishable with imprisonment. This would appear to mean that the court must have the legal right to impose a term of imprisonment on this particular offender, even if this right is restricted because of age. A community service order should not be imposed by a magistrates' court for an offence which constitutes breach of a Crown Court suspended sentence, such matters being referred to the Crown Court.[1]

The nature of a CPO involved an offender being required to participate in work. Potential issues arise under the European Convention. It has already been noted that a potential problem arises under Art 4.[2] However, it is unlikely that any challenge will succeed, unless the requirements of the order are unfair or disproportionate.[3]

---

1   *R v Stewart (Kevin John)* (1984) 6 Cr App R (S) 166.
2   See para **4.24**.
3   See para **1.34**.

5.94   Custody and a CPO should not be combined, whether for the same or different offences: the mixing of sentences of different types is to be discouraged.[1] However, if community services orders are made by a court for a series of offences, the making of an order does not prevent another court imposing a term of imprisonment for offences committed before the community service order was made.[2]

A CPO and community rehabilitation order (CRO) can be imposed for the same offence only in the form of a combination order (CPRO). The same position exists in the context of sentences for different offences. However, there appears to be no sentencing objection in combining a community service order (if the offender is under 21) with an attendance centre order, provided there is no unavoidable clash between the reporting requirements. However, questions as to the maturity of the offender arise, and may affect the ability of the offender to cope with the demands of two different court orders. The likelihood of completion should be borne in mind. Similar comments may be made in respect of curfew orders.

In respect of CPO and supervision orders, this combination might theoretically be available if the offender is 16 or 17. In addition, however, the restriction on combining probation and community service except in the form of a combination order is analogous and suggests that this combination of sentence is also impermissible.

---

1   *R v McElhorne* (1983) 5 Cr App R (S) 53.
2   *R v Bennett (Derek Ronald)* (1980) 2 Cr App R (S) 96.

Hours

5.95   The number of hours must be specified in the order and in aggregate must be:

(a)   not less than 40, and
(b)   not more than 240.

The hours provisions apply to the aggregate of hours under all the orders. An order may be concurrent or consecutive, or additional to those being served, but must not in any way exceed the statutory maximum (2000 Act, s 46(8)). Theoretically, therefore, consecutive orders each individually of less than 40 hours are permissible, but may well be undesirable. It is also possible to award community service of whatever length (not exceedings 60 hours) for breach of most community orders (para 6(3)).

The appropriate length of a community service order will depend on the seriousness of the offence. CPOs have been regarded since 1991 as sentences in their own right, not alternatives to custody. Nevertheless, the length of the order should reflect the seriousness of the offence. The number of hours should reflect the degree of restriction of liberty commensurate with the nature of the offence committed.

Where a community service order is being substituted for a custodial sentence on appeal, the court may well take into account the period of custody served in determining the number of hours. Thus in *R v Jackson (Jane); R v Jackson (Trevor)*,[1] orders of 100 and 80 hours were imposed on a man and wife of previous good character, who had been given 15 months' imprisonment for obtaining goods worth £4,000 by the use of stolen store credit cards.

No problems arise in making orders that are concurrent, although the position if the offender is found in breach of one needs careful consideration and difficulties arise where orders are to run consecutively to each other. The court should state clearly whether orders are concurrent or consecutive. Consecutive orders can be made, but within certain hours restrictions. In *R v Evans (David)*,[2] the Court of Appeal stated that a consecutive order was permissible in law, but that it was highly desirable that no more than 240 hours are outstanding at the same time in respect of the same offender. This was interpreted in *R v Anderson (Tim Joel)*[3] as meaning that it was impermissible to impose a consecutive order where the total number of hours under the orders exceeds 240. This view was not supported by the Court of Appeal in *R v Silha*.[4] Two hundred and forty hours is the maximum that can be imposed on a single occasion, but nothing in *R v Evans* prevents the making of a second order which would take the total above 240 hours when aggregated with the original order, but which would not do so if aggregated with the remaining hours to be worked. What s 14(2) of the 2000 Act prohibits is a court on the same occasion making orders which in aggregate exceed 240 hours. In short, therefore, any number of orders may be imposed consecutively, provided the total outstanding at any one time does not exceed 240 hours. Whatever the length of order imposed, an appeal court will only rarely interfere with the length of a CPO imposed.[5]

1   (1992) 13 Cr App R (S) 22.
2   [1977] 1 WLR 27.
3   (1989) 11 Cr App R (S) 417.
4   *R v Bushell (David Stephen)* (1987) 9 Cr App R (S) 537.
5   (1992) 156 JP 629.

5.96   Where a person is subject to a CPO, then, by s 47 of the 2000 Act, they must:

> '(a) keep in touch with the responsible officer in accordance with such instructions as he may from time to time be given and notify him of any change of address;
> (b) perform such work as may be specified for such hours as may be specified in the order.'

As is usual, the instructions must, so far as practicable, avoid any conflict with the offender's religious beliefs or with the requirements of any other community order, and avoid interference with the times, if any, at which he normally works or attends school or any other educational establishment (s 47(2)).

Breach, revocation and variation

5.97   The provisions of Sch 3 to the 2000 Act apply equally to a CPO, and reference should be made to paras **5.79–5.90**.

COMMUNITY PROTECTION AND REHABILITATION ORDERS (COMBINATION ORDERS)

5.98   These orders are now governed by ss 51 to 54 of the 2000 Act. A community protection and rehabilitation order (CPRO or combination order) is, by s 51(1) of the 2000 Act, an order which requires the offender:

(a) to be under the supervision of a probation order for a period of not less than 12 months or more than three years; and
(b) to perform unpaid work for a specified number of hours, being not less than 40 or more than 100.

The effect of s 51(4) is that the probation element is to be treated as a probation order, and the unpaid work element as a community service order. The two elements together form a single order and sentence.

The offender must be aged 16 or over, and convicted of an offence punishable with imprisonment. In addition, by s 11(2) of the 2000 Act the court must be of the view that the making of such an order is desirable in the interests of:

'(a) securing the rehabilitation of the offender; or

(b) protecting the public from harm from him or preventing the commmission by him of further offences.'

These offences do not have to be offences of the same type for which the offender is being sentenced.

It is unclear whether a court may impose consecutive combination orders. There appears to be no legal prohibition against doing so, but it does prolong the period of probation supervision beyond the period set out in the statutory requirements.

It is inappropriate to combine combination orders with a custodial sentence. Nor can it be combined with a discharge. To mix a combination order with a supervision order seems wrong in principle. To combine them would subject an offender to two different supervisory regimes. There appears to be no objection to combining combinations orders with attendance centre orders, for 16- to 21-year-olds. Such an order would appear to be an extremely onerous course of action and may not be an attractive sentencing option.

5.99 The wording of s 51(4) is wide enough to permit the imposition of requirements on the probation order element of the order. Particular caution should be used before imposing requirements of specified activities or attendance centres, because the restrictions on liberty caused by the community service element of the order will already impinge on the offenders' available time. Care should be taken in the definition of the different elements of the order: courts need to ensure that any requirements in a probation element are staggered so as not to conflict with the community service obligation. A combination order ought not to be used where probation or community service are appropriate in their own right (see the National Standard).

CURFEW ORDERS

5.100 By s 37 of the 2000 Act, where a person is convicted of an offence, the court by or before which he is convicted may make an order requiring him to remain, for periods specified in the order, at a specified place. It mirrors the new power, when that power is brought into force, to impose a curfew requirement in a probation order[1] and the new exclusion order.[2]

This order, introduced initially in 1991 for offenders aged 16 or over, now potentially is available to offenders of any age. The extension of curfew orders to those under 16, available since 1997, raises significant issues linked, as it is, to the question of electronic monitoring. Possible arguments arise as to whether electronic tagging of young offenders may amount to inhuman or degrading treatment within the meaning of Art 3 of the European Convention on Human Rights.

1   See para **5.75**.
2   See para **5.116**.

5.101   By s 37(1) a curfew order may specify different places or different periods for different days, but must not specify:

'(a)   periods which fall outside the period of six months beginning on the day the order is made; or

(b)   periods which amount to less than two hours or more than twelve hours in any one day.'

The periods of restriction are limited by the 2000 Act. They must not be less than two hours or more than 12 hours in any one day. The requirements must, so far as practicable, be such as to avoid any conflicts with the offender's religious beliefs, or with the requirements of any other community order, and should avoid interference with the times, if any, at which the offender normally works or attends school or other educational establishment (s 37(3)).

The effect of the order has to be explained to the offender, in ordinary language, and also the consequences of non compliance. The offender must also be told of the power the court has to review the order. An order is not to be made unless:

(a)   the court considers information about the place proposed to be specified in the order, including information about the attitude of persons likely to be affected by the offender's presence;

(b)   in the case of an offender under 16, the court must consider the attitude of persons likely to be affected by the enforced presence of the offender.

By s 38, a curfew order may include requirements for securing the electronic monitoring of the offender's whereabouts during the curfew period specified in the order. The court must be satisfied that electronic monitoring arrangements are in place in the area in which the place proposed to be specified is situated.

5.102   Breach of a curfew order is governed by Sch 3 to the 2000 Act, and reference should be made to paras **5.79–5.90**. Therefore, although applicable to young offenders aged 16 to 17, it is also applicable to adult offenders.

DRUG TREATMENT AND TESTING ORDERS

5.103   Section 52 of the 2000 Act provides for a community order (a 'drug treatment and testing order') for offenders aged 16 and over who are dependent on or have a propensity to misuse drugs. This was introduced by the Crime and Disorder Act 1998, and is available in respect of an offence committed on or after 1 October 1998 (s 52(1)).

5.104   Any person aged at least 16 may be subject to an order. Section 61(1) of the 2000 Act provides that the court by or before which the offender is convicted may make an order (a 'drug treatment and testing order') which:

'(a) has effect for a period specified in the order of not less than six months nor more than three years ('the treatment and testing period'); and

(b) includes the requirements and provisions mentioned in sections 53 and 54.'

A court must not make a drug treatment and testing order unless it has been notified by the Home Secretary that arrangements for implementing such orders are available in the area proposed to be specified in the order and the notice has not been withdrawn (2000 Act, s 52(5)). Once such a notification has been given, and has not been withdrawn, the power to impose a requirement in respect of drug dependency in a probation order no longer arises.[1] Instead the court will have to make a drug treatment and testing order.

---

1   See para **5.70**.

5.105   A drug treatment and testing order is a community order and thus the threshold for the making of a community order contained in s 39 of the 2000 Act applies.[1] Like some, although not all, provisions relating to community orders, an order cannot be made unless the offender expresses his willingness to comply with its requirements (2000 Act, s 52(7)). However, if an offender fails to express his willingness to comply with its requirements, the court will be entitled to impose a custodial sentence irrespective of the fact that the offence itself does not reach the custody threshold. Alternatively, a community order not requiring consent could be made. These include a curfew order, and a probation order, although not one containing requirements for medical treatment, or for treatment in respect of alcohol.[2]

When a drug treatment and testing order is made, its effects and its requirements, the consequences of non compliance, and availability of powers of review must be explained to the offender in ordinary language (s 52(6)).

---

1   See para **5.2**.
2   See para **5.68**.

Combination of drug treatment and testing order with other orders and disposals

5.106   The order is a community order (2000 Act, s 61(4)). That not only means that the seriousness threshold for a community order under s 79 of the 2000 Act has to be crossed, but also that it is inappropriate to combine on the same occasion the order with a custodial sentence passed in respect of another offence.[1] It is not possible to, say, combine a short custodial sentence with a drug treatment and testing order to address the addiction or drug misuse that motivated and underpinned the crime. However, there is nothing to prevent its combination with other community sentences. The Consultation Paper, *Breaking the Vicious Circle*[2] clearly envisaged such combinations, particularly the combination of detention and treatment order and curfew and tagging. It noted that there was anecdotal evidence from chaotic drug misusers that electronic tagging has helped impose a degree of discipline on their lives as well as specific benefits of preventing them from going out to their dealers at particularly vulnerable moments.

---

1 See *R v McElhorne* (1983) 5 Cr App R (S) 53.
2 *Breaking the Vicious Circle*, op cit.

Restriction on making a drug treatment and testing order

5.107 By s 52(3) of the 2000 Act, a court must not make a drug treatment and testing order in respect of the offender unless it is satisfied:

'(a) that he is dependent on or has a propensity to misuse drugs; and
(b) that his dependency or propensity is such as requires and may be susceptible to treatment.'

These pre-conditions do not differ in material respects from the definition of drug dependency used in Sch 2 in respect of requirements in probation orders.[1] It will be for the court to determine whether a person is, or has a propensity to misuse drugs. For this purpose, alcohol is not a drug.

---

1 See para **5.70**.

Establishing misuse or propensity to misuse drugs

5.108 Section 52(4) of the 2000 Act provides that, for the purpose of ascertaining for the purposes of s 52(4) whether the offender has any drug in his body, the court may by order require him to provide samples of such description as it may specify, but the court must not make such an order unless the offender expresses his willingness to comply with its requirements.

Clearly, such an order can only be made against an 'offender'. There is thus no power whatsoever to make an order under s 52(4). Nor does the court have to make such an order, and it is not envisaged that it will often be necessary to test before a drug treatment and testing order is made, on financial, logistical and practical grounds.[1] The pre-conditions for the making of a drug treatment and testing order do not of themselves require there to be evidence of the presence of a drug, or a particular level of drug, at any particular time, although, clearly, if a person is dependent or has a propensity to misuse then he or she may be unlikely to have no trace of drug, or drug misuse, when tested. Certain drugs have a quick metabolisation rate, whilst, of course, arrest and trial for the offence may occur a considerable period after the offence itself. It may be the offence itself rather than the offender's current bodily state or behaviour that indicates a propensity to misuse drugs. However, the offence itself does not have to be a drugs offence. It might, for example, be a burglary committed with the motivation of obtaining cash to purchase drugs.

The crucial question is not whether there is evidence of the presence of a drug, but rather whether the court is satisfied that the conditions in s 52(3)(a) and (b) are met. This could be by the result of a test, or by any other evidence before the court, including the details of the offence for which the offender is being sentenced. It could be by the opinion formed by the writer of a pre-sentence report.[2] There is no requirement in the legislation for a judicial finding to be made, nor any obligation to identify which drugs the offender has a dependency on or a propensity to misuse. The assessment of the offender by the probation service is therefore crucial. Any disputes about that assessment should be dealt with by a sentencing court in the normal way it would deal with challenges to the findings of, or statements in, a pre-sentence report. The Home Office has indicated that consideration should be given to the use of specialist probation assessors with effective contacts in police stations to assist in informal early assessments.[3] The order is aimed at drug misusers who are known to commit a high level of crime in order to fund their habit or who are violent and who show some willingness to co-operate with treatment.[4]

---

1   See para **5.109**.
2   For the need for a pre-sentence report, see para **3.1**.
3   *Breaking the Vicious Circle*, op cit.
4   Ibid, para 6. See also Lord Falconer of Thornton, Solicitor-General, HL Committee, col 637.

5.109   Where a court has requested the consent of the offender to a test prior to the making of the order, under s 52(4), his failure to consent does not of itself debar the court from making a drug treatment and testing order if there is other evidence of drug misuse or propensity of misuse. Of course, it is unlikely that if such other evidence existed that the court would have sought to test at that stage in any event. In addition, such refusal makes it highly unlikely that the offender would be suitable for such an order, either because of an unwillingness to consent to the making of the order iself or because the refusal to undergo the test may indicate to the court that there is no real willingness to co-operate. The courts should only make an order where the offender is assessed as suitable for it.[1]

---

1   Lord Falconer of Thornton, Solicitor-General, HL Committee, col 637.

5.110   Section 52(5) of the 2000 Act imposes a further restriction on the making of an order. A court shall not make a drug treatment and testing order unless it is satisfied that arrangements have been or can be made for the treatment intended to be specified in the order (including arrangements for the reception of the offender where he is to be required to submit to treatment as a resident).

Requirements in drug treatment and testing orders

5.111   Section 53(1) of the 2000 Act provides that a drug treatment and testing order must include a requirement ('the treatment requirement') that the offender submit, during the whole of the treatment and testing period, to treatment by or under the direction of a specified person having the necessary qualifications or experience ('the treatment provider') with a view to the reduction or elimination of the offender's dependency on or propensity to misuse drugs. The required treatment for any period must be:

(a) treatment as a resident in such institution or place as may be specified in the order; or

(b) treatment as a non-resident in or at such institution or place, and at such intervals, as may be so specified,

but the nature of the treatment must not be specified in the order except as specified by section 53(2)(a) and (b) (ie it will specify the place at which the treatment will be conducted).

The court will need to specify itself that arrangements can be, or have been, made for the specified treatment (including arrangements for the reception of the offender where he is to be required to submit for treatment as a resident) (s 53(3)).

5.112 The 2000 Act imposes a duty on a court making an order for it to impose a testing requirement (s 53(4)). This is a requirement that, for the purpose of ascertaining whether he has any drug in his body during the treatment and testing period, the offender must provide during that period, at such times or in such circumstances as may (subject to the provisions of the order) be determined by the treatment provider, samples of such description as may be so determined. The question of what samples, when given and in what circumstances, is a matter for the treatment provider, not the court, save only that the testing requirement must specify for each month the minimum number of occasions on which samples are to be provided (s 53(5)). The order will also specify the petty sessions area in which it appears to the court making the order that the offender resides or will reside (s 54(1)).

5.113 A drug treatment and testing order must:

(a) provide that, for the treatment and testing period, the offender be under the supervision of a responsible officer, that is to say, a probation officer appointed for or assigned to the petty sessions area specified in the order;

(b) require the offender to keep in touch with the responsible officer in accordance with such instructions as he may from time to time be given by that officer, and to notify him of any change of address; and

(c) provide that the results of the tests carried out on the samples provided by the offender in pursuance of the testing requirement be communicated to the responsible officer.

The supervising probation officer does not, in the case of a 16- or 17-year-old, have to be a member of a YOT, although he or she might be.[1] The Government intend to issue guidance on the co-ordiantion that will need to occur if a drug treatment and testing order is made alongside another community order supervised by the youth offending team.

The levels of supervision are intended to be sufficient only for specified purposes. These are specified by s 54(5) of the 2000 Act, and are to the extent necessary to enable him to report on the offender's progress, or on any failure, or to determine whether revocation or amendment of the order is appropriate (s 54(5)). However, the potential co-ordinating role set out above needs also to be borne in mind.

---

1   See para **1.19**.

Review of a drug treatment and testing order

5.114   A drug treatment and testing order must be kept under periodic review. By s 54(6) of the 2000 Act the order must:

> '(a)   provide for the order to be reviewed periodically at intervals of not less than one month;
> (b)   provide for each review of the order to be made at a hearing held for the purpose by the court making the order (a 'review hearing');
> (c)   require the offender to attend each review hearing;
> (d)   provide for the responsible officer to make to the court, before each review, a report in writing on the offender's progress under the order; and
> (e)   provide for each such report to include the test results communicated to the responsible officer under section 62(7)(c) and the views of the treatment provider as to the treatment and testing of the offender.'

The words 'not less than month' should not be misunderstood: it is intended that the minimum frequency, and the right frequency, is monthly, although a longer frequency does not appear to be ruled out by the wording of s 63(1)(a).

The italicised word 'the' makes it clear that the review is undertaken by the court that made the order, but in any event the position is put beyond doubt by the terms of s 63(1)(b). Surprisingly, there is no explicit power to vary the reviewing court to take account of, for example, the offender moving to the other end of the country. It is true that, by s 62(7)(a), the order will specify the responsible officer and state the petty sessions area. These can be amended under s 63(2), and one argument might be that by amendment of those matters the reviewing court itself can be changed. That argument, however, faces the inconvenient obstacle of the clear words of s 63(7).

Although an offender must be present at a review hearing, there is, to that rule, one exception. By s 54(7), if at a review hearing the court, after considering the responsible officer's report, is of the opinion that the offender's progress under the order is satisfactory, it may amend the order to provide for each subsequent review to be made by a court without a hearing. A 'review without a hearing' is defined by s 63(10), in the case of the Crown Court, as a reference to a judge of the court, and, in the case of a magistrates' court, as a reference to a justice of the peace acting for the commission area for which the court acts.

Subsequent review hearings may therefore be held in the absence of the offender, but only if his progress is satisfactory. If at a review without a hearing the court, after considering the responsible officer's report, is of the opinion that the offender's progress under the order is no longer satisfactory, the court may require the offender to attend a hearing of the court at a specified time and place (s 54(8)). At that subsequent hearing the court, after considering that report, may exercise powers available at a review hearing, and may amend the order as to provide for each subsequent review to be made at a review hearing (s 54(9)).

Amendment of an order

5.115 At a review hearing the court, after considering the responsible officer's report, may amend any requirement or provision of the order (2000 Act, s 55). The order may also be amended at other hearings without the offender present, but only in accordance with s 55(9) (ie to provide for each subsequent review to be a review hearing).

By s 55(2) the court:

'(a) must not amend the treatment or testing requirement unless the offender expresses his willingness to comply with the requirement as amended;
(b) must not amend any provision of the order so as to reduce the treatment and testing period below the minimum specified in section 55(2), or to increase it above the maximum so specified; and
(c) except with the consent of the offender, shall not amend any requirement or provision of the order while an appeal against the order is pending.'

If the offender fails to express his willingness to comply with the treatment or testing requirement as proposed to be amended by the court, the court may by s 55(4):

'(a) revoke the order; and
(b) may, unless the offender was 16 or 17 when the order was made, deal with him, for the offence in respect of which that order was made, in any manner in which it could deal with him if he had just been convicted by the court of the offence.'

In so dealing with him the court must take into account the extent to which the offender has complied with the requirements of the order, and may impose a custodial sentence irrespective of offence seriousness (s 55(5)). There will be no requirement for a pre-sentence report (although a court may require one), but obviously the responsible officer will have reported on the progress under the order. However, in the absence of a pre-sentence report there will not necessarily be a report on the offender's wider circumstances.

The powers of a court in respect of a person aged[1] under 18 at the date of the making of the order, and in respect of an offence triable only in indictment in the case of an adult, are limited, by s 55(5), to one of the following:

'(a) a fine not exceeding £5,000; or
(b) to deal with the offender for that offence in any way in which it could deal with him if it had just convicted him of any offence punishable with imprisonment for a term not exceeding six months.'

1   See para **1.2**.

Breach

5.116   As a community order, Sch 3 to the 2000 Act has effect, and reference should be made to paras **5.70–5.98**.

Chapter 6

SENTENCES: CUSTODIAL SENTENCES

Restrictions on Sentencing Power of Youth Court or Magistrates' Court – Detention and Training Orders

INTRODUCTION

6.1 A variety of custodial penalties for offenders aged 10 to 17 is available. The alternative custodial disposals are set out below. Not all of them are available to a youth court or a magistrates' court.

(a) Detention at Her Majesty's pleasure, formerly under s 53(1) of the Children and Young Persons Act 1933 and now under s 90 of the 2000 Act, for murder or any other offence the sentence for which is fixed by law as life imprisonment.[1] The sentence may be served in local authority secure accommodation or prison service accommodation, depending on the age and vulnerability of the offender and the availability of accommodation.

(b) Long-term detention, formerly under s 53(2) of the Children and Young Persons Act 1933, and now governed by s 91 of the 2000 Act, up to the adult maximum. This sentence may be served in either local authority secure accommodation or prison service accommodation.

(c) Detention and training order, under s 100 of the 2000 Act. This sentence is served in appropriate secure accommodation, whether local authority or prison service.

Only (c) above is available to the youth court.

---

1   As amended by the Criminal Justice and Courts Services Act 2000 (in force 30 November 2000).

RESTRICTIONS ON SENTENCING POWER OF YOUTH COURT OR MAGISTRATES' COURT

6.2 The youth court has hitherto been limited to the power to impose a custodial term of six months, which increases to a maximum of 12 months in respect of two or more indictable offences.[1] This restriction has been removed, following the passage of the Crime and Disorder Act 1998 and the introduction of the detention and training order. That order on its face appears to confer

authority on a youth court to impose a custodial term of up to 24 months.
Section 133 of the Magistrates' Courts Act 1980 provides:

'(1) Subject to section 102 of the Crime and Disorder Act 1998, a magistrates'
     court imposing imprisonment or detention in a young offender institution
     on any person may order that the term of imprisonment or detention in a
     young offender institution shall commence on the expiration of any other
     term of imprisonment or detention in a young offender institution imposed
     by that or any other court; but where a magistrates' court imposes two or more
     terms of imprisonment or detention in a young offender institution to run
     consecutively the aggregate of such terms shall not, subject to the provisions
     of this section, exceed 6 months.

(2) If two or more of the terms imposed by the court are imposed in respect of an
     offence triable either way which was tried summarily otherwise than in
     pursuance of section 22(2) above, the aggregate of the terms so imposed and
     any other terms imposed by the court may exceed 6 months but shall not,
     subject to the following provisions of this section, exceed 12 months.

(2A) In relation to the imposition of terms of detention in a young offender
     institution subsection (2) above shall have effect as if the reference to an
     offence triable either way were a reference to such an offence or an offence
     triable only on indictment.

(3) The limitations imposed by the preceding subsections shall not operate to
     reduce the aggregate of the terms that the court may impose in respect of any
     offences below the term which the court has power to impose in respect of any
     one of those offences.'[1]

Nothing in s 133 prevented the operation of the plain words of s 73 of the 1998
Act, and, indeed, in that context, the effect of s 133(3) of the 1980 Act was to
permit a term of 24 months for consecutive sentences. The fact that this is the
result was strengthened by the repeal of s 37 of the 1980 Act, depriving the
youth court of the power to commit offenders for sentence. The correctness of
this conclusion is confirmed by recent case-law. In *R v Medway Youth Court, ex
parte A*,[2] a Divisional Court concluded that the now defunct secure training
centre order[3] was not included in the sentences the length of which were
restricted to the traditional magistrates' court limit of six months. It was
possible for such an order to be made up to the maximum specified by the 1994
Act (which governed such orders) of two years. Section 101(1) of the 2000 Act
lists the lengths of time for which a detention and training order can be passed,
and, in its terms states that it applies to an order made by a magistrates' court or
otherwise.

---

1   Magistrates' Court Act 1980, ss 31, 133.
2   (1999) 164 JP 111, DC.
3   See para **6.6**

DETENTION AND TRAINING ORDERS

6.3   Section 73 introduced a new custodial sentence which will initially apply to those aged 12 or over but under 18, and which potentially can be extended to 10- and 11-year-olds. The detention and training order requires the offender to be subject to a period of detention and training, followed by a period of supervision. The detention and training order replaces the secure training centre order, introduced by ss 1–4 of the Criminal Justice and Public Order Act 1994. Those provisions are repealed. The provisions of the 1998 Act are now repealed and consolidated by the 2000 Act, to which reference is now made.

6.4   The power to make a detention and training order arises where the offender is convicted of an offence punishable with imprisonment in the case of a person aged 21 or over[1] (2000 Act, s 100(1)). It is the date of conviction that determines the availability of the order, not the date of the offence, which may be prior to the commencement date.

---

1   This age reduces to 18 when the provisions of s 74 of the Criminal Justice and Court
     Services Act 2000 came into force.

Background

6.5   There were four pre-existing powers to impose a custodial sentence on children and young persons. First, detention at Her Majesty's pleasure, under s 53(1) of the Administration of Justice Act 1933, on conviction for murder. Secondly, detention for certain serious offences, under s 53(2) of the 1933 Act, served either in local authority secure accommodation or in prison service accommodation. Thirdly, detention of young offenders aged 15, 16 or 17, for periods of between two months and two years in a young offender institution, pursuant to s 8 of the Criminal Justice Act 1982. Fourthly, the secure training order, which permitted detention of 12- to 14-year-olds for periods of between six months and two years, in a secure training centre.

6.6   The secure training order provisions contained in ss 1 to 4 of the Criminal Justice and Public Order Act 1994 were amongst the most controversial provisions in that Act, because they moved away from the principle inherent in earlier legislation that custodial sentences served no useful purpose for children and young persons, and that rehabilitation and educative work should be undertaken within the community. Some 36 different organisations, including the Law Society criticised the extension of custodial powers for 12- to 14-year-olds.[1] The Law Society observed that it was not the lack of powers which caused the then perceived problem, but rather the lack of facilities and resources, particularly in respect of local authority secure accommodation. Despite this level of criticism, the secure training centre order formed a central part of Part I of the 1994 Act, with other provisions dealing with establishment of secure training centres. The intention was that five regional secure training centres be created, each capable of taking about 40 children.[2] One, at Medway, Kent, is currently in operation.

---

1   Home Affairs Select Committee, 6th Report, Juvenile Offenders, HC 44–I, para 147.
2   David Maclean, MP, Minister of State, Home Office, HC Standing Committee B (1993) cols 98–102.

6.7   The secure training centre order was opposed by the then Labour opposition during the passage of the 1994 Act. When the Labour Government took office, it indicated that it intended to review the implementation of ss 1 to 4 of the 1994 Act.[1]

The result of that review was a decision to introduce those provisions, which therefore came into effect. However, the Government considered the position relating to custodial sentences for young offenders to be unsatisfactory, for four distinct reasons.[1] First, the available accommodation is fragmented, and with regimes varying both in quality and cost. Secondly, courts' powers to remand young persons to secure facilities were inadequate and inappropriate. Thirdly, the sentencing framework could lead to arbitrary outcomes, with the kind of institution in which the sentence is served being to a large extent determined by the powers under which the young person was being sentenced rather than the needs of the young person. Finally, the structure of sentences did not allow for sufficient emphasis to be placed on preventing offending or responding to progress.

The response to this analysis was to establish a review of the availability and type of secure accommodation, the conferment of new powers on the proposed Youth Justice Board, changes in the powers and arrangements in respect of remands to secure accommodation,[2] and the new detention and training order. This is intended to replace the secure training centre order, and also the sentence of detention in a young offenders' institution with a more constructive and flexible custodial sentence providing a clear focus on preventing offending. The aim is to ensure that custodial sentences, where they are necessary, are more effective in preventing further crime.[3] Such custodial sentences are needed to protect the public by removing the young offender temporarily from the opportunity to re-offend. The increased emphasis on supervision after release, on a clear sentence plan to tackle the causes of offending behaviour and on continuity of supervision before and after release, are intended to complement the other provisions in the new Act for more effective community penalties.

---

1   *No More Excuses—A New Approach to Tackling Youth Crime in England and Wales* Cm 3809 (1997), para 6.2.
2   Ibid, para 6.11. See also Alun Michael, MP, Minister of State, Home Office, HC Committee, col 599.
3   Ibid, para. 6.20.

The power to make the order

6.8 Section 100 provides that, subject to ss 90, 91 and 93, and to the restrictions contained in s 100(2), where:

'(a) a child or young person (that is to say, any person aged under 18) is convicted of an offence which is punishable with imprisonment in the case of a person aged 21 or over; and

(b) the court is of the opinion that either or both of paragraphs (a) or (b) of section 79(2) apply or the case falls within section 79(3),

the sentence that the court is to pass is a detention and training order.'

The references to s 79 of the 2000 Act have the effect of maintaining the principles inherent in the 1991 Act, and re-enacted by the 2000 Act, namely that custody should be imposed only where the offence (together with associated offences) is so serious that only custody can be justified, or, in the case of a violent or sexual offence, where only custody would be adequate to protect the public from harm. Custody can none the less be imposed where the offender fails to express his willingness to comply with any requirement in a probation or supervision order that requires such willingness, or willingness to comply with a requirement in a drug treatment and testing order.[1] The detention and training order is a custodial sentence.

---

1   See para **5.103**.

6.9   The effect of s 100(1) is, therefore, that if a custodial sentence is imposed on a child or young person, it must be by way of detention or training order unless imposed under what was formerly s 53(1) or (2) of the Children and Young Persons Act 1933[1] or s 8 of the Criminal Justice Act 1982. There are, however, further pre-conditions.

Section 100(2) states that a court must not make a detention and training order:

'(a) in the case of an offender under the age of 15[2] at the time of the conviction, unless it is of the opinion that he is a persistent offender;

(b) in the case of an offender under the age of 12 at that time, unless –

(i)   it is of the opinion that only a custodial sentence would be adequate to protect the public from further offending by him; and

(ii)   the offence was committed on or after such date as the Secretary of State may by order appoint.'

In respect of 15-, 16- and 17-year-olds, the only pre-condition is that the seriousness conditions or the unwillingness to consent to the relevant community order when consent is necessary apply. In respect of those aged 13 and 14, the court must form the opinion that the offender is a persistent offender.

---

1   See para **6.1**.
2   See para **1.3**.

6.10   The term 'persistent offender' is not defined. It is a question of fact in each case, to be judged by his past course of conduct, not necessarily by the likelihood of, or level of seriousness of, future offending. Clearly, however, a detention and training order might well be inappropriate in a case where there was no such likelihood of future offences of a level justifying custody.

The offences do not have to be offences in respect of which the offender has been convicted; they might be conduct for which a reprimand or final warning has been given, or which are admitted. Of course, a court should not make a finding of persistence in respect of matters which are denied.

The nature of 'persistence' is the continuance in a course of action.[1] Clearly, for that purpose more than one offence is required, but even two offences could scarcely be described with conviction as a course of conduct. Obviously, the more offences there are the clearer is the behavioural pattern and thus the easier it is to ascribe the label 'persistent'. In *No More Excuses*, reference is made, in another context, to persistence as involving at least three offences.

A further question arises: persistence in what? A 14-year-old may have a pattern of offending involving 'joy-riding' in motor vehicles. Clearly, he is a persistent offender if there is an on-going pattern of such crimes. What, however, if his offending propensity is more varied, involving shoplifting, wanton vandalism and football hooliganism? He is, nevertheless, a persistent criminal, albeit that he may not 'persist' in types of particular crime. This conclusion fits with the general intent of the new order, namely, that a period of detention, training and supervision are necessary to divert the offender from offending behaviour, but may not be an approach favoured by the courts. The case-law gives a wide interpretation to the term 'offender'. A person can be a persistent offender with no previous convictions, but with a string of convictions being dealt with at the same time. This was the approach of the court in *R v Smith*[3] where a 14-year-old pleaded guilty to three offences of robbery, two involving possession of an offensive weapon and one of false imprisonment, all of which were committed over a two-day period. Clearly the term 'offender' is being interpreted as referring to the commission of offences, not to previous appearances before the court, a conclusion which sits with the objectives of the legislation outlined above. Of course, different considerations would apply if the offences had not been admitted. Again, the same approach was taken in *Re C (Young Person: Persistent Offender)*[4] with some five offences being dealt with on the instant occasion. It fits also with other constructions of 'persistent': the courts have held that whether a person is 'persistent' is a matter of fact and degree. In *Re Arctic Engineering Ltd (No 2)*[5] it was held that on the true construction of s 188 of the Companies 1948 Act 'persistently' required some degree of continuance or repetition. If the court is of the opinion that the offender is a persistent offender, it must state so in open court (s 100(4)), as well as complying with the requirements of s 79(4) of the 2000 Act.

---

1   The *Oxford English Dictionary* defines the word 'persist' as 'To continue firmly or obstinately in a state, opinion, purpose or course of action'.
2   [2000] Crim LR 613; (2000) 164 JP 681, CA.
3   (2000) *The Times*, 11 October.
4   [1986] 2 All ER 346, ChD.

6.11   Section 73(2)(b) applies to offenders aged 10 and 11. The detention and training order will not be available for this age-group until an order has been made by the Home Secretary. Its potential availability met fierce criticism in Parliament on the basis that it is wrong in principle, and a significant extention of the law, to impose custodial sentences on 10- and 11-year-olds for anything other than the most grave of offences.[1] The Government agreed that the need for such an extention had not been incontrovertibly established.[2] The intention, at this stage, is to provide a convenient legislative power should the need to extend the order to 10- and 11-year-olds become clear.

If and when this provision comes into effect, a court which proposes to impose a detention and training order must first be of the opinion that only a custodial sentence would be adequate to protect the public from further offending by him. If it is of that opinion, it must say so in open court (s 100(1)), as well as complying with the requirements of s 79(4) of the 2000 Act. It is not enough that custody be the best way, or the most convenient way, of adequately protecting the public from further offending: it must be the only way of so doing. The wording of s 100(2)(b) does not require that the further offending has to be in respect of offences of a level of seriousness which would themselves justify the imposition of a custodial sentence. However, because that is the threshold for the making of an order it ought surely to be the case that the further offending envisaged is of the same level of seriousness.

---

1   For criticism, see James Clappison, MP, HC Committee, cols 595–596. For the powers in respect of grave crimes, see Adminsitration of Justice Act 1933, s 53(2).
2   Alun Michael, MP, Minister of State, Home Office, HC Committee, col 599.

Length of the order

6.12   A detention and training order is an order that the offender in respect of whom it is made shall be subject, for the term specified in the order, to a period of detention and training followed by a period of supervision. Subject to the limitation as to overall length contained in s 101(4), the term of a detention and training order shall be 4, 6, 8, 10, 12, 18 or 24 months. As noted below, this provision is an exception to the general limitation on youth court powers. One effect of the minimum length of the order may be to raise the custody threshold, given it was possible hitherto to impose a shorter peirod of detention in a young offender institution on offenders aged 16 and 17, the ages of those being sentenced in *R v Inner London Crown Court, ex parte N and S*.[1] The court must not take into account that four months is the minimum custodial sentence, albeit that only two months will be served in detention.

The total length of the order (comprising both the period of detention and training and also the period of supervision) may not exceed the maximum term of imprisonment that a Crown Court could impose on an adult offender (s 101(2)). This conclusion is self-evident, given that the term 'detention and training order' includes both the elements of detention and of supervision. In respect of an offender being convicted of more than one offence, a court may make more than one order, either concurrent or consecutive, provided that the term does not exceed 24 months (s 101(3)). For this purpose, the terms of wholly or partly concurrent orders are to be regarded as a single term. If made on the same occasion or if made on different occasions, the offender has not been released (s 101(3)). It is unclear whether the consecutive orders in total have to comply with the statutorily stated sentence lengths.

---

1   [2000] Crim LR 871, CA.

The making of an order in respect of a person detained in a young offender institution

6.13   Where an order is made in respect of a person subject to a sentence of detention in a young offender institution, the rules are somewhat complex. If he has been released pursuant to Part II of the Criminal Justice Act 1991, then the order takes effect immediately.[1] If, by contrast, he is still in detention, then the new sentence takes effect on the day he would (but for the new sentence) be released on licence (s 106(2)). In calculating dates of release, the rules governing concurrent orders, set out in para **6.12**, apply equally in this context.

---

1   It should be noted that, when implemented, s 74 of the Civil Justice and Court Services Act 2000 repeals this order.

The position in respect of the conviction of an offender already subject to an order

6.14   The position in respect of the conviction of an offender already subject to a detention and training order is more complex. If the offender is still serving the detention and training element of the first order, then a subsequent detention or training order, wholly or partly concurrent to the first, is to be treated as part of a single term (s 101(3)). If, by contrast, the offender has been released and is under supervision, the subsequent detention and training order is not to be regarded as part of a single term with the first (s 101(3)(b)).

If a court inadvertently makes an order the effect of which is that the aggregate term of the total order exceeds 24 months, the excess shall be treated as remitted (s 101(5)). This provision, which replicated similar provisions in other statutes,[1] caused debate during the passage of the Act as to the effects of a court not making its wishes clear. It might simply order a period of detention, in the form of 'sentence to detention for [x]', without making it clear that it is detention under s 53(2) of the Children and Young Persons Act 1933 that the court had in mind.[2] Clearly, there is a need for sentencers to be precise and clear.

---

1   See Criminal Justice Act 1982, s 1B(5).
2   See Stephen Hawkins, MP, HC Committee col 605, citing the opinion of Dr David Thomas QC.

Examples

6.15   The following examples illustrate the effect of the above provisions.

Example 1: In a case where a s 100 order is being imposed for offences A and B, a court may make two orders, each of 24 months, to run concurrently. It may not impose two orders of 24 months consecutively. If it wishes to impose consecutive orders, the total length in aggregate must not exceed 24 months.

Example 2: An offender was made subject to a 12-month order on 1 January. On 1 April, the offender (who is still detained in custody) is before the court for a further offence. It may impose an order of no greater than 12 months to run consecutively from the end of the first order, or an 18-month order (or less) to run concurrently from 1 April.

Example 3: An offender is made subject to an 18-month order on 1 January. After 12 months he is released, and is then subject to a period of 12 months supervision. After another six months (ie 1 June, the following year) he is sentenced for another offence. The court may impose a concurrent term of 24 months.

6.16   A person who is subject to a detention and training order may subsequently be sentenced to detention in a young offender institution. This may be because of his age, or because of the effect of s 106(6) which provides that where a person who has attained the age of 18 is being dealt with in a manner in which a court on a previous occasion could have dealt with him, and is sentenced to a detention and training order, that person shall be treated as if he had been sentenced to detention in a young offender institution. If a person is already subject to a detention and training order, and is then sentenced to detention in a young offender institution, that second sentence comes into effect at a time which depends on whether the offender has been released from the custodial element of the order. If he has, then the second sentence commences on the day on which it was passed (s 106(2)). If, by contrast, the offender is still being detained, the order of detention will commence on the date when, by virtue of s 101 the offender would otherwise be released from the custodial element of the order (s 106(2)). In any case where the offender is subject concurrently to a detention and training order and to a sentence of detention in a young offender institution, he is to be treated for the purposes of ss 75 to 78 of the new Act, for the purposes of s 1C of the Criminal Justice Act 1982 and for the purposes of Part II of the Criminal Justice Act 1991 as if the offender were subject only to one of those terms, that term being the one imposed on the later occasion (s 101(4)). However, the effect of s 101(5) is that the offender shall not be released in respect of either the order or the sentence unless and until he is required to be released in respect of each of them.

Length of the order

6.17 It will have been noted that s 101(1) limits the permissible length of an order to certain specified, even-numbered months (4, 6, 8, 10, 12, 18 and 24). The even numbers can perhaps be explained on the basis that the normal split of time between detention and training on the one hand, and supervision on the other, is 50:50 (s 102(2)). More seriously, the question arises as to why other options are not left to the court. The explanation[1] given for these discrete periods was, first, that they make the sentence simpler and easier for the young offender to understand. Secondly, it is desired that supervisors in the youth offending team and those who deal with the young person in custody are able to produce a constructive sentence plan that is based on a fixed predetermined period. A fixed period aids such sentence planning. Thirdly, the fixed periods chosen are designed to ensure that those who receive a lengthy order, but who receive the benefit of early release, do not serve less than those who are made the subject of shorter orders. These explanations may provide some justification for the approach taken (although whether a convincing justification is a different matter), but do not address all the concerns that arise. Section 48 of the Criminal Justice and Public Order Act 1994 introduced an entitlement for an accused who pleads guilty to receive a discount on the sentence that would otherwise be imposed. This is now governed by s 152 of the 2000 Act. Clearly, the effect of the fixed point approach taken by s 101(1) is that discount, if it is to be given, must reflect that scale, thus distorting both the discount which a court may wish to grant and the whole sentencing levels for other offenders in a case of multiple defendants. In *R v F and W*,[1] the Court of Appeal considered, but rejected on the facts, a submission that an early guilty plea meant that the defendant should not have received the maximum 24-month order. The court concluded that, for various offences including burglary, a sentence of detention under the then s 53 of the 1933 Act would have been appropriate. The court was not obliged to make the reduction sought for the early plea and for time spent in custody. To this extent, these provisions might be seen by some as unfair, in giving no credit for the guilty plea, although the reality may be that the court considered the sentence in any event lenient.

---

1   (2000) 165 JP 77, CA.
2   See Alun Michael, MP, Minister of State, Home Office, HC Committee, col 607.

6.18 In determining the length of a detention and training order, the court is under a duty to take account of any period for which the offender has been remanded in custody in connection with the offence, or any other offence the charge for which was founded on the same facts or evidence (s 101(8)). Because the custodial element of the order is only, usually,[1] one-half of the total length of the order, if the period of time spent in custody is to be reflected in accordance with s 101(8), the order should be reduced by a period equal to twice the period of time spent on remand. This is not to be regarded as an exact calculation, by reference to perhaps two or three days in custody.[1] Further, it is a duty to consider, not a duty to reduce.[2] The wording of s 101(8) ('... determining the term of a detention and training order') makes it quite clear that the allowance for time spent on remand should be against the total length of the order, not against the period to be spent in custody. The court must then, having made the appropriate deduction from what is otherwise considered to be the appropriate length of order, make a further adjustment to take the order to the nearest, and lower, permitted order length, a conclusion highlighting the lack of flexibility in the order lengths and discussed earlier.[1] It is clear, however, that the practice followed in respect of adults who spend time on remand, where time spent on remand is automatically credited to the offender, cannot be followed in the case of young offenders. The effect of doing so would be that an order which either did not fit the regime chosen, rightly or wrongly, by the Government in respect of order length or, alternatively, shorten the custodial element of the order in a way that might negate the training aspect of the period of detention.

---

1   *R v Inner London Crown Court, ex parte N and S* [2000] Crim LR 871, DC.
2   *R v Inner London Crown Court, ex parte I* (2000) *The Times*, 12 May.

The period of detention and training

6.19   Section 102(1) provides that an offender shall serve the period of detention and training under a detention and training order in such secure accommodation as may be determined by the Home Secretary or by such other person as may be authorised by him for that purpose. That could be a secure training centre, a young offender institution, local authority secure accommodation, or a youth treatment centre. The accommodation in which the offender is detained will depend on the age of the offender and the availability of accommodation.[1] Attempts were made during the passage of the Act[2] to introduce changes the effect of which would have been to require separate provision of offenders aged under 15[3] from those aged 15 or above. As the law currently stood, 12-, 13- and 14-year-olds served terms of custody in different accommodation from those aged 15 or above. This approach was resisted by the Government. *No More Excuses* had indicated that how the new arrangements would work would in part depend upon the review of the secure accommodation estate currently being undertaken by the Government. It is intended that the Youth Justice Board will review the regimes put in place. However, flexibility in available regimes is considered important.[3] The precise accommodation should depend on the maturity of the offender and his or her needs. The provisions are also intended to permit different regimes to provide, for example, mental treatment for a young sex offender, and to keep open possibilities for innovative regimes for the future. Younger offenders will normally be dealt with discretely and differently from older offenders, but not always.[4] Different children mature at different rates, and chronological age is not an indicator of either maturity or vulnerability.

---

1   See *No More Excuses: A New Approach to Tackling Youth Crime in England and Wales* Cm 3809 (1997), para 6.18.
2   See James Clappison, MP, HC Committee, col 619.
3   Alun Michael, MP, Minister of State, Home Office, HC Committee, col 629.
4   Ibid, col 630

6.20   The period of detention and training under a detention and training order shall be one-half of the term of the order (s 102(2)). The Home Secretary may at any time release the offender if he is satisfied that exceptional circumstances exist which justify the offender's release on compassionate grounds (s 102(3)).

In addition, the Act contains provisions permitting early release and also extended periods of detention. The purpose of these provisions in s 102 is to provide some flexibility to reward good behaviour and progress, or to provide some sanction for poor behaviour and lack of progress. No guidelines have yet been established to give guidance as to how these powers are to be exercised.

By s 102(4), the Home Secretary may release the offender:

'(a)   in the case of an order for a term of 8 months or more but less than 18 months, one month before the half-way point of the term of the order; and
(b)   in the case of an order for a term of 18 months or more, one month or two months before that point.'

The converse situation is where an offender has not behaved or progressed under the order. In that case, there is clearly no possibility of extending the period to be served by executive order. Section 102(5) provides that, if an application is made by the Home Secretary and the youth court orders, the period of detention may be extended. If such an application is granted, the Home Secretary must release the offender:

'(a)   in the case of an order for a term of 8 months or more but less than 18 months, one month after the half-way point of the term of the order; and
(b)   in the case of an order for a term of 18 months or more, one month or two months after that point.'

The Act does not specify to which youth court such an application should be made. The Act is silent on this point. Although s 104 defines the relevant petty session areas for the purposes of breach proceedings as the area in which the youth court which made the order is situated, or the area in which the offender resides for the time being, it is unclear that this is the position with regard to applications under s 102(5). The phrase used is '*the* youth court' (our emphasis). Arguably, the relevant youth court is the court which made the order.

The effect of these provisions relating to the period of detention can be seen from Table 2 below.

Table 2

Length of order	Minimum period possible	Maximum period possible*
4 months	2 months	2 months
6 months	3 months	3 months
8 months	3 months	5 months
10 months	4 months	6 months
12 months	5 months	7 months
18 months	7 months	11 months
24 months	10 months	14 months

* Pre-supposes youth court order under s 75(5).

Whilst it is true that these figures presuppose good behaviour and progress, the fact that, potentially, the difference between a six and 10-month order is only one month actually in custody, and that between six months and 24 months only seven is striking.

Period of supervision

6.21 On release from the period of detention and training, the offender is subject to a period of supervision. By s 103(1), the period of supervision of an offender who is subject to a detention and training order:

(a) begins with the offender's release, at whatever point that occurs; and

(b) subject to s 103(2), ends when the term of the order ends. Thus, for example, an offender sentenced to an order of 10 months in length, who is released at the earliest possible moment (ie four months), will be subject to a supervision period of six months.

However, s 103(2) empowers the Home Secretary to make an order providing that the period of supervision shall end at such point as may be specified in the order. That point must be during the term of such an order, and thus there is no question of the Home Secretary extending the period of supervision.

6.22 Supervision of the offender under the order may be by a probation officer, local authority social worker or a member of a youth offending team[1] (s 103(3)–(5)). The category of person who is appointed to supervise which orders will be determined by the Home Secretary. Before the commencement of the period of supervision or the alteration in details of category of supervisor or change of requirements, the offender must be given a statutory notice setting out the category of person responsible for supervision and any requirements with which the offender must for the time being comply (s 103(6) and (7)). The Act does not expressly authorise the imposition of requirements by a court, or, indeed, by the Home Secretary, but the terms of s 103(6) assume the right of the Home Secretary to impose conditions. There appears to be no limit, other than that of reasonableness or proportionality, on the requirements that may be imposed by the Home Secretary, but the human rights context must be borne in mind. Obviously, the imposition of conditions could, in an appropriate case, be subject to judicial review on normal judicial review principles.

---

1   See para **1.18**.

6.23   The implicit power to impose requirements has already been noted. By s 104(1), where a detention and training order is in force in respect of an offender, and it appears on information to a justice of the peace acting for a relevant petty sessions area that the offender has failed to comply with requirements under section 103(6)(b) above, the justice may:

(a) issue a summons requiring the offender to appear at the place and time specified in the summons before a youth court acting for the area; or

(b) if the information is in writing and on oath, issue a warrant for the offender's arrest requiring him to be brought before such a court.

The 'relevant petty sessions area' for this purpose is the area in respect of which the order was made by a youth court acting for it; or in which the offender resides for the time being (s 104(3)).

If it is provided to the satisfaction of the youth court before which an offender appears or is brought under that he has failed to comply with requirements, that court may deal with the offender in accordance with s 104(3). There does not appear to be any power on any other youth court to deal with any breach of requirements, or to discharge or vary the supervision requirements.

Where an offender appears, or is brought, before a youth court pursuant to s 104(1), that court may under s 104(3):

'(a) order the offender to be detained, in such secure accommodation as the Secretary of State may determine, for such period, not exceeding the shorter of three months or the remainder of the term of the detention and training order, as the court may specify; or

(b) impose on the offender a fine not exceeding level 3 on the standard scale.'

The period of detention may thus be a potentially very short one. There is a no minimum length of detention for breach of requirements. Clearly, if the breach occurs at the very end of the supervision period, the short nature of the potential detention for breach will be a factor a court will bear in mind in determining whether to make an order under s 104(3)(a). If detention is ordered under that subsection, the secure accommodation in which the fresh period of detention is to be served does not, inevitably, have to be of the same type as that in which the original period of detention was served.

INDEX

References are to paragraph numbers.